THE PSYCHO-BIOLOGY OF LANGUAGE

THE PSYCHO-BIOLOGY
OF LANGUAGE

An Introduction to Dynamic Philology

GEORGE KINGSLEY ZIPF

* * *

Introduction by
George A. Miller

THE M.I.T. PRESS

Massachusetts Institute of Technology
Cambridge, Massachusetts

P 105. Z 7 1965

First Edition 1935 by
Houghton Mifflin Company

First M.I.T. Press Paperback Edition, August, 1965

Printed in the United States of America

INTRODUCTION

The Psycho-Biology of Language is not calculated to please every taste. Zipf was the kind of man who would take roses apart to count their petals; if it violates your sense of values to tabulate the different words in a Shakespearean sonnet, this is not a book for you. Zipf took a scientist's view of language — and for him that meant the statistical analysis of language as a biological, psychological, social process. If such analysis repels you, then leave your language alone and avoid George Kingsley Zipf like the plague. You will be much happier reading Mark Twain: "There are liars, damned liars, and statisticians." Or W. H. Auden: "Thou shalt not sit with statisticians nor commit a social science."

However, for those who do not flinch to see beauty murdered in a good cause, Zipf's scientific exertions yielded some wonderfully unexpected results to boggle the mind and tease the imagination. Language *is* — among other things — a biological, psychological, social process; to apply statistics to it merely acknowledges its essential unpredictability, without which it would be useless. But who would have thought that in the very heart of all the freedom language allows us Zipf would find an invariant as solid and reliable as the law of gravitation?

Over the years Zipf's name has been linked to this particular statistical phenomenon until today one hears "Zipf curves" mentioned in the same offhand manner as "Bohr atoms" or "Skinner boxes" or "Bunsen burners." We pick up such tags and use them all too easily, often with little thought for the man or the work behind them. Yet each such term stands as an abbreviation for some important episode in the history of science. When a man's contribution is sufficient to earn him immortality — even this kind of anonymous terminological immortality — it is probably worth reprinting occasionally, if only to keep the record straight.

A "Zipf curve" expresses either (*a*) a relation between the frequency of occurrence of an event and the number of different events occurring with that frequency, or (*b*) a relation between the frequency of occurrence of an event and its rank when the events are ordered with respect to frequency of occurrence. All this is explained and illustrated in Chapter 2, and need not be repeated here. The point is that (for word events) Zipf found these curves to have a uniform shape under a remarkable variety of circumstances — for different topics, different authors, even for different languages — and he devoted most of his intellectual life to exploring and explaining what this regularity might signify. Although he was not the first to notice the fact, his many publications and ambitious hypotheses brought the matter to the attention of everyone with any scientific interest in language and eventually earned him the honor of having his name identified with the phenomenon he so diligently publicized.

Faced with this massive statistical regularity, you have two alternatives. Either you can assume that it reflects some universal property of the human mind, or you can assume that it represents some necessary consequence of the laws of probability. Zipf chose the synthetic hypothesis and searched for a principle of least effort that would explain the apparent equilibrium between uniformity and diversity in our use of words. Most others who were subsequently attracted to the problems chose the analytic hypothesis and searched for a probabilistic explanation. Now, thirty years later, it seems clear that the others were right. Zipf's curves are merely one way to express a necessary consequence of regarding a message source as a stochastic process.

Put it this way. Suppose that we acquired a dozen monkeys and chained them to typewriters until they had produced some very long and random sequence of characters. Suppose further that we defined a "word" in this monkey-text as any sequence of letters occurring between successive spaces. And suppose finally that we counted the occurrences of these "words" in just the way Zipf and others counted the occurrences of real words in meaningful texts. When we plot our results in the same manner, we will find exactly the same "Zipf curves" for the monkeys as for the human authors. Since we are not likely to argue that the poor monkeys were searching for some equilibrium between uniformity and diversity in expressing their ideas, such explanations seem equally inappropriate for human authors.

A mathematical rationalization for this result has been provided by Benoit Mandelbrot. The crux of it is that if we assume that word-boundary markers (spaces) are scattered randomly through a text, then there will necessarily be more occurrences of short than long words. Add to this fact the further observation that the variety of different words available increases exponentially with their length and the phenomenon Zipf reported becomes inescapable: a few short words will be used an enormous number of times while a vast number of longer words will occur infrequently or not at all.

So Zipf was wrong. His facts were right enough, but not his explanations. In a broader sense he was right, however, for he called attention to a stochastic process that is frequently seen in the social sciences, and by accumulating statistical data that cried out for some better explanation he challenged his colleagues and his successors to explore an important new type of probability distribution. Zipf belongs among those rare but stimulating men whose failures are more profitable than most men's successes.

The mathematical explanation for the form of the "Zipf

curve" leaves the whole question of word frequencies in an
anomalous theoretical position. On the one hand we know
that the form of his curves follows necessarily from the assumption that word-length is a random variable — or, in
Zipf's words, that "a speaker selects his words not according to their lengths, but solely according to the meanings
of the words and ideas he wishes to convey" — so that no
further assumptions about an equilibrium between hypothetical forces working toward uniformity and toward
variety of expression need be invoked. But, on the other
hand, we recognize that any language in which short words
were not the most frequent would be grossly inefficient.
Moreover, psychologists have demonstrated that the frequency with which a word is used can powerfully influence
the accuracy with which we hear it, read it, memorize it,
associate to it, or use it appropriately in our own speech.
It is impossible to believe that nothing more is at work to
guide our choice of letter sequences than whatever random
processes might control a monkey's choice, or that the
highly plausible arguments Zipf puts forward have no rele-
vance at all. In order to avoid overstating the case, therefore, we should put it negatively: whatever the social or
psychological influences may be that move us toward effi-
ciency in our use of words, the shape of the "Zipf curve" is
irrelevant to them. If a statistical test cannot distinguish
rational from random behavior, clearly it cannot be used
to prove that the behavior is rational. But, conversely,
neither can it be used to prove that the behavior is random.
The argument marches neither forward nor backward.

Because his fame has been so closely tied to the puzzle of
the curves, the fact that these curves were but one facet of
Zipf's work is often forgotten. He was above all else a
man with a vision — a naturalistic vision — of human language, a vision he attempted to actualize in statistical form.
Without the support his word counts gave it, his vision

must now seem less compelling to us than it did to him, but it is still worthy of study and discussion.

Begin with the assumption that a concept is a bundle of semantic features, or "genes of meaning," as Zipf called them. If a particular bundle occurs frequently in the cognitive life of a community, they will assign to it some phonological representation, or "word." If it occurs infrequently, no word will be available, so the bundle will have to be made up as needed from strings of words arranged in phrases. As the language evolves, a relation will develop between the lengths of the phonological representations and the frequencies of occurrence of the bundles they express. These ideas still have considerable currency among students of psycholinguistics, on grounds having little or nothing to do with "Zipf curves" or probability theory. It is difficult to see how to develop or test them without a much better theory of syntax than was available in 1935, but nevertheless they are ideas that merit consideration in their own right. It is even possible that statistical analysis may yet prove relevant if we can learn how to look behind those surface symptoms called "words" to the deeper cognitive processes that underlie them.

So it is good to have this book in print again. Perhaps now we are ready to look beyond its statistical puzzles to some of the underlying issues it raises concerning the cognitive aspects of linguistic behavior. That may not be a prospect to inspire a poet, but it is difficult to imagine any way a scientist could probe closer to what is uniquely human about human beings.

George Kingsley Zipf was born in Freeport, Illinois, on January 7, 1902. He graduated *summa cum laude* from Harvard College in 1924 and spent the following year in Germany, studying at Bonn and Berlin. He returned to Harvard and received his Ph.D. in Comparative Philology in 1930; then became Instructor in German until 1936, Assistant Professor of German until 1939, and University Lecturer until 1950.

His Ph.D. dissertation was concerned with relative frequency of use as a determinant of phonetic change in the evolution of language, a topic revisited in Chapter 3 of the present book. *The Psycho-Biology of Language* was his first attempt to relate his linguistic ideas to man's experience as a whole. In 1941 he published *National Unity and Disunity,* which applied his statistical methods to the study of the sizes of cities and movements of population. His most ambitious work, *Human Behavior and the Principle of Least Effort* (1949), was a further study of semantics, psychology, sociology, geography; it abounds with illustrations of the probability distributions he first noticed in his statistical studies of vocabulary.

Zipf died on September 25, 1950.

GEORGE A. MILLER

Harvard University
April, 1965

PREFACE

NEARLY ten years ago, while studying linguistics at the University of Berlin, it occurred to me that it might be fruitful to investigate speech as a natural phenomenon, much as a physiologist may study the beating of the heart, or an entomologist the tropisms of an insect, or an ornithologist the nesting-habits of a bird. That is, speech was to be regarded as a peculiar form of behavior of a very unusual extant species; it was to be investigated, in the manner of the exact sciences, by the direct application of statistical principles to the objective speech-phenomena. The stream of speech, whatever it might represent to the historical grammarian, the comparative philologist, or the descriptive phoneticist, was to be viewed as but a series of communicative gestures. The findings of the extensive investigation that resulted are now presented in full. They are presented, moreover, intentionally in such a manner that they will, I think, be readily available, not only to the professional linguist, but to any serious reader interested in linguistic phenomena, whether his interest be from the angle of the biological, sociological, or psychological sciences, or from the angle of aesthetics and *belles lettres*.

Perhaps nothing will more conveniently illustrate the nature, scope, and appeal of the material about to be discussed than the brief presentation of a few typical examples from our findings. For example, it can be shown that the length of a word, far from being a random matter, is closely related to the frequency of its usage — the greater the frequency, the shorter the word. It can furthermore be shown either from speech-sounds, or from roots and affixes, or from words or phrases, that the more complex any speech-element is phonetically, the less frequently it occurs. As an illustration of the high degree of orderliness with which linguistic forces operate, the frequency distribution of words in English may be conveniently cited. In any extensive sample of connected English, it will, in all probability, be found that the most frequent word in the sample will occur on the average once in approximately every 10 words, the second most frequent word once in every 20 words, the third most frequent word once in every 30 words, the 100th most frequent word once in every 1000 words, the nth most frequent word once in every $10n$ words; in brief, the distribution of words in English approximates with remarkable precision an harmonic series. Similarly, one finds in English (or Latin or Chinese) the following striking correlation. If the number of different words occurring once in a given sample is taken as x, the number of different words occurring twice, three times, four times, n times, in the same sample, is respectively $1/2^2$, $1/3^2$, $1/4^2$,.... $1/n^2$ of x, up to, though not including, the few most frequently used words; that is, we find an unmistakable progression according to the inverse square, valid for well over 95% of all the different words used in the sample.

The above evidence, as well as all the other evidence, points quite conclusively to the existence of a fundamental condition of equilibrium between the form and function of speech-habits, or speech-patterns, in any language. And it has been the chief concern of this investigation to assemble sufficient data to establish this finding as a condition probably generally present in speech. In addition, however, almost equal effort has been devoted to discovering and establishing the probable effect of this condition of equilibrium upon the evolutionary development of a given language. In the light of the data collected it appears that the impulse to preserve or restore this condition of equilibrium is the underlying cause of linguistic change which, as is commonly known, is constantly occurring, leading to dialectal divergences, if not to wide linguistic cleavages. By change is meant not only changes in phonetic form and accent, but changes in meaning, in emotional intensity, in syntactical arrangement.

Of course, during this entire investigation, a very understandable human question has continuously lurked in the background. What person in speaking ever selects or arranges his words for the sake of preserving or restoring any imaginable condition of equilibrium in the resultant frequency-distribution of the elements of his speech? Clearly we select words according to their meanings, and according to the ideas and feelings which we wish to convey; both content and direction of our speech are dictated almost solely by exigencies of meaning and emotion. What, then, is the nature of meaning and emotion that their manifestation in the production of speech reveals such a high degree of orderliness as we find? A study of language is certainly incomplete which totally disregards all questions of meaning and emotion even though these refer to the most elusive of mental phenomena. Therefore I have ventured a cautious inspection of the problems of meaning, emotion, and of mental behavior in general, as they appear in light of the new data empirically derived from the stream of speech. The inspection of these problems has not, however, been undertaken *a priori*. On the contrary; much as a physicist might investigate the intangible forces of gravitation by observing their influence on the perceptible, so too I have attempted, as far as the evidence will permit, to investigate the forces of the mind by viewing linguistic phenomena in the stream of speech as manifestations of the forces of the mind in the process of functioning. It is hoped that this discussion of meaning and emotion will serve to bring our new linguistic data into a rational perspective with the rest of human behavior. In this last phase of the investigation, as in the investigation as a whole, I trust it will be remembered that the entire study is but a beginning, and a beginning along only one of possibly many different valid lines of approach to the general subject of speech-dynamics.

In this introduction to a new manner if not to a new field of study a few practical problems had to be considered.

For example, this study is, on the one hand, greatly indebted
for impulse and material to the formal linguistic fields of
comparative philology, historical grammar, and descriptive
phonetics. On the other hand, I have become clearly aware
of the fact that my investigation has gradually diverged in
aims, methods, and interests very far from the customary
aims, methods, and interests of the linguistic fields in which
this investigation first had its origin. My recognition of
this fact is explicit in my use of the term Dynamic Philology,
a field of investigation to which this study is tendered as an
introduction. Of equal importance is my indebtedness to
the theories and findings of more closely related fields,
notably those of biology and psychology. The work of
investigators in these other fields has often served as welcome
blazes along a difficult trail; in return it may be said without
exaggeration that some of the theories and findings of these
others receive at times substantial corroboration from the
present linguistic data. It has not been, however, within
the scope of this introductory study to call attention to
any correspondences with the findings in other fields, especially since appeal to these correspondences has not seemed
necessary for the interpretation of our data.

In attempting to make this material readily available to
the reader without special linguistic or mathematical train-
ing I have not disguised from myself the difficulties in the
way; whether I have been successful in the presentation can
be decided only by the reader himself. Welcome light has
been shed for me on the exposition of certain knotty problems by the frequently penetrating questions of former students in my course at Harvard University on this general
subject. In the actual development of the manuscript in
its various stages I am indebted to Dr. Allan Evans, Dr.
Margaret Bailey Lieder, Professor Francis P. Magoun, Jr.,
and Dr. John C. Whitehorn; these have read the manuscript
in whole or in part, in the earlier or in the final stages of
composition, and, without commitments, have tendered

valuable suggestions, of which some have been adopted. I also take this occasion to thank Dean George H. Chase of the Graduate School of Arts and Sciences of Harvard University for his encouragement and practical advice during the last ten years. This investigation is greatly indebted to the General Education Board from whose grant to Harvard University liberal sums have been made available to me. With these sums I have been able to conduct and publish in full the extensive statistical researches referred to in the present text. For help either in locating, or in making available, or in utilizing material I wish to thank Professor M. A. Buchanan of the University of Toronto, Professor R. H. Fife, Jr., of Columbia University, Professor V. A. C. Henmon of the University of Wisconsin, Professor Martin Heepe of the University of Berlin, and Professor Otto Mauser of the University of Munich. The assembling of much of the new phonetic material now published for the first time was made possible through the kindness of Professor Paul Menzerath, director of the Phonetic Institute of the University of Bonn, who in the summer of 1933 kindly put at my disposal the library and facilities of the Institute, the services of a trained assistant, and much of his own valuable time for the discussion of many pertinent phonetic problems. Should the future find anything of value in this study, it is dedicated gratefully and respectfully to these many persons whom I have found to be true guides, counsellors, and friends.

G. K. Z.

CAMBRIDGE, MASSACHUSETTS
   December 19, 1934

NOTE: The term PSYCHO-BIOLOGY is employed in the title because it seems to designate more concisely and accurately than any other term the present treatment of linguistic behavior in reference to: (1) man's experience, and (2) the rest of man's bodily functions.

CONTENTS

THE PSYCHO-BIOLOGY OF LANGUAGE

I

INTRODUCTION

I. PRELIMINARY CONSIDERATIONS

DYNAMIC PHILOLOGY has the ultimate goal of bringing the study of language more into line with the exact sciences. To this end it views speech-production as a natural psychological and biological phenomenon to be investigated in the objective spirit of the exact sciences from which its methods have been taken. Our chief method of procedure is the application of statistical principles to the observable phenomena of the stream of speech.

In this introductory study our primary aim is the observation, measurement, and, as far as it is possible, the formulation into tentative laws of the underlying forces which impel and direct linguistic expression. Our first interest will be in the relationship which exists between the form of the various speech-elements and their behavior, in so far as this relationship is revealed statistically. The findings which result from this initial interest may be viewed as dynamic laws of speech with general applicability, though they are offered, of course, subject to future corrective experimentation. These dynamic laws can presumably be similarly demonstrated from the material of any known language.

Our second interest will be to relate the above dynamic laws with the familiar phenomena of meaning and emotional intensity which have generally proved elusive to direct quantitative analysis. The findings resulting from this second phase of our investigation may be taken only as inferential conclusions; their validity can be apprehended against the general statistical background of the dynamic laws, yet the conclusions themselves can probably never be established numerically because of the nature of the phenomena involved.

In turning now to an investigation of the dynamics of speech we are but taking the next logical step in the development of linguistic study. Previous studies of language which have made this step inevitable have also furnished the student of speech-dynamics with a large body of historical and comparative material so accurate that he may now expect to fare both well and far, even in an introductory investigation. Indeed, perhaps nothing can more expeditiously familiarize the reader both with the objectives to be sought and with the material to be used, than a very brief survey of the main aims and achievements of the formal linguistic disciplines — historical grammar, comparative philology, and descriptive phonetics — in which the present investigation had its origin.

Not until during the last hundred years have the historical facts of language been studied with scholarly accuracy. To the early scholars of this comparatively short period we owe much of our knowledge about the historical relationships of the many and diverse Indo-European languages.* These early scholars, or as we might say, early philologists, also propounded far-reaching questions involving an aesthetic, cultural, ethnological, and psychological evaluation of their newly discovered linguistic facts.[1] However, with the coming of a new generation of students of language, interest gradually became restricted to the detailed comparisons and explanations of single words, forms, and sounds. With this second step the older philology became *linguistics*, while linguistic study became the very accurately descrip-

---

* Frequently termed the *Aryan* or the *Indo-Germanic* languages. Throughout this investigation we shall employ the term *Indo-European*, which has found wide acceptance in English-speaking countries, to designate the large family of languages in question.

tive field of specialized historical research as we know it today. Whether because of the perhaps premature nature of the generalizations of the early philologists, or whether because of the absorbing interest of a series of brilliant discoveries [1] which resulted solely from the detailed comparisons of sounds and forms, the larger significance of language, both in respect to other cultural activities, as well as in respect to the rest of human behavior, was now lost sight of.

It was only natural that the later linguists should have been severely censured for their extreme specialization in interests and technique, especially since the expressions of some modern linguists have indicated a firm belief that any comprehensive scientific linguistic generalization was in itself a downright evil.[2] Of course not all students of language have followed the restricted paths of linguistics. Indeed one of them, Otto Jespersen, eminent alike for achievements in philology and linguistics, has chided the modern linguists in no uncertain words for putting entirely out of court all questions relating to the cultural and psychological implications of their field of research.*

However, in spite of the frequent censure of linguistics, it is difficult to believe that linguistics has been entirely mistaken in the direction it gave to language study. Certainly no student of speech-dynamics can for a moment regret the stringency of the historical and comparative disciplines which have provided him with immediately available material. Furthermore, he cannot forget that these same censured linguists were the ones who proved conclusively, as we shall see at a more opportune time, that phonetic development, whatever its amorphous and random appear-

* Otto Jespersen: 'These great questions have to be put over and over again, till a complete solution is found; and the refusal to face these difficulties has produced a certain barrenness in modern linguistics, which must strike any impartial observer, however much he admits the fertility of the science in detailed investigations. Breadth of vision is not conspicuous in modern linguistics, and to my mind this lack is chiefly due to the fact that linguists have neglected all problems connected with a valuation of language.' [3]

ance may be, is essentially an orderly process with a high degree of precision.   Without this previous auspicious knowledge that phonetic development is orderly, few persons would today dare to undertake an investigation of the causal laws behind speech-activity.   Just as the student of astro-physical laws cannot with propriety contemn the laborious, careful, and ingenious camera-work of the observers and recorders of the historical acts of astro-process without which his own more general studies would be impossible, so too the student of speech-dynamics, in acknowledging his great indebtedness to linguistics, can only hope that linguistics will in the future continue just as stringently along the same fruitful paths.

In the present investigation, however, and under the heading of Dynamic Philology,* we are returning to the comprehensive views of language held by the early philologists who believed that speech-phenomena cannot be isolated from the content of speech, nor from the personal, social, and cultural backgrounds of the speaker.   Naturally, we are returning with more data than they possessed, and with the equipment of some scientific methods and information doubtless unknown to them.   From an observation of extensive data we now know definitely that (1) the patterns of everyday speech are by no means essentially incommensurable with (2) the patterns of style, of metrics, even of music, and that a sober study of the dynamics of the former may well lead to a profounder comprehension of the dynamics of the latter.   Having been constantly reminded by psychologists that language is a delicate indicator of the activity of the mind, we must not forget that the laws governing the formation and behavior of speech-patterns may also subtly reflect the laws governing other patterns of behavior.   If it is not for us to divert our main attention to the findings of

---

* The term *Dynamic Philology* is preferable to *Dynamic Linguistics* because the former avoids the implication that our aims and methods are restricted to those reflected in the achievements of the latter.

investigators of these non-linguistic patterns of behavior, it is nevertheless our duty to explain our findings in such terms that investigators in these same fields of non-linguistic behavior may be able to follow — especially since Dynamic Philology is more closely related in aims and methods to these psychological, biological, sociological, and aesthetic fields than it is to the formal disciplines of historical linguistics.

With this preliminary discussion behind us, let us now briefly view the manner in which we shall approach the study of speech-dynamics and consider the advantages of our particular method in dealing with the problems which will arise.

2. MANNER OF APPROACH AND METHODS OF ANALYSIS OF DYNAMIC PHILOLOGY

The manner with which one approaches the study of a field of inquiry determines to a considerable extent the particular method to be employed. Both our manner of approach and method of analysis are each only one of possibly many different valid approaches and methods.

a. The View of Language as an Implement of Behavior

In spite of the abundant uses to which speech is put and despite the numerous angles from which speech may be viewed, nothing has ever been found in the nature of speech in any of its manifestations which is not completely comprised in the statement that speech is but a form of human behavior. To appreciate the implications of this statement, which will be of importance to us later, let us for the moment view language against the general background of all behavior of which it is but a part.

To begin, it may be said that every organism is placed in an environment against which it must defend itself and from which it must gain its support. For this battle of self-defense and self-support, every organism is equipped with what may be termed implements or tools — in the case of man, with hands, ears, feet, and so on. Each of these tools is a product of biological evolution, and the particular behavior of each is presumably co-ordinated in some way, first, with the activity of the mind, conscious or instinctive, and second with the activity of other tools. In respect to being a tool of defense and aggression whose behavior is co-ordinated with the behavior of other tools, language is no exception. This view of language as a tool of behavior we shall find a more fruitful angle of departure for dynamic studies than the more usual view of language as an elaborate system of signalling and communication, though language is, of course, both.

The chief difference between language and many other tools of behavior, say a hand, is that language is primarily social in its use while the behavior of the hand is primarily individualistic or non-social. The occurrence of speech generally presupposes some second person who stands in some relationship to the speaker's problems and their solution; the behavior of the hand is usually more immediate in its effectiveness, and generally attempts to solve the individual's problems without recourse to another person. If acts of the hand (e.g. beckoning) can easily be discovered which are of a social nature, these are nevertheless more the exception than the rule. If, when a person talks or thinks over his problems by himself, his use of language is primarily individualistic, this function of language, however important, is by no means so important a function as language in its social use. The predominating social use of language is that which distinguishes the use of language from the behavior of the hand or of any other tool.

The analogy of language to the hand, though obviously

incomplete, is in many respects surprisingly appropriate. Yet the analogy is complete only if we compare the vocal organs that produce speech to the hand, or else the speech produced by the vocal organs to the activity of the hand, or, if one will, the total phenomenon of vocal organs in activity to the total phenomenon of hand in activity. No matter in which of these ways the analogy is stated, the two tools have this in common: each is a tool in use, and the use of each tool is attended by some degree of purpose, insight, intelligence, and experience. With this analogy of the hand in mind let us turn to the problem of measurement.

b. The Problem of Measuring Behavior

Until some means has been devised for measuring the phenomena of a given field, one can neither make of that field an exact science nor study the dynamics of the field with any mentionable degree of precision. Hence the discovery of a method suitable for measuring the chief phenomena of speech is of immediate concern to Dynamic Philology. It is at this point — in the quest of a measuring rod for speech — that the analogy of the hand to the vocal organs and language will be helpful. For, instead of inquiring how language may best be measured, let us ask how one would measure the hand. By considering the hand before we consider the vocal apparatus we shall gain a welcome objectivity as well as a refreshing liberation from the numerous small prejudices and biases which have colored and distorted our views on language from earliest school-days, and which frequently becloud the fundamental problems at issue.

How, then, would one measure a hand? As to the physical measurements of the hand, one might, by the judicious employment of customary methods, obtain a fairly accurate knowledge of the hand's volume, mean temperature, weight, area, dimensions, and the like. Yet, however accurate these physical measurements might be, they would yield quite as inadequate an idea of the total phenomenon of the hand in action as would similar measurements of the vocal organs give of the total phenomenon of speech. A mere physical measurement of the hand would provide no indication of the numerous aggressive and defensive gestures of which the hand is capable and for the sake of which the hand presumably exists. The chief task in measuring the entire phenomenon of the hand would, therefore, be to find a means of measuring all the significant acts of any given hand (and *mutatis mutandis* in measuring speech).

What is to be understood under the term 'significant acts of a hand' is merely a matter of definition. One might give the term a general meaning and call every act of the hand significant, whether the act fulfilled a need or not. Or one might limit the term and apply it only to acts of the hand, like pointing or beckoning, which are significant in a very literal sense, that is, which are signals or acts of communication. There is, however, a third definition which is neither so general as the first nor so narrow as the second, and which, in view of the analogy of a hand to the vocal organs, seems recommended: any act of the hand is significant if, directly or indirectly, it is useful for the satisfaction of a need. Hence, when the hand beckons, the act is significant; when the hand unlocks a door or lights a cigarette, the act is significant; but when, say, a person turns in his sleep and his hand accidentally slips over the edge of the bed, this act is probably not significant, for it seems to be in no way useful to the satisfaction of a need.

With this definition of a significant act, i.e. an act directly or indirectly useful in the satisfaction of a need, let us approach the general problem of measuring the significant acts of behavior. For convenience we may at times refer to these simply as acts of behavior, for the present study will not deal with any action of behavior which is not significant

in the sense of being directly or indirectly useful in the
satisfaction of a need.

At least on one point it is possible to make with certainty
an inclusive statement about the significant acts of any
tool of behavior: the number of significant acts actually
made by any tool, say the right hand of a given person,
from birth to death is finite, and the kinds of these acts,
though manifold, are limited. Hence if there is no other
means of measuring the significant action of a tool of
behavior, its acts could conceivably be counted and arranged among themselves according to the relative frequency
of their occurrence over a reasonable period of time. Furthermore, with a reasonable degree of accuracy, it might be
possible to determine whether a certain act is made over a
given period of time more often than another. Such a
system of measurement would comprehend all significant
acts produced by any implement of behavior, linguistic or
non-linguistic.

The several apparent insufficiencies of this system of
measurement (i.e. statistics), which seems to consist of
little more than mere counting, are familiar and deserve
mention only to show that they cease to be of serious consequence when the acts of behavior to be measured are the
gestures of the stream of speech.

The one general criticism of our contemplated system of
measurement is that it entirely ignores in its objectivity
the differences in intelligence, value, and experience evinced
by the various acts of behavior. Everyone will rightly
insist, moreover, that the qualities of intelligence, value,
and experience are especially vital factors in speech-behavior.
Nevertheless, in view of our present limited knowledge about
the nature of these qualities, it seems a far more prudent
procedure to select a measuring rod without any reference
to these seemingly variable and highly elusive factors, than
to attempt to devise one which will take them into consideration. The least that we may expect from the application of

our method is the establishment of a domain of speech-behavior where the disturbing effect of these elusive factors is negligible. And in addition there always remains the possibility (indeed, as we shall see, the strong probability) that the dynamics of these elusive factors may in turn be apprehended against the background of our statistics, and that ultimately their dynamic behavior may be measured quantitatively, if not directly, at least by ratios in so far as it motivates changes in other behavior that is measurable. In short, our method of statistical measurement may well prove itself of considerable service in studying objectively the otherwise highly subjective phenomena of meaning, value, and experience.

In addition to this general criticism of our method which we have just discussed and found unimportant in our case, there are several other secondary objections that we shall now only mention. For instance, the statistical method of measurement seems to ignore the palpable fact that most, if not all, acts of behavior are but parts of elaborate complexes of action in which the activities of other implements of behavior frequently come into play; many acts of behavior are truly meaningless when isolated from the whole into which they are co-ordinated. In the entire action of playing tennis, for example, the grip of the hand, though important, is by no means the only act, nor necessarily the most important act in the complete co-ordination. Furthermore, even if an isolation of the behavior of a single implement were permissible, there would still remain practical difficulties to hinder the successful employment of the method: (1) Every act of behavior may be viewed both as a complex of ever smaller acts, and as a component in ever larger complexes of action; we might well be in doubt as to the proper size to select as a unit. (2) Granted that the proper size of the unit were determinable, there would remain the problem of establishing criteria of comparison to determine how similar two acts of behavior must be before they can be considered the same, and how dissimilar they must be before being classed as distinctly different. (3) There would finally remain the almost insuperable task of observing and recording all the gestures of a given implement of behavior without making self-conscious the person whose behavior was under consideration.

But these secondary objections just mentioned, however serious they might be if the method were applied to other acts of behavior, become of minimal consequence, indeed for practical purposes disappear, once the method is applied to the acts of speech. In now discussing the application of the statistical method to the phenomena of speech we shall in fact be forcibly reminded of the unusual advantages which the study of speech-dynamics possesses over the study of the dynamics of any other type of behavior, advantages which seem in many respects to be unique in the whole range of biological and psychological phenomena.

c. The Statistical Method When Applied to the Phenomena of Speech

The phenomena of speech which we wish to measure are not those represented by an extensive list of alphabetized words in a dictionary, nor those represented by pages of paradigms and syntactical rules in a grammar. They are rather the phenomena of speech in the process of being uttered; they represent the stream of speech that may appropriately be viewed as a succession or a continuum of communicative gestures, produced by the vocal organs occurring in arrangements that are essentially permutations.

If we view language as a continuum of gestures, many serious practical difficulties in the way of statistical measurement have already been solved for us. First of all, the general problem of labelling becomes minimal: so great is the rate of repetitiveness of most of the gestures that the necessary variety of different labels is correspondingly small. Moreover, though actual variation is great in pitch, amplitude, timbre, and speed, there is nevertheless in most cases little doubt as to significant differences and similarities, and hence little doubt as to the suitable label of classification for a given speech-gesture. To devise a scheme for labelling the different gestures occurring in the stream of speech (which is the same as to devise a system of writing) is by no means an *a priori* impossibility. Furthermore, the observation and the recording of the gestures of the stream of speech, by use of these labels, without making unduly self-conscious the speaker under observation, appears never to have amounted to an insuperable obstacle in the past.

Indeed, skill in writing is so old and has been so much employed even in the remote past that we already possess an enormous body of recorded speech-gestures, which includes almost every type of speech, and which has been produced in the course of the centuries, unbiased by the needs of Dynamic Philology. If the labelling in this older material is at times not so precise in many respects as the comparative philologist might wish, it is unquestionably, even at its worst, far more accurate than could be devised for the acts of any other implement of behavior. Moreover, we are not bound, like the paleontologist, to records of the past. The dynamic philologist, with the help of phonology (see pages 54–58) may devise his own system of labelling, and may record his own speech, or the speech of his contemporaries; since the dynamic forces of language are presumably manifest in all speech, the selection of samples of language may be dictated at least to a considerable extent by the investigator's convenience.

Although many gestures of the stream of speech can be subdivided into subsidiary gestures and hence can be viewed as a sequence or sequences of smaller gestures (e.g. a sentence as a sequence of words which are in turn sequences of speech-sounds), this sequential nature of speech-gestures offers no serious impediment to speech-labelling. For even the larger sequences of speech-gestures have often such a high rate of repetitiveness and stability in the stream of speech that many of them could be labelled as units in themselves if it were expedient. To illustrate, taking English as an example, we might first label each of the successive speech-sounds (i.e. *phonemes*, see page 49 ff.) by the use of a phonemic alphabet.[1] For example, the English word *untruthfulness* may be reviewed as a sequence of twelve phonemes, if one chooses to select the phoneme as a unit, i.e. *u-n-t-r-u-th-f-u-l-n-e-ss*. Or one may view the same word as a sequence of five units which we shall term *morphemes* (see pages 132 ff.), i.e. *un-tru-th-ful-ness*, and devise a morphemic alphabet [2] to label all the different morphemes (e.g. prefixes, roots, suffixes, and endings) of a language. Again one might anatomize the stream of speech into syllables,[3] devising a label for each different syllable. Or one might anatomize the stream of speech into words in their full inflected form, and for each different word in full inflected form devise a special label,[4] e.g. one for *boy*, one for *boys*, one for *man*, one for *men*. Naturally as one takes larger and larger sequences for units — phrases, clauses, sentences — variety increases with a concomitant diminution in the average rate of repetitiveness, to the general effect that an ever larger sample must be taken from the stream of speech before repetitions are sufficiently abundant to justify the application of statistical principles. Though the task of labelling and counting these larger sequences of gestures would doubtless be difficult in the extreme, it is by no means impossible.

It would, of course, be incorrect to imply that one would at no time be in any doubt as to how a speech-gesture should best be labelled. In many districts in America the pronunciation of *latter*, for example, is so similar to that of *ladder* that one may reasonably hesitate between the use of *t* or *d* in the labelling of the dental of *latter*. Yet doubtful forms of this sort are proportionately so rare in the stream of speech that they are comparatively insignificant statistically, although, as we shall see (page 106 ff.), they do afford interesting problems to dynamic studies. If, from the point of view of the perfectionist, every gesture of the stream of speech cannot be labelled with perfect accuracy, nevertheless from the point of view of a biologist or psychologist investigating the significant action of any other tool of behavior, the gestures of speech must seem ideally suitable for labelling.

Likewise in respect to another general problem, the student of language is favored. As was observable from our previous analogy of the hand, the significant act of any one tool of behavior is frequently not merely sequential but also a part of some larger complex of gestures; thus the act of the hand, in gripping the tennis racket, is but a part of the total tennis stroke in the performance of which the behavior of many other members of the body take part. So, too, the stream of speech is often accompanied by gestures of other members (e.g. beckoning with the hand or winking with the eye). But though acts of other tools may accompany speech-gestures, they are in no wise an obligatory accompaniment of speech. The reason why speech is comparatively free from the necessity of concomitant acts of other tools of behavior is possibly because of the social nature of language. For, language is a medium for the young and the old, the halt and the blind, and one which must be serviceable in darkness as well as in daylight, in immediate proximity and over a considerable distance; its social utility would clearly be diminished were it encumbered with many other obligatory gestures. Such other acts of behavior as do accompany those of speech fall mainly into two classes: the constant and the random. The constant acts, such as the beating of the heart, the functioning of the liver, and the like, acts without which there would be no speech, can, because of the comparatively high degree of constancy in their behavior, be temporarily disregarded until more is known about the peculiar structure and behavior of the stream of speech itself, even as the engineer in surveying a piece of land can with impunity disregard the constant rotation of the earth. The random acts, such as pointing and winking, though frequently important in speech, can be disregarded at present on the very grounds of their randomness. Of all the acts of human behavior the stream of speech alone seems to constitute a continuum which with the minimum of distortion can be isolated from the total background of behavior and at the same time be labelled and studied statistically with a high degree of accuracy.

Of course, after all is said, while it may be readily conceded that the stream of speech is a continuum of gestures which can be anatomized or dissected in a way entirely suitable for the application of statistical principles, nevertheless the belief is hard to combat that dissection of this sort annihilates the most significant and important aspects of language. For language is more than a continuum of gestures; it is a continuum of gestures in arrangement, and in an arrangement which is of vital importance for the conveyance of meaning and emotion. One feels instinctively that it is rather in the configurations of language than in the atoms that meaning and intensity lie, and that configurations do not seem to lend themselves to mere addition, subtraction, multiplication, and division. Yet the dynamic philologist in using the methods of statistical analysis does not for a moment ignore the existence nor the importance of configurational arrangement. On the contrary, his anatomization is to be viewed solely as a device whereby the structure and forces of configurational arrangement can be better approached. The dynamic philologist is in a position analogous to that of the chemist who anatomizes so that through analysis of the parts he may better comprehend the total phenomenon. The justification of our contemplated empirical analysis of the stream of speech into its parts will be, I hope, the synthesis of those parts again, not into the stream of speech from which they were derived, but into the totality of a person's behavior of which the stream of speech is but a part; but this attempt at synthesis will first be undertaken (Chapter VI) after our analysis of the parts has been completed (in Chapters II–V).

3. PROSPECTUS

That the reader may at no time be confused in the ensuing empirical investigation of the dynamics of speech, it is perhaps expedient to enumerate in advance the major steps in the presentation. We shall, as suggested previously, analyze samples of the stream of speech of many languages into their component parts, we shall study the frequency distributions of these parts, and shall attempt to correlate these empirically observed phenomena with the significant phenomena of meaning, emotional intensity, and configurational arrangement. But we shall not investigate the frequency distributions of all the different speech-elements at once. We shall begin (Chapter II) by restricting our investigation to the form and behavior of words; thence we shall proceed (Chapter III) to a discussion of the smallest speech-unit, the phoneme (sometimes termed speech-sound); in Chapter IV we shall devote our attention to the morpheme (i.e. prefixes, roots, suffixes, and endings) and the syllable, with special emphasis upon the relationship between relative frequency and accent. With the accumulated evidences of the previous chapters we shall, in Chapter V, be in a position to study the dynamics of sentence structure in reference both to the question of relative frequency and to the question of meaning, emotional intensity, and configurational arrangement. At this point our investigation ceases to be primarily empirical, and in Chapter VI the attempt is made speculatively to comprehend the significance of all preceding findings in their relationship to the totality of behavior. Since Chapter VI is largely speculative, it is hoped that the contents of that chapter will not be considered as on the same plane with the major portions of the preceding chapters in support of which data, empirically derived, are advanced. Since all linguistic phenomena appear to be closely interrelated, this investigation can probably be grasped only as a whole; as we progress from chapter to chapter, the accumulating evidence will strengthen what has gone before. That the reader may be informed of whither this investigation is proceeding, it may profitably be stated in advance — though the entire significance of the statement will be only later apparent — that all our data seem to point conclusively to two fundamental conditions present in all speech-elements or language-patterns: (1) whether viewed as a whole or in part, the form of all speech-elements or speech-patterns is intimately associated with their behavior, the one changing with the other, so that all seems to be relative and nothing absolute in linguistic expression; and (2) all speech-elements or language-patterns are impelled and directed in their behavior by a fundamental law of economy in which is the desire to maintain an equilibrium between form and behavior.

II

THE FORM AND BEHAVIOR OF WORDS

THERE is a decided advantage in beginning our investigation of language by restricting our attention to the form and behavior of words, since the essential phenomena in the dynamics of words are far more clearly apparent and readily apprehended than those of the smaller or larger speech-elements. If it cannot be truthfully averred, as is sometimes felt, that the stream of speech is primarily a stream of words rather than a stream of, say, phonemes or sentences, the word does seem, nevertheless, to occupy a middle terrain between the smaller elements which are its components and the larger phrasal, clausal, and sentence elements of which the word is in turn but a part. In studying the dynamics of words, then, we are studying what represents simultaneously either an aggregate of, or the component of, other speech-elements, and are hence incidentally approaching the dynamic problems of these other speech-elements at their most accessible side.

PART I

THE QUESTION OF FORM

I. THE LENGTH OF WORDS AND THEIR FREQUENCY OF USAGE

Probably the most striking feature of words is difference in length. A word may consist of a single phoneme (e.g. English *a* in *a book*), or it may represent a phoneme-sequence of considerable magnitude (e.g. English *transcendentalism*, *constitutionality*, *quintessentially*). The question naturally arises as to what, if any, is the significance of these observable differences in length.

If there is any connection between the length of a word and its meaning, the nature of the connection is certainly not at once apparent. The same idea is found adequately conveyed in different languages by words of decidedly different length (e.g. English *trade*, German *Handwerk*; English *work*, German *Arbeit*). Hence, at least for the present, we may disregard considerations of meaning in examining the significance of the factor of length in the form of words.

The question is natural as to the number of different long and short words in the vocabulary of a given person, or of a given dialect. As far as any *a priori* statement is permissible on this subject, it seems deducible only from the law of permutations which clearly gives the presumption in favor of a greater abundance of different longer words than of shorter. For, the possible permutations of a given number of phonemes taken, say, five at a time is far greater than those when only two are taken at a time. If some permutations of phonemes would be too difficult to pronounce with convenience (e.g. *tp* or *tpbgd* in English), unpronounce-ability is not restricted to long or short words. That is, short permutations may be unpronounceable as well as long permutations. If long permutations offer greater opportunity for unpronounceable arrangements of phonemes than do smaller configurations, they also offer, by the same token, greater opportunity for pronounceable arrangements. Hence, the palpable fact that some combinations of phonemes are impossible to articulate does not in itself invalidate the *a priori* statement which has just been made.

Nevertheless, empirical evidence does preclude the use of this *a priori* statement, for it would be accurately descriptive only if every language availed itself progressively of every possible legitimate short permutation before employing a larger permutation, a condition which is by no means the case. In English, for example, the long permutation *constitutionality* is a meaningful word while the shorter and equally pronounceable permutations *puv*, *za*, *ut* have no meaning. Hence, the one *a priori* statement which it seems possible to make about the length of words may be discarded at the outset.

Interesting light might be shed empirically upon the significance in the length of words if it were possible to make a list of all words in the active-passive vocabulary of an individual or of a speech-community to ascertain the actual number of different words representing each of the different degrees of length. But a list of this type for any single language is impossible. Dictionary lists are generally inadequate because of their inclusion of obsolescent and obsolete words, and because of their exclusion of highly useful neologisms. And it seems practically impossible ever to make a completely adequate list, even of the vocabulary of an individual person, because so many words exist in the passive vocabulary which are used rarely, if at all, in the stream of speech which is alone perceptible. Then, too, the active-passive vocabulary, whether of individuals or of speech-groups, differs so in size and content and varies so from time to time, that an attempt even to estimate merely the limits of a vocabulary at any time is largely a matter of guesswork.[1] Hence we are obliged at the very beginning of our investigation to restrict our attention exclusively to the objective evidence of the stream of speech itself which, during the entire course of our investigation, will be the sole source of our data.

Now, in so far as data are already available from the stream of speech, it seems reasonably clear that shorter words are distinctly more favored in usage than longer words. That is, however large the stock of short and long words may be, the evidence of language seems to indicate unequivocally that the larger a word is in length, the less likely it is to be used. To illustrate this point, the data gathered by F. W. Kaeding [2] from samplings of connected written German, totalling 10,910,777 words (or 20 million syllables) in length, are presented. Kaeding selected the syllable as the unit of length, and, in the following tabulation of his results, the left-hand column indicates the magnitude of each class of words as estimated by the number of syllables; the center column presents the number of occurrences (including repetitions) of words of each magnitude; and the column at the right notes the percentage of the occurrences of all the words (including repetitions) of each magnitude to the total number of words (10,910,777).

Number of Syllables in Word	Number of Occurrences (Including Repetitions) of Words	Percentage of the Whole
1	5,426,326	49.76%
2	3,156,448	28.94
3	1,410,494	12.93
4	646,971	5.93
5	187,738	1.72
6	54,436	.50
7	16,993	
8	5,038	
9	1,225	
10	461	
11	59	.22
12	35	
13	8	
14	2	
15	1	
	10,906,235*	100.00%

These figures indicate that in German there is a decided preference in usage for short words, and that the magnitude of words stands in an inverse (not necessarily proportionate) relationship to the number of occurrences (including repetitions) of all words possessing that magnitude.

Though these statistics from Kaeding seem clear for all occurrences of all words when arranged in classes according to differences in syllabic magnitude it provides no information about the number of different words in each class. We do not know from the statistics for example whether the

* Subsequently corrected by Kaeding [1] to 10,910,777.

five million odd occurrences of words of one syllable represent the single occurrence of that many different words, or that many different occurrences of a single word. While Kaeding gives enough additional information in his entire treatise for us to determine with reasonable accuracy the general tendencies involved, we shall in lieu of this Kaeding material (which may be consulted in the notes [1]) present the results of three separate investigations, one of Plautine Latin,[2] one of modern colloquial Chinese [3] (Peiping dialect), and one of English,[4] which are far more precise than the Kaeding material on this subject, and which are corroborated in their main tendencies by the data of the Kaeding material.

The material for the investigation of colloquial Chinese of Peiping consists of twenty different samplings of connected speech, each a thousand syllables long. The number of different words * occurring in these 20,000 Chinese syllables are arranged in the ensuing table (p. 26) according to the relative frequency of their occurrence. The left-hand column of the Chinese statistics gives the times of occurrences; the center column presents the number of words assignable to a given frequency of occurrence; and the right-hand column, in parentheses, indicates the number of words in each frequency grouped according to the number of syllables (designated by a superior number). Thus, of the 2046 Chinese words of single occurrences, 315 contained only one syllable, 1571 two syllables, etc.

In the investigation of the Latin of Plautus a different procedure was adopted. With all the words of four Plautine plays (*Aulularia, Mostellaria, Pseudolus,* and *Trinummus*) selected for material, the average number of syllables in each frequency category was computed (p. 27). The

---

* It is commonly asserted that Chinese is a monosyllabic language in the sense that Chinese words on the whole represent compounds of monosyllabic roots (e.g. English *cupboard*) some of which do not occur except in compounds. That Chinese is not monosyllabic in the sense that every Chinese word is a monosyllable, is clear from the tabulation.

respective averages are in parentheses at the right. Thus, the average number of syllables of all words occurring once was 3.23, of those occurring twice, 2.92, etc.

The third investigation was made by R. C. Eldridge of four samples of American newspaper English totalling 43,989 words in length and representing the occurrences of 6002 different words.* The figures in parentheses at the right (p. 28) of the two columns represent the average number of phonemes in each frequency category. For example, the average number of phonemes in all words occurring once in this investigation is 6.656; this figure was derived by dividing the sum total (i.e. 19,809) of all phonemes (estimated according to the phonemic system in use in Cambridge, Massachusetts) of all words occurring once, by the number of words occurring once (i.e. 2976).

Thus in the investigations of the three different languages, three different yet apparently equally valid units of length were employed: the morpheme in Chinese, the average number of syllables in Plautine Latin, and the average number of phonemes in American newspaper English. The difference in the unit of magnitude does not disguise the presence of the prevailing tendency which, as we shall now clearly see, is equally manifest in each of the three languages. From the evidence of these tables it is clear: (1) that the magnitude of words tends, on the whole, to stand in an inverse (not necessarily proportionate) relationship to the number of occurrences; and (2) that the number of different words (i.e. variety) seems to be ever larger as the frequency of occurrence becomes ever smaller. That is, a statistical

---

* This material was in part re-examined to determine as far as possible the degree of its accuracy. Instead of the figures given above it was found that the investigation represented 5995 different words (instead of 6002) which aggregated in their occurrences 43,990 (instead of 43,989). If all the steps in Eldridge's entire investigation were conducted with the remarkably high degree of accuracy as evidenced in this one instance, which is presumable, the investigation is eminently trustworthy. Regrettably it is, however, not entirely adequate for our purposes because it disregards the occurrences of all numerals and proper nouns.

CHINESE OF PEIPING

Number of Occurrences	Number of Words	Number of Words with their Syllables
1	2046	$(315^1\ \ 1571^2\ \ 144^3\ \ 14^4\ \ 1^5\ \ 1^6)$
2	494	$(110^1\ \ 358^2\ \ 23^3\ \ 3^4)$
3	216	$(\ 59^1\ \ 147^2\ \ 9^3\ \ 1^4)$
4	100	$(\ 24^1\ \ 73^2\ \ 3^3)$
5	99	$(\ 39^1\ \ 58^2\ \ 2^3)$
6	66	$(\ 24^1\ \ 41^2\ \ 1^3)$
7	41	$(\ 16^1\ \ 25^2)$
8	25	$(\ 10^1\ \ 14^2\ \ 1^3)$
9	30	$(\ 13^1\ \ 15^2\ \ 1^3\ \ 1^4)$
10	20	$(\ 13^1\ \ 7^2)$
11	25	$(\ 14^1\ \ 11^2)$
12	22	$(\ 15^1\ \ 7^2)$
13	10	$(\ 6^1\ \ 4^2)$
14	14	$(\ 7^1\ \ 7^2)$
15	13	$(\ 5^1\ \ 8^2)$
16	10	$(\ 4^1\ \ 5^2\ \ 1^4)$
17	10	$(\ 6^1\ \ 4^2)$
18	6	$(\ 2^1\ \ 4^2)$
19	5	$(\ 4^1\ \ 1^2)$
20	5	$(\ 5^2)$
21	4	$(\ 3^1\ \ 1^2)$
22	2	$(\ 2^1)$
23	5	$(\ 4^1\ \ 1^3)$
26	3	$(\ 2^1\ \ 1^2)$
28	4	$(\ 3^1\ \ 1^2)$
29	4	$(\ 1^1\ \ 3^2)$
30	6	$(\ 4^1\ \ 2^2)$
32	6	$(\ 4^1\ \ 2^2)$
33	2	$(\ 1^1\ \ 1^2)$
34	1	$(\ 1^1)$
35	1	$(\ 1^1)$
36	1	$(\ 1^1)$
37	1	$(\ 1^2)$
38	1	$(\ 1^2)$
41	4	$(\ 4^1)$
43	2	$(\ 2^2)$
44	2	$(\ 1^1\ \ 1^2)$
45	3	$(\ 1^1\ \ 2^2)$
46	1	$(\ 1^1)$
47	2	$(\ 2^1)$
50	1	$(\ 1^2)$
52	1	$(\ 1^1)$
55	2	$(\ 2^1)$
57	1	$(\ 1^1)$
58	1	$(\ 1^1)$
60	1	$(\ 1^1)$
66	2	$(\ 1^1\ \ 1^2)$
68	1	$(\ 1^1)$
72	1	$(\ 1^1)$
73	1	$(\ 1^1)$
75	1	$(\ 1^1)$
78	1	$(\ 1^1)$
81	1	$(\ 1^1)$
83	1	$(\ 1^1)$
101	2	$(\ 2^1)$
102–905	12	$(\ 12^1)$
13,248	3,332	

LATIN OF PLAUTUS

Number of Occurrences	Number of Words	Average Number of Syllables	Number of Occurrences	Number of Words	Average Number of Syllables
1	5429	(3.23)	31	8	
2	1198	(2.92)	32	3	
3	492	(2.77)	33	4	
4	299	(2.05)	34	6	(2.05)
5	161	(2.60)	35	3	
6	126	(2.53)	36	5	
7	87	(2.39)	37	7	
8	69	(2.44)	38	2	
9	54	(2.35)	39	4	
10	43	(2.32)	40	3	
11	44	(2.29)	41	3	
12	36	(2.30)	43	4	
13	33	(2.30)	44	1	
14	31	(2.09)	45	1	
15	13	(2.07)	46	1	
16	25	(2.40)	47	3	(1.70)
17	21	(2.09)	48	1	
18	21	(2.04)	49	1	
19	11	(2.18)	50	2	
20	15		51	2	
21	10		53	4	
22	8	(2.08)	54	1	
23	8		55	1	
24	9		56	2	
25	11		58	1	
26	7		61	3	
27	9	(2.00)	62–514	71	(1.40)
28	12		33,094	8,437	
29	4				
30	4				

relationship has been established between high frequency, small variety, and shortness in length, a relationship which is presumably valid for language in general.

AMERICAN NEWSPAPER ENGLISH
(According to R. C. Eldridge)

Number of Occurrences	Number of Words	Average Number of Phonemes	Number of Occurrences	Number of Words	Average Number of Phonemes
1	2976	(6.656)	31	6	
2	1079	(6.151)	32	4	
3	516	(6.015)	33	6	
4	294	(6.081)	34	2	
5	212	(5.589)	35	5	
6	151	(5.768)	36	3	
7	105	(5.333)	37	2	
8	84	(5.654)	39	2	
9	86	(5.174)	40	4	
10	45	(5.377)	41	1	(3.903)
11	40	(4.825)	42	7	
12	37	(5.459)	43	1	
13	25	(5.560)	44	4	
14	28	(5.00)	45	1	
15	26	(4.807)	46	2	
16	17	(5.058)	47	5	
17	18	(4.166)	48	1	
18	10	(6.100)	49	3	
19	15	(4.733)	50	3	
20	16	(4.687)	51	1	
21	13		52	3	
22	11		54	1	
23	6		55	1	(3.333)
24	8		56	1	
25	6		58	2	
26	10	(3.455)	60	1	
27	9		61–4290	71	(2.666)
28	6				
29	5				
30	4				

2. THE QUESTION OF A CAUSAL RELATIONSHIP BETWEEN THE LENGTH AND FREQUENCY OF WORDS

The question now arises as to the nature of a possible causal relationship between the length of a word on the one hand, and the relative frequency of its occurrence on the other. If there is a causal relationship between relative frequency and length which accounts for the statistical relationship just discussed, there are only two possible explanations: (1) the length is a cause of the frequency of usage, or (2) the frequency of usage is a cause of the length. That is, for example, the shortness of, say, the most frequent English word, *the*, is either (1) a cause of its high frequency of occurrence, or (2) a result of its high frequency of occurrence.

It seems that on the whole the comparative length or shortness of a word cannot be the cause of its relative frequency of occurrence because a speaker selects his words not according to their lengths, but solely according to the meanings of the words and the ideas he wishes to convey. Occasionally, of course, out of respect for the youth, inexperience, or low mentality of a particular auditor, a given speaker may seek to avoid long or unusual words. On the other hand, speakers are sometimes found who seem to prefer the longer and more unusual words, even when shorter more usual words are available. Yet in neither case are the preferences for brevity or length followed without respect for the meanings of the words which are selected. Hence there seems no cogent reason for believing that the small magnitude of a word is the cause of its high frequency of usage.

There are, however, copious examples of a decrease in the magnitude of a word which results, as far as one can judge, solely from an increase in the relative frequency of its occurrence, as estimated either from the speech of an individual in which the shortening may occur, or in the language of a minor group, or of the major speech-group. Shortenings of this sort may be termed abbreviations; these are of two types: (1) truncations, (2) substitutions, whether permanent or temporary. A consideration of these two types of abbreviation reveals that they account for practically the entire statistical relationship between magnitude and frequency, and suggest unmistakably that high frequency is the cause of small magnitude.

a. Abbreviatory Acts of Truncation

That truncation occurs primarily with frequent long words, presumably for the purpose of saving time and effort, is a proposition which is too self-evident to require demonstration. When any object, act, relationship, or quality becomes so frequent in the experience of a speech-community that the word that names it develops a high frequency of occurrence in the stream of speech, the word will probably become truncated. A development of this sort is reflected in the histories of the words *movies, talkies, gas,* which are shortenings of *moving pictures, talking pictures, gasoline.* The shortenings result from frequent usage, a frequency due to the rapid increase of frequency of movies, talkies, and gas in our daily experience.* Longer words than these, such as *constitutionality, quintessentially, idiosyncrasy* are not truncated because they are not frequently used.

There are, however, two aspects of truncation which deserve mention at this time: first, the risk of a possible homonymy arising from truncation, and second, the influence of small speech-groups upon truncations within the larger speech-community. Though the two are essentially unrelated phenomena, yet the influence of the small speech-group in minimizing the risk of homonymy, which may in turn conceivably restrain truncation, justifies their being treated together.

That the truncation of a longer word may result in an abbreviation which is homonymous with another word already in the language is not inconceivable nor will it of necessity lead to a confusion of meaning. One may safely assume that all languages have homonyms, such as English

* Frequently used proper names are very susceptible to truncation (e.g. *Whitsuntide* from *Whitsunday-tide* or *Dorchester* from *Dornwara-ceaster*). The truncation of place-names is especially interesting because often the middle member of the composition is truncated (see Otto Ritter, *Vermischte Beiträge zur englischen Sprachgeschichte,* Halle: Niemeyer, 1922, pp. 88–90).

hole and *whole*, *hear* and *here*, which are of identical phonetic form but of different usage. The differences in usages seem in most instances sufficient to obviate any serious confusion in meaning.

But though differences in syntactical usage are frequently sufficient to keep separate and distinct two words of like form and different meaning, this is not always the case. The simple statement 'I want some gas,' could in itself signify a desire for illuminating gas, for gasoline, or for 'laughing gas' (nitrous oxide). Another instance is the two homonyms *hypo*, both of which are the results of truncations: *hypo* may be a truncation of a *hypodermic injection* (*A* below), or it may be an abbreviation of '*hyposulphite of soda*' (*B* below), a name erroneously applied by early photographers to a well-known fixative (hypothiosulphate of soda). Both *hypos* (*A* and *B*) are of the same part of speech; in real life a confusion of the two might easily be disastrous. To photographers *hypo* means one thing, to physicians and trained nurses another, to perhaps the majority of English speakers it is without any meaning at all. If we were examining the vocabularies of photographers, physicians, and the general public in respect to *hypo*, we should find at least one salient difference in usage. Photographers use *hypo* (*B*) in their speech presumably much more frequently than *hypo* (*A*); physicians use *hypo* (*A*) more frequently than *hypo* (*B*); the public uses either rarely if ever. A patient suffering from heavy metal-poisoning would be more likely to receive a 'hypo of hypothiosulphate of soda' than a 'hypodermic injection of hypo' although both amount to the same thing; he certainly would not receive a 'hypo of hypo.'

From the above we may perhaps conclude that a longer word may be truncated if it enjoys a high relative frequency, not only if this high relative frequency obtains throughout the entire speech-community (*movies* for *moving pictures*) but if its use (as *hypo A* and *B*) is frequent within any special group inside this large and inclusive speech-community. To the photographer, *hypo* means 'fixative' and he very likely calls a *hypodermic injection* by its full name. At a filling station, *gas* means 'gasoline'; at a plant producing illuminating gas, *gas* means 'illuminating gas'; in a dental clinic, *gas* means 'nitrous oxide.' And the mutually exclusive nature of many groups tend to minimize the danger of confusion which might otherwise arise from homonymy resulting from truncations.

The influence of the special group also doubtless explains the short form of many words of comparatively rare occurrence in the general stream of speech, such as English *volt*, a unit of measure of electricity. Though rare in the general speech it is doubtless of high frequency in the group of electricians and physicists by whom the word *volt* was introduced into the general stream of usage.[1] To understand its short form we must remember its high frequency in this special group in which the impetus toward brevity took place. Though a speech-community is a unit group in itself, it is also a complex of many different minor social, political, professional, economic, and even geographical groups, in each one of which there are deviations in relative frequency of usage of words from that found in the general vocabulary of the total speech community. Not only do truncations of words occur and persist in these minor groups, as we have seen in *hypo A* and *B*, but a truncated form originating in a minor group may become adopted into the language of the large community. Viewed from the average language of the larger group, the rare word appears to be unjustifiably short; yet viewed from the special group where the word is used, the word has a frequency sufficiently high to justify its shortness. The influence of minor groups, then, as we shall repeatedly observe, must be borne in mind as a possible modifying factor in the behavior of the stream of speech of the general speech-community.

Occasionally homonyms of identical usage but of decidedly

different meaning may arise through some process of linguistic change, either in a special group or in the whole speech community. What then? An example of this is the Shakespearean *let* 'to hinder' and *let* 'to allow' — words of the same part of speech and of almost opposite meaning. Today the verb *let* 'to hinder' is obsolete. On the ground of being less frequent and on occasion susceptible to confusion with *let* 'to allow,' *let* 'to hinder' was presumably dropped in favor of the synonymous, unambiguous, equally familiar, and incidentally longer *hinder*.

In concluding our brief discussion of the phenomenon of truncation, it may be said that abbreviatory acts of truncation seem to arise on the whole as a consequence of the increased frequency in usage of a word, whether within the entire speech-community or within certain minor groups thereof. The accumulated effects of abbreviatory acts of truncation during the long periods of years in which language has slowly evolved are probably responsible for the shortness of many of the frequently occurring words in speech today, and responsible, as we shall presently see, in many other ways than that which we have just observed.

b. Abbreviatory Acts of Substitution

The substitution of shorter words for longer words, such as *car* for *automobile*, or *it* for *Christmas*, has much the same net effect as truncation on the magnitude of words, and doubtless contributes extensively to the preponderance in usage of short frequent words in the stream of speech. The abbreviatory acts of substitution fall into two types: (1) the more durable substitutions which often involve a change in meaning, and (2) the temporary substitutions which we shall see are largely contextual in nature.

i. *Durable Abbreviatory Substitutions*

Durable abbreviatory substitutions may occur throughout the entire speech-community (e.g. *car* for *automobile*) or within minor groups within the entire speech-community (e.g. *juice* for *electricity*, *soup* for *nitroglycerine*, *spuds* for *potatoes*). Though one effect of substitutions of this sort may be a more or less permanent renaming (see page 274), we are now chiefly interested in the effect of such substitutions on the frequency-magnitude relationship of words in the stream of speech. If it cannot be directly proved by means of statistics that abbreviatory acts of substitution are the direct result of high relative frequency of occurrence, we can nevertheless apprehend the existence and nature of this causal relationship between high frequency and abbreviatory substitution by viewing typical examples of abbreviatory substitution against the general background of the statistics already presented.

The influence of high frequency upon the more durable substitutions is most readily observable in the substitution of a single word for a complex of words. For example, let us take the two complexes, *sweet potatoes* and *Irish potatoes*, which designate two distinctly different vegetables familiar both in the northern and southern states of the United States. In the northern states, sweet potatoes are called *sweet potatoes*, but Irish potatoes simply *potatoes*; in the southern states the reverse is true. In the South *potatoes*, 'sweet potatoes,' has been dialectally and colloquially abbreviated to *taters*; in the North *potatoes*, 'Irish potatoes,' has been similarly abbreviated to *spuds*. In the South, the sweet potato is a far more familiar article of diet than the Irish potato, and being more familiar in experience is undoubtedly more frequent in the stream of speech; in the North, the reverse is true. Surely in these two instances where all significant factors are constant except differences in frequency, one cannot but believe that the preponderant frequency in each case has led to the shortening.

In the two transitive phrases, *strike with the chin* and *strike with the foot*, there is no difference in the degree of complexity of verbal arrangement or of clarity of meaning of the concept. Yet is not the greater frequency of the second (*to strike with the foot*) indicated by the very existence of a convenient abbreviatory substitute, *kick*, which is lacking to the first? In the two concepts, *brother* and *uncle's second wife's tenth child by her first marriage*, we find the first described by one word, the second by nine. The difference in frequency of these concepts in the normal stream of speech seems alone to account for the differences in length; were the second as frequent in occurrence as the first, we should doubtless possess a single word for it — an abbreviatory substitution caused by high frequency. Though the longer example seems to be an "inherently more complex" concept than that of the single word, yet what we may term "inherent complexity of the concept" does not seem alone capable of preserving the speech-element from abbreviation; few things are more complex in nature than electricity, yet we not only have a single word for the total phenomenon but even a colloquial substitute, *juice*, a substitution presumably made because of the high frequency of usage of the concept without any respect for its complexity whatsoever.

In the minor speech-groups within the large speech-community, abbreviatory substitutions occur more frequently; witness the technical jargon and slang of the various professional, social, political, and commercial groups.[1] To the outsider the most striking aspects of the jargon, aside from its picturesqueness, are the shortness of the clique-terms, the frequency of their usage, and the unusualness of the meanings which they convey. But to the insider, the meanings are familiar and the high frequency and short length unnoticed.

It does not, of course, follow that every substitution constitutes a shortening, or that the primary conscious impulse thereto is always one of time-saving. Substitutions may be made for the sake of increased vividness of expression,[1] or of increased articulatedness of meaning. Nevertheless the frequent use of slang and technical terms, words on the whole apparently more convenient than standard language, takes place because it saves time in expression; slang and technical terms save time because these terms represent, by and large, abbreviatory substitutions for frequent concepts which, if fully articulated in standard language, would be excessively long.

The sole point of present concern, however, is not a consideration of the question of change in meaning, which will be treated later (see page 274), nor of the influence of the group upon the speech of the whole community, but rather the fact that many substitutions are shortenings resulting from high frequency. Until it can be shown that lengthenings occur from frequency or shortenings from rarity, we may reasonably presume: (1) that, where frequency and abbreviatory substitution are connected, the frequency is the cause of the abbreviatory substitution; and (2) that the accumulated effect of acts of durable abbreviatory substitution during the evolution of a language is in part reflected by the frequency-magnitude relationship of words today.

ii. *Temporary Abbreviatory Substitutions*

Substitutions of the second type, such as a pronoun for a noun (e.g. *it* for *Christmas*) or a simple adverb for an adverbial phrase, are likewise the result of high frequency. But they differ from the first (more durable) type of substitutions in one salient respect: the more durable substitutions of the first type reflect a general increase in the average relative frequency of a concept within the entire speech-

community or within a minor group, while the temporary or
transitory substitutions of the second type reflect merely a
temporary increase in relative frequency resulting from the
topic of conversation.   Thus in the substitution of *car* for
automobile, there is a high average frequency of occurrence
of the concept; but in the substitution of *it* for *Christmas*
in the sentence 'Christmas is a great day, *it* comes but once
a year,' the substitution is the result of only a high temporary
frequency which is occasioned by the nature of the context.
Similarly with the substitution *there* for *down in Florida* in
the sentence 'They are *down in Florida* because it is so warm
there.' If substitutions of the first type are intimately connected with the phenomena of naming, substitutions of the
second type will be found closely bound up with questions of
syntax and style (see Chapter V).

Likewise with temporary abbreviatory substitutions one
cannot prove statistically that frequency is the inevitable
cause of all substitutions of shorter forms.   Nevertheless,
our feelings assure us that the substitutions of *it* for *Christmas* and *there* for *down in Florida* in the above typical sentences were made to avoid a too great repetitiveness or frequency of *Christmas* and *down in Florida* within a short
period of time.   The unusual frequency of occurrence of
the concepts precipitated the substitutions which were in
fact shorter words.   It is unquestionably true that from the
point of view of grammar, either the chief or a major function of many of these shorter words, such as pronouns, adverbs, and auxiliaries, is to act as substitutes.   But for our
present purposes it is sufficient to observe that their use
may generally be viewed as abbreviatory substitutions
which result from a high though transitory frequency of
occurrence of the concepts for which they stand.

3. CONCLUSION: THE LAW OF ABBREVIATION

In view of the evidence of the stream of speech we may say that the length of a word tends to bear an inverse relationship * to its relative frequency; and in view of the influence of high frequency on the shortenings from truncation and from durable and temporary abbreviatory substitution, it seems a plausible deduction that, as the relative frequency of a word increases, it tends to diminish in magnitude. This tendency of a decreasing magnitude to result from an increase in relative frequency, may be tentatively named the Law of Abbreviation.

The law of abbreviation seems to reflect on the one hand an impulse in language toward the maintenance of an equilibrium between length and frequency, and on the other hand an underlying law of economy as the *causa causans* of this impulse toward equilibrium. That the maintenance of equilibrium is involved is clear from the very nature of the statistics. That economy, or the saving of time and effort, is probably the underlying cause of the maintenance of equilibrium is apparent from the fact that the purpose of all truncations and transitory contextual substitutions is almost admittedly the saving of time and effort. If one cannot argue with complete certainty in favor of economy as the sole cause of the more durable abbreviatory substitutions, one cannot readily advance any other factor as a general precipitating cause, nor escape the inference that the result of durable abbreviatory substitutions is frequently an economy of time and effort, even though this may conceivably not be the purpose. Unquestionably other factors are involved in the general phenomena of abbreviation, some of which will be subsequently discussed in considerable detail as they manifest themselves in the typical

* Not necessarily *proportionate*; possibly some non-linear mathematical function.

behavior of the phoneme, morpheme, and sentence. And from these several angles we shall also observe that the law of abbreviation is by no means restricted in its scope to the length of words.

Part II

The Behavior of Words

I. The Frequency Distribution of Words in the Stream of Speech

Manifestations of a tendency toward the maintenance of equilibrium in the behavior of words is not restricted to the relationship between their length and the frequency of their usage; the orderliness of the frequency distribution of the words themselves in the stream of speech suggests an analogous tendency toward the maintenance of equilibrium. But before turning to the evidence in support of this statement, let us momentarily digress in order to define a certain aspect of the term *word*.

a. The Word and the Lexical Unit

In the statistical analyses of Chinese, English, and Plautine Latin (pages 26 f.) and in the Kaeding analysis of German (pages 22 f.) the unit into which the streams of speech were anatomized was the word. For example, in English the word *child* may be considered as one word, *children* as another, *give* a third, *gives* a fourth, *given* a fifth, — five different words for each of which the respective frequencies in a given sample may be established. On the other hand, a dictionary compiled on the basis of this evidence would view *child* and *children* as but two forms of one word, and *give, gives, given* as but three forms of one word;

the five different words above would appear in the dictionary list under the word *child* and the word *give*, — two
words.   The sole difference between these two uses of the
term *word* is that the former considers only a word *in its
fully inflected form* as a unit of speech, whereas the lexicog-
raphers are inclined to take the word either in its non-
inflected form, or in some one arbitrarily selected and tradi-
tionally maintained inflected form (e.g. in German, the
nominative singular for substantives, the infinitive for
verbs) as the unit.   For the sake of keeping these two units
distinct, let us henceforth call the lexicographer's unit the
lexical unit and the other unit, that is, the word in its fully
inflected form, the *word*.   Although both terms are popu-
larly considered *words*, slight reflection on the subject will
convince the reader that a statistical analysis of the stream
of speech into fully inflected *words* and into *lexical units* will
yield significantly different quantitative results, as we have
just seen in the case of *child, children, give, gives, given*.

In the present investigation the term *word* will always
designate a word in its fully inflected form as it occurs in
the stream of speech.   In the rare instances where the sense
of *lexical unit* is intended (not until Chapter V) this unusual
sense of the term will be plainly stated.   The Kaeding,
Chinese, Plautine investigations and the Eldridge investigation of English are each an analysis of the frequency distribution of words in fully inflected form, i.e. *words* and not
lexical units.

b. The Orderliness of the Distribution of Words; the $ab^2 = k$ *relationship*

Earlier in this chapter (pages 26–28) we observed that in
the streams of speech of the colloquial dialect of Peiping,
and of Plautine Latin, and of American newspaper English,
a few words occur with very high frequency while many

words occur but rarely. If we refer again to the data of these languages in the tables (pages 26–28), we find the strikingly evident phenomenon that, as the number of occurrences increases, the number of different words possessing that number of occurrences decreases. Yet the significant feature in the diminution of variety which attends upon an increase in frequency of usage is the orderliness with which the one decreases as the other increases — an orderliness which includes an overwhelming majority of the total number of different words of the vocabulary used in these samplings, especially in the less frequent range.

To objectify the orderliness of this distribution for the less frequent range we shall plot upon double logarithmic graph paper the words which occur from 1 to 45 times inclusive for Chinese, which occur from 1 to 45 times inclusive in English, and from 1 to 45 times inclusive in Plautine Latin. Plates I, II, and III are the graphical representations of these quantities. To elucidate in reference to these graphs the manner in which the quantities were plotted, let us take the frequency distribution of English words as a typical example. In Eldridge's English samplings, 2976 words were found to occur but once; this point is located at 2976 on the abscissa (number of words) and 1 on the ordinate (number of occurrences). Similarly, 1079 words occur twice; this point is located at 1079 on the abscissa and 2 on the ordinate. The 516 words which occur 3 times are represented by the point 516 on the abscissa and 3 on the ordinate. And so on for English, and similarly for Latin and Chinese. The reader is reminded that both the abscissae and the ordinates are on the logarithmic scale.

Now, the line drawn approximately through the center of the points in each chart represents in each case the formula $ab^2 = k$ in which a represents the number of words of a given occurrence and b the number of occurrences. That is, the product of the number of words of a given occurrence, when multiplied by the square of their occurrences, remains constant for the great majority of the different words of the vocabulary in use, though not for those of highest frequency. To be more specific, the $ab^2 = k$ relationship includes: in Chinese, 97.7% of the total number of different words (*vocabulary*) used, and 59.3% of the entire *bulk* of the occurrences; in English 98% of the *vocabulary* and 42.4% of the *bulk* of occurrences; in Latin, 99% of the *vocabulary* and 62.5% of the *bulk*.

It is apparent in the chart for English that the words of single occurrence which total only 2976 fall considerably short (by approximately 1700) of the point indicated by the formula. The probable explanation of this irregularity is that Eldridge did not include the occurrences of numerals and proper names (quite legitimate words) which in the newspaper English from which he selected his material would have added appreciably to the number of words occurring with extreme rarity.

The few enormously frequent words of each list which were not charted do not follow this $ab^2 = k$ relationship. As can be seen from the tables on pages 26–28, these words of highest frequency are distributed close to, if not upon, 1 on the abscissa; the most frequent in Chinese being at 905 on the ordinate and at 1 on the abscissa; the most frequent in English being 4290 on the ordinate and 1 on the abscissa; the most frequent in Latin at 514 and 1, respectively. If one extended the diagonal line on each chart to include these words of great frequency, the line would bend up sharply. Hence the $ab^2 = k$ relationship is valid only for the less frequently occurring words which, however, represent the greater part of the vocabulary in use, though not always a great majority of the occurrences. Nevertheless, the upper portion of this curve, which is not plotted, is equally interesting in understanding and measuring the dynamics of expression, and we shall return to it at a more opportune time in Chapter V.

It is perhaps worth pointing out that the $ab^2 = k$ relationship which appears valid for the frequency distribution of the less frequent words would demand fractional words when applied to the speech-elements of highest occurrence, such as *the* in English. To elucidate this point, the word *the* occurs 4290 times in Eldridge's material and if placed in the formula we should have $a(4290)^2 = k$. Now, the size of k, as deduced from the data of our curve of English words, is approximately 4200; hence the formula can be expanded to $a(4290)^2 = 4200$. The quantity, a, then, which represents the number of words occurring 4290 times would be $\dfrac{4200}{(4290)^2}$; that is, *the*, in English would represent .000025 of a word — a very absurd statement no matter how a word is defined. To avoid the use of such a concept as 25 millionths of a word, let us simply say that our formula, $ab^2 = k$, is apparently valid only for words in the lower range of frequency, and remember that these words where the formula is valid represent very close to 100 per cent of the words of a vocabulary in use in the stream of speech.

One has the feeling that the exponent of b may well differ with differences in the size of the bulk examined. It seems scarcely credible that a frequency distribution within a bulk of 1000 words, as within a bulk of one hundred million words, would invariably reveal the exponent [2] for b. With smaller bulks one would expect a smaller repetitiveness and hence a larger exponent than the square; by plotting Eldridge's lists [1] Nos. 1, 2, 3, and 4 which represent bulks of 13,825; 11,538; 9,608; and 9,018, respectively, and which together constitute list No. 5 [2] (bulk 43,989 words), which is plotted on Plate II, we obtain the following exponents: 2.15, 2.05, 2.1, and 2.15, respectively, which are indeed larger than the square.* With an enormous bulk of one hundred million, one would expect to find that words of

---

* But only negligibly so at best, nor are these differences from the square necessarily significant in this case because the data omit consideration of proper names and numerals which might seriously change the exponents.

very rare occurrence (say occurrences of 1, 2, and 3) would have been considerably reduced in number. In brief, one anticipates *a priori* that a point will be reached in extending the size of the bulk where new additions of samplings will add proportionately far more to the repetitions than to the new words.[1]

The problem of the relationship of the exponent of b to the total bulk merits extensive statistical investigation for the light it may shed on the psychology of behavior. It is conceivable that an exponent of b which is larger than the square may represent the frequency distribution in bulks that may be viewed as incomplete discussions of a topic. It is also conceivable that bulks extending into millions upon millions of words of colloquial discourse may be so rich in neologisms and slang expressions — coined on the spur of the moment and adding greatly to the words of very rare occurrence — that the $ab^2 = k$ relationship might possibly still be valid. On these two points, further statistical investigations can alone shed light.

c. The Standard Curve of English

There is, however, another method of viewing and plotting these frequency distributions which is less dependent upon the size of the bulk and which reveals an additional feature. As suggested by a friend, one can consider the words of a vocabulary as ranked in the order of their frequency, e.g. the first most frequent word, the second most frequent, the third most frequent, the five-hundredth most frequent, the thousandth most frequent, etc. We can indicate on the abscissa of a double logarithmic chart the number of the word in the series and on the ordinate its frequency. Thus, in Eldridge's English count, the most frequent word occurs 4290 times, and is represented by 1 on the abscissa and 4290 on the ordinate; the second word is

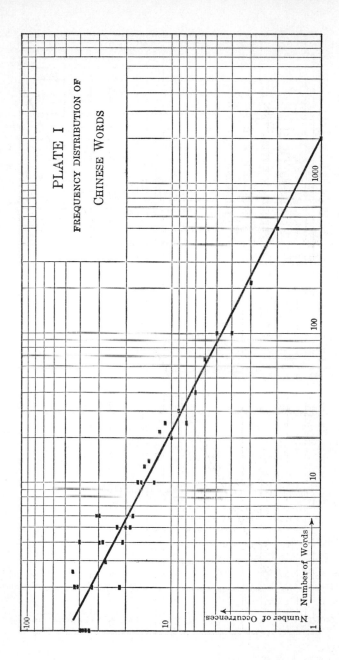

PLATE I

FREQUENCY DISTRIBUTION OF

CHINESE WORDS

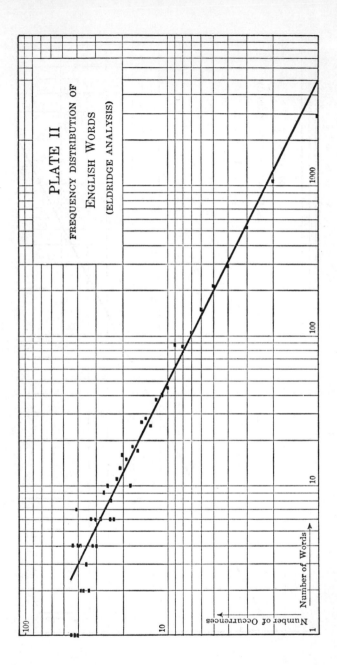

PLATE II

FREQUENCY DISTRIBUTION OF
ENGLISH WORDS
(ELDRIDGE ANALYSIS)

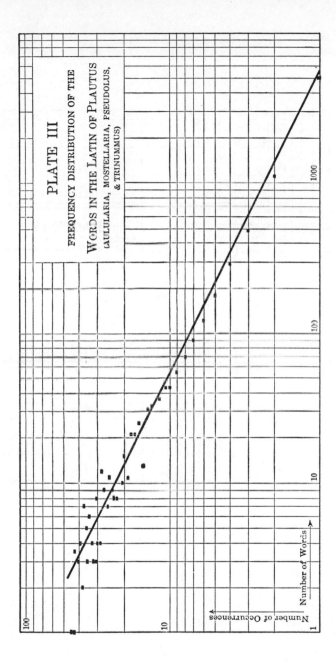

PLATE III

FREQUENCY DISTRIBUTION OF THE

WORDS IN THE LATIN OF PLAUTUS

(AULULARIA, MOSTELLARIA, PSEUDOLUS, & TRINUMMUS)

Number of Words →

← Number of Occurrences

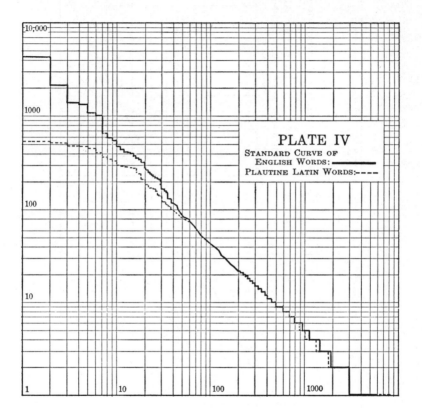

PLATE IV

STANDARD CURVE OF
ENGLISH WORDS: ──────
PLAUTINE LATIN WORDS:─ ─ ─

2122 and is represented by 2 on the abscissa and 2122 on the ordinate. The words from 239 through 253 each occur 19 times, hence from 239 through 253 on the abscissa the ordinate is 19, and this group of words of like frequency would appear on the chart as a straight line running at 19 on the ordinate from 239 to 253 on the abscissa. For illustration, the English count of Eldridge and the count of Plautine Latin are plotted in this fashion on the graph of Plate IV; English is represented by the heavy line, and Latin by the light broken line.

Now, when the words of a vocabulary are ranked in the order of frequency, the average 'wave lengths' * (the reciprocals of the frequency) are approximately successive multiples of ten; that is, the wave length of the nth word is 10 n. For example (on the basis of Eldridge's table of 43,989 English words)

the first	word has a 'wave length' of	10 (actually	10.2)
" second	" " " " " "	20 ("	20.4)
" third	" " " " " "	30 ("	32.1)
" tenth	" " " " " "	100 ("	91.)
" twentieth	" " " " " "	200 ("	163.)
" fortieth	" " " " " "	400 ("	382.6)
" 100th	" " " " " "	1000 ("	1047.6)
" 195th	" " " " " "	1950 ("	2000.)
" 500th	" " " " " "	5000 ("	4888.88)
" 920th	" " " " " "	9200 ("	8800.)
" 1950th	" " " " " "	19500 ("	22000.)
" 3000th	" " " " " "	30000 ("	43989.)

The latter figures in this list are calculated on the first word of a given frequency; e.g. the words in the series from 920 to 1130 (the 920th to the 1130th words) each have the same frequency of occurrence (i.e. five times each) and 920

---

* The 'wave length' of a word is the average number of words occurring between its average occurrences. Being highly variable and at best only an approximation, this 'wave length' is not to be confused with the wave lengths of physics.

is taken as the representative of this group. If we recalculate from the 200th word on, selecting from the graph the middle of a given frequency series instead of the first word of the series, we have in place of the 195th word, the 199th word; or, in tabulation: *

the	199th word has a	'wave length' of	1990	(actually	2000	)
"	530th	" " " " " "	5300	("	4888.8)	
"	1000th	" " " " " "	10000	("	8800.	)
"	2400th	" " " " " "	24000	("	22000.	)
"	4300th	" " " " " "	43000	("	43989.	)

In saying that the 'wave length' of the nth word is 10 n we are speaking in terms of a harmonic series; hence, in this sense, English is a harmonic language nearly over its whole extent. Plautine Latin is harmonic up to about its 40 most frequent words, i.e. the point on the graph where the dotted line bends away from the English to the left. If one plots similarly the frequencies for the Chinese of Peiping, one obtains a line falling between Latin and English in the upper ranges, but more nearly approaching English than Latin.

One value of this method of plotting is that the average 'wave lengths' of the most frequent words remain approximately the same regardless of the extent of the samplings, provided of course that a sampling is taken of sufficient length and variety (say, ten thousand words) to be statistically significant. Thus the average interval between occurrences of the most frequent word will be approximately the same whether one counts 5000 or 10,000, 100,000 or ten million words of connected English speech, that is, approxi-

---

* By the aid of standard deviations computed for the various words in a series of equal frequency selected as representatives of the series in which they occur, it would probably be possible to determine which element (e.g. the first, middle, or last) represents on the whole the smallest deviation throughout. But for significant information on this point the Eldridge material is not sufficiently accurate (see page 42).

mately 10.* Of course as one proceeds to the more rarely occurring words in the frequency-list, there will be a proportionately greater randomness in the occurrence of a given word and accordingly a greater variability in the length of the interval between occurrences. Nevertheless, as we saw from Plate I–IV, it is in the frequency distribution of the rarer words that we find the closest approximation to the $ab^2 = k$ relationship.

The chief value of the 'wave length' method of viewing a language is that it provides Dynamic Philology with *a standard curve of distribution* in reference to which the frequency distribution of any other language can be described. If the curve of the frequency distribution of a given language conforms at any point with the standard harmonic curve or if it deviates at any point either slightly or seriously above or below, these facts may shed welcome light on significant factors in the structure of the language. Thus the deviation of the most frequent words of Latin below the standard curve of English may well be connected with the greater degree of inflection of Latin (see Chapter V) or with the facts that Eldridge's count was based on written prose while the Plautine count was based on verse to be declaimed. These suggested problems merit future investigation.

d. Equilibrium in the Distribution of Words

The high degree of orderliness of the distribution of words in the stream of speech points unmistakably to a tendency to maintain an equilibrium in the stream of speech

---

* For example, Eldridge's list No. 1 (page 22) represents a total bulk of 13,825 words; list No. 2 (page 30) a total bulk of 11,538 words; list No. 3 (page 37) a total bulk of 9608 words; list No. 4 (page 43) a total bulk of 9018 words. In these four lists the most frequent word (*the*) has the following 'wave length' (i.e. bulk divided by frequency) respectively: 10.8; 9.2; 10.6; 10.6.

between frequency on the one hand and what may tentatively be termed variety on the other.

Perhaps the most interesting feature of this high degree of orderliness in the distribution of words in the stream of speech is this: we select and arrange our words according to their meanings with little or no conscious reference to the relative frequency of occurrence of those words in the stream of speech, yet we find that words thus selected and arranged have a frequency distribution of great orderliness which for a large portion of the curve seems to be constant for language in general. The question arises as to the nature of meaning or meanings which leads automatically to this orderly frequency distribution. Whether this question can ever be completely solved quantitatively is probably doubtful, for meaning or meanings do not lend themselves to quantitative measurement. Yet, by the isolation of other factors which can be measured, we may gain a considerable insight into the nature of meaning, and perhaps finally apprehend something of its nature and behavior.

III

THE FORM AND BEHAVIOR
OF PHONEMES

THE purpose of the present chapter in our study is to investigate the relationship between the form of a phoneme and the relative frequency of its occurrence. In the course of the investigation we shall obtain abundant evidence in support of the following conclusions: (1) that there exists an equilibrium between the magnitude or degree of complexity of a phoneme and the relative frequency of its occurrence, in the sense that the magnitude or degree of complexity of a phoneme bears an inverse * relationship to the relative frequency of its occurrence; (2) that, by means of a process partly analogous to the process of abbreviatory truncation in words (see page 30 ff.), the phonemic system of a language is constantly striving to maintain this state of equilibrium; (3) that the preservation of this equilibrium is the probable cause of phonetic changes which lead to dialect cleavages resulting in new dialects and, ultimately, new languages.

For greater clarity of exposition the material of this chapter will be presented in two parts which will differ primarily in point of view. In Part I we shall study the various phenomena of the phoneme primarily as they appear in a cross-section of the stream of speech, that is, in a steady state. In Part II we shall study the various phenomena of the phoneme primarily as they appear in the stream of speech itself. From this latter point of view which is possible only because of the findings obtained from the former point of view, we shall gain considerable insight into the dynamics of the phoneme as revealed by its form and behavior.

---

* Not necessarily *proportionate*, possibly some nonlinear mathematical function.

PART I

EQUILIBRIUM OR STEADY STATE
IN A PHONEMIC SYSTEM

I. THE SPEECH-SYMBOL, THE SPEECH-
SOUND, AND THE PHONEME

Before embarking upon our investigation of the dynamics of phonemes, it is well to anticipate a possible confusion by defining in advance the three different terms which will be employed in the course of our ensuing investigation: the *speech-symbol*,[1] the *speech-sound*,[2] and the *phoneme*.[3] Since language consists both of speech-sounds and phonemes, and, when written, is represented by speech-symbols, these three terms will refer to practically identical phenomena in the many instances when we view a record of the stream of speech instead of the vocal stream of speech itself. For example, the record of an utterance of the English word *sit* may be viewed as consisting of three speech-symbols, and of three speech-sounds, and of what we shall later describe as three phonemes: in each case an *s*, a short *i* and a *t*. Yet in many cases of recorded language these three are not the same, as we shall presently see, nor in the case of merely spoken language do speech-sound and phoneme always refer to identical phenomena. In elucidating the significant differences between the three terms whose usage must be unambiguous in all discussions of the pertinent phenomena in language, we shall first discuss cursorily the general problems and methods of recording any linguistic phenomena, whether graphically or otherwise. This discussion of the question of recording will lead automatically to a discussion of the material to be recorded, a discussion which will provide both the reason for our employment of the two terms (*speech-sound* and *phoneme*) and the linguistic criteria whereby the use of these two terms may be clearly defined.

a. *The Question of Record and Graphic Representation*

The task of inventing a set of symbols to represent the observable or inferable phenomena of nature confronts every field of science and is comparatively simple. The true problem involved concerns the application of a set of arbitrarily devised symbols to the phenomena of nature so that the distinctive features may be recorded, transmitted to others, and scrutinized at leisure. The contrivance of a system of symbols to represent linguistic phenomena is aided, though not accomplished, by the use of mechanical apparatus.

Thanks to the invention and perfection of the phonograph, the gross acoustic effects of the stream of speech of an individual can be recorded with a high degree of accuracy. The phonographic instrument records not only features of the speech which are shared in common with all speakers of the language, but even the peculiar nuances arising from a speaker's local dialect, or from the peculiar construction or use of an individual speaker's vocal organs, which distinguishes his voice from that of another; further, it records the variations in pitch and amplitude and speed resulting from the speaker's temperament and mood, or from the exigencies of the situation, or from the requirements of the context. In short, the phonograph records what is spoken as it is spoken; it records what we shall term the *speech-sounds* of a discourse, and records them accurately and permanently, and is invaluable for field work. Yet for the purposes of Dynamic Philology the record of the phonograph is (for two reasons) inadequate as the final representation of speech.

The first inadequacy of phonographic recording for our purposes is that the record is not in a form immediately available for statistical analysis. Before the record can be analyzed statistically, it must be transcribed into written symbols. Hence the value of phonographic recording over an immediate written notation of the stream of speech is chiefly that the phonographic record of a given sample of the ephemeral stream of speech is permanently available for graphic transcription irrespective of time or place.

The second inadequacy of phonographic recording is that in many respects the record is too detailed in its recordings. That is, in recording all the nuances which occur in the stream of speech, it records many personal features of a speaker which from the point of view of the entire speech-community are unessential if not indeed fortuitous. A record of these fine nuances, though possibly of considerable importance in studying the psychology and anatomy of the individual or his personality, is by no means prerequisite to an understanding of the basic linguistic forms and patterns of linguistic behavior which are common to all speakers in the entire speech-community; in fact, a preliminary study of the common basic fabric of speech, if possible, is a better approach to an understanding of peculiarly individualistic elaborations and distortions of the common basic fabric than a reversal of the procedure. That is, an understanding of the phoneme which is common property leads more quickly to an understanding of the peculiarities of individual speech-sounds than will be the case if the order of procedure is reversed. Yet there are more fundamental differences between speech-sounds and phonemes than the mere fact that the former are more individualistic than the latter.

b. The Phoneme as a Norm Approximated by Speech-Sounds; Variant Forms of a Phoneme

The chief feature of a *phoneme* is that it represents a norm which the individual speech-sounds may be said to approximate. To objectify this relationship, we might, with considerable appropriateness, use the target as an analogy [1]: the bull's eye of the target represents, say, the phoneme *k* in English, and the shots aimed at the target are the speech-sounds. That is, the actual articulations of *k* in the stream of speech by speakers of the language are shots aimed at the norm which is the phoneme. The speech-sounds, distributed about the norm of the phoneme, give significance to the phoneme, just as the norm of the phoneme gives meaning to the speech-sounds which approximate it. The one without the other is unthinkable.

However, it is often observable in language that individual phonemes may possess several subsidiary norms instead of merely one norm, and that the speech sounds approximate one or another of these subsidiary norms according to conditions prevailing in the stream of speech at the time. These subsidiary norms of a given phoneme may be termed the *variant forms* [2] of that phoneme, and the speech-sounds, which constitute the occurrences of the phoneme in the stream of speech, approximate one subsidiary norm or another according to the particular conditions under which the speech sound is produced. For example, the initial *k*-sounds as pronounced by English speakers in the English words *keel*, *call*, and *cool* are neither acoustically nor phonetically identical in the subsidiary norms which they approximate. In English the velar *k* is closed farther forward in the mouth in *keel* than in *call*, and farther forward in *call* than in *cool*: the *k* of *keel* is palatal, the *k* of *cool* is velar, and the *k* of *call* falls in between. The norms which these three different *k*-sounds approximate are conditioned in each case entirely by the nature of the following vowel sound. Indeed it is practically impossible for the average English speaker to pronounce the palatal *k* of *keel* before the vowel of *cool*, or the velar *k* of *cool* before the vowel of *keel*, nor will this alternate pronunciation be necessary for the proper pronunciation of any word in English. As a parallel example, the spirant in German, usually written as *ch*, has two variant forms: (1) the palatal, as pronounced in German *ich*, and (2) the velar, as in German *Buch*. These two forms of *ch* are not identical in position of articulation and each consistently approximates its own norm. But in the case of German *ch*, the determining factor is the preceding vowel sound and not the succeeding vowel, as was the case above with *k* in English. The German speech-sound, written *ch*, when following an *a* or a back vowel, is automatically and invariably velar in German, and approximates what may be termed the velar norm of the phoneme (e.g. *Bach, hoch, Buch*); yet when following a front vowel in German, the *ch* is automatically and invariably palatal, and approximates what may be termed the palatal norm of the German phoneme *ch* (e.g. *sich, Blech*).

These two typical examples from English and German illustrate the manner in which specific surrounding sounds may sufficiently influence the articulation of a phoneme as to make it deviate consistently under specific conditions in the direction of one of several variant forms. The variant form of a speech-sound is not of random occurrence in the stream of speech; wherever the environmental conditions are correct for the occurrence of a particular variant form, that variant form appears, and from its appearance we may in turn be certain that the prerequisite environmental conditions are present.

c. The Phoneme as the Smallest Unit of Distinctive Significance

One may wish to inquire into the particular criteria whereby it is determined whether a given form is to be viewed as an independent phoneme or as a variant form of an independent phoneme. That is, by what criteria can one determine that the palatal and velar pronunciations of *k* in English are but variants of the phoneme *k* and not phonemes in their own right? For, a variant form of a phoneme is also a norm which is approximated by speech-sounds. The mere fact that a phoneme is a norm is clearly not a sufficient definition of a phoneme.

The chief distinction, and a sufficient distinction, between phonemes and the variant forms of phonemes is this: phonemes are capable of distinguishing one word of a language from other words of the same language, whereas the different variant forms and speech-sounds which appertain to one phoneme do not distinguish one word from another. The consistent failure of a foreigner to distinguish between the different appurtenant variant forms of one phoneme may result in a foreign accent, but very probably not in unintelligibility. Yet the consistent failure to distinguish between different phonemes will inevitably lead to unintelligibility. For example, we should probably understand a foreigner who pronounced *cool* with the palatal *k*-sound of *keel*, although his pronunciation would be marked with 'a foreign accent'; yet we should very probably not understand him if in pronouncing the *k*-sound of *cool* he indiscriminately used the *r*-sound of *room*. In this latter instance we should very probably understand the word *rule* instead of *cool*, for he has substituted for the correct form of the phoneme not an alternate variant form, but a different phoneme.

A phoneme is then the smallest unit of distinctive significance.[1] Like phonemes in a language are phonemes which behave alike in reference to the meanings of all words in that language. Two sounds of a language may be considered either as identical or as appertaining to the same phoneme, if a substitution of one for the other throughout the entire language will not lead to the confusion of meaning of a single word. Thus, the substitution of palatal *k* for velar *k* in English will lead to no confusion of meaning. But two sounds of a language must be considered phonemically different (i.e. as approximating different phonemic norms) if a substitution of one for the other throughout the language will lead to the confusion of meaning between a single pair of words in that language. Thus, the substitution of the *k*-sound of *cool* for the *r*-sound of *room* will lead to a confusion of meaning in at least the one pair: *rule — cool*. In English *k* and *r* are therefore different phonemes; similarly, *l* and *r* in English are different phonemes (e.g. *lack, rack*); in some periods of Sanskrit,[1] however, *l* and *r* seem to have been but variants of one phoneme,* (e.g. *rih-, lih-* 'lick').

There is one aspect of a phoneme which deserves constant remembrance: a feature which is significant in segregating words in one language may be insignificant in another. In Northern Chinese, for example, there is the sound *k* without aspiration, and the sound *k* with aspiration (written *kʰ*); the absence or presence of the slight puff of air after the *k*-sound which distinguishes the unaspirated *k* from the aspirate *kʰ* is sufficient in Northern Chinese to keep apart words of widely different meaning which are otherwise phonetically identical. In Northern Chinese, then, *k* and *kʰ* are different phonemes, and the aspiration *ʰ* is *phonemically* significant. In English, too, both the non-aspirate *k* and the aspirate *kʰ* occur; for example, the initial *k* of *kick* is aspirated, but the *k* of *skin* is unaspirated.† Yet nowhere in the English vocabulary can two words of different meaning be found which are phonetically identical except for

---

* To determine whether two different sounds belong to the same or different phonemes, one need only search the vocabulary for a single pair of words which are different in meaning, and which are differentiated phonetically solely by the difference between the two sounds to be tested. Thus, to determine whether the *th*-sound (þ) of English *think*, and the *th*-sound (ð) of English *the* represent the same or different phonemes, one need only consider the pair of words *mouth — mouthe* to perceive that the presence or absence of voicing which distinguishes þ from ð is sufficient to keep distinct two different words, and that þ and ð are therefore two separate phonemes in English. By the extension of this method of comparison it is possible to isolate all the different phonemes of a language which constitute the *phonemic system* of that language.[2]

† Similarly English *p* and *t*, though generally aspirated, are regularly not aspirated after *s*, e.g. *spin* and *stone*.

this aspiration, and which are kept separate solely by this aspiration. In English, therefore, k and k^h do not represent different phonemes, but approximate the same phonemic norm.

Hence the term phoneme is understandable only in reference to some specific language in which it is the smallest unit of distinctive significance. Since phonemic differences exist only when actually demonstrable in a language, the comparison of similar phonemes in different languages may be undertaken only with extreme caution. If, for example, we choose to believe that t is phonemic in both English and French, the 'foreign accent' either of the average Frenchman while speaking English, or of the average Englishman while speaking French, reminds us forcibly that the t in English is more aspirated than the t in French.[1] And we shall presently observe that the presence or absence, or difference in degree, of aspiration may possibly reflect an appreciable modification in the behavior of a phoneme.

To summarize our discussion of the phoneme to this point, it may be said that the speech sounds of a language are approximations of norms, which are either those of the variant forms of phonemes or of phonemes themselves. In deciding whether two different norms are to be viewed as belonging to the same or different phonemes, one need only determine whether a substitution of one for another will lead to any confusion of meaning in a single word; unless they can be interchanged without confusing the meaning of two words they represent differences which are phonemic. The question of selecting a system of symbols for representing these various speech-phenomena depends to a considerable extent upon the artistic taste or cunning of the investigator; for simplicity we shall use, unless otherwise stated, symbols which have presumably been familiar to the reader since school-boy days; and we shall call attention to the presence of length in a vowel by a macron (e.g. long $a = \bar{a}$) to the presence of shortness in a vowel by a breve (e.g.

short $a = \breve{a}$), to the presence of accent (stress) by an acute accent mark above the vowel of the accented (stressed) element (e.g. *áccent*). Though in time Dynamic Philology will doubtless find it expedient to employ in its problems a more elaborate system of symbols — that of the International Phonetic Association is eminently satisfactory — in the present introductory study the employment of an elaborate system is not necessary for an adequate representation of the phenomena under consideration, and would only intrude upon the reader's attention an unnecessary refinement.

2. THE COMPARATIVE MAGNITUDE
OF COMPLEXITY OF A PHONEME

a. The Question of Quantitative Measurement of Phonemes

Our chief problem in the study of the dynamics of the form and behavior of phonemes is to devise a system whereby phonemes can be compared quantitatively. It is one thing to describe phonetically the place and manner of articulation of *g* and *k* in English, or to determine whether indeed the two are phonemically different in English, but it is quite another matter to establish significant quantitative differences between the two, or to discover a scale according to which the magnitudes of all phonemes of a language can be measured.

To commence, it does not seem that any mechanical apparatus for physical measurement will be of help in the quantitative measurement of phonemes even though the apparatus of experimental phonetics may conceivably be sufficiently refined some day to cope with the enormous task of complete mechanical measurement of individual speech-sounds. For the speech-sounds of a given phoneme in a given language differ so widely in expiratory force, duration, pitch, amplitude, and the like in the stream of speech that even a reasonably accurate computation of an average norm seems a practical impossibility. And even if it were ultimately possible to compute with accuracy the average amount of physical force expended in the production of any given phoneme in any given language, there would still be no cogent reason for believing that all the dynamic processes involved in the production of a phoneme are entirely represented quantitatively by a measurement of their average expenditure of physical force. Hence there is little point in urging an investigation in a direction which promises to be fruitless.

There is, however, a method of viewing phonemes, which, though in no strict sense quantitative, is nevertheless useful in arranging specific phonemes in respect to differences that are by no means inconsiderable in the totality of their manifestation; and the use of this method ultimately receives, as we shall see, the pragmatic sanction from the stream of speech. If the method is not in itself quantitative, its adoption leads immediately to quantitative study.

b. *A Phoneme Viewed as a Complex of Sequences of Articulatory Sub-Gestures*

Any phoneme [1] can be viewed as a complex or configuration of articulatory sub-gestures in sequential arrangement. The complex sequential nature of a phoneme can perhaps be most readily comprehended if one performs an imaginary experiment. For example, let us imagine that while a person is speaking we take, with the help of X-rays, a slow-motion picture of all his speech organs in activity; or, expressed differently, take pictures so rapidly of his speech organs that a projection of the film on a screen would show the activity of the speech organs much retarded in speed.

In the utterance of *t* for example we should see, among other things, the tip of the tongue rising, say, to the top of the back of the upper teeth to form an *occlusion* after which the tip of the tongue is withdrawn. This sequence or series of gestures, really a continuum of an infinite number of events, may for convenience be represented by the sequence of symbols *a b c d*. The utterance of *d* would be somewhat similar, though in addition to and simultaneous with the *a b c d* gestures of the tongue, there would also be a contraction, vibration, and relaxation of the vocal cords to produce *voicing*. The sequence representing voicing might for convenience be designated by the sequence of symbols *m n l o*. In the articulation of both *t* and *d* there would be a sequence, say *r s t u*, to designate the closing and opening of the nasal passages (a sequence not present in the production of nasals). Similarly one might devise nominal sequences to represent the activity of the various organs of speech which come into play in the production of all other speech-sounds in any language.

The point of concern at present, however, is not to devise a system of symbols whereby the sequences of sub-gestures constituting a speech-sound can be noted, but rather to remark that speech-sounds and phonemes may be viewed as constellations, or configurations, of articulatory sub-gestures, arranged partly or completely in sequential order, some sequences running concurrently with others (e.g. the *occlusion* is concurrent with the *voicing* of *d*). Though there is not a single speech-sound, or a variant form, of a phoneme in any language which cannot be conceived of as a constellation or configuration of the type envisaged above, yet a complete and accurate description of even a single speech-sound in terms of sequences is practically impossible. However, by conceiving of phonemes as constellations of this order, we have found a very useful method of comparing a number of specific phoneme pairs which have essential sequences in common. These pairs are (1) *the aspirated* and *unaspirated stops,** (2) the *lenes* and *fortes stops* and (3) the *voiceless* and *voiced* stops. A consideration of each of these pairs in turn will illustrate the value of this method of comparison.

i. *The Aspirated and Unaspirated Stops*

As observed previously (page 56), the aspiration (represented by ^{h}) of a consonant as in the case of many Chinese dialects (e.g. that of Peiping) may be phonemically significant. That is, the chief difference between the two phonemes in the dialect of Peiping which we shall represent as k and k^h, is the aspiration ^{h}. Whether it can be said that the k^h of this dialect equals precisely the sum of k plus the aspiration ^{h}, cannot now be answered one way or the other quantitatively; it may or it may not. If the instinctive opinion of the average speaker of Peiping Chinese on this subject would be as worthless as the opinion of an average American on an analogous subject in English phonetics (e.g. the voicing and voicelessness of p and b), this is probably because he would consider the two as totally different phenomena which occur in totally different words.† The only direct evidence on the subject is provided by the observations of experimental phoneticists [1] which suggest that the k appears at times less vigorously stressed when unaspirated (i.e. as simple k) than when aspirated (i.e. as k^h), though it must be added that opinion is by no means unanimous in respect to all the corresponding aspirates and non-aspirates in this dialect.

* A speech-sound may be termed a *stop* if at any time during its production the complete stoppage of the passage of air is an essential characteristic, e.g. $k — k^h$, p, b, b^h, t, etc. A *stop* may occur at the beginning, middle, or at the end of a word.[2]

† Of course the symbol k^h is more complex than the symbol k, yet we are interested solely in the differences of complexity of the phenomena and not in that of the symbols of which k^h merely happens to be the more complex of the two, and might readily be represented as the less complex of the two by selecting two other symbols (e.g. $k = \infty$, and $k^h = \cdot$).

Since there is no conclusive evidence on the comparative magnitudes of k and k^h and since whatever evidence there is suggests that k^h has not only an aspiration not present in k but also at times a more vigorous stress, it would not seem, then, to be an undue distortion of the phenomena either to say that the aspirated stop (k^h) represented a greater magnitude than the non-aspirated stop (k), or to say that the first possessed a higher degree of complexity than the second. And, if we view the two phonemes represented symbolically by k and k^h as sequences of articulatory sub-gestures, we may with considerable propriety indicate the non-aspirate (k) with such a sequence as $l\ m\ n\ o$, and the aspirate (k^h) as $l\ m\ n\ o\ p\ q$ in which the additional $p\ q$ may be considered as representing the aspiration. If each phoneme is to be viewed as a crystallized configuration and not as the sum of its parts, this fact may be indicated by the use of parentheses, e.g. ($l\ m\ n\ o$) and ($l\ m\ n\ o\ p\ q$).

Now the dialect of Peiping has a series of these pairs of aspirated and unaspirated stops, each member of each pair being an independent phoneme. In the table below, these pairs are arranged vertically, each aspirated stop above its corresponding unaspirated stop.

Aspirated stops	t^h	p^h	k^h	ς^h	$t\!\int^h$	ts^h
Unaspirated stops	t	p	k	ς	$t\!\int$	ts

The chief interest of this series for our present purposes is not a phonetic description of how these phonemes are articulated, for this is available in special treatises on the subject [1]; it is sufficient to notice that we have here six pairs of phonemes, and that in each pair the aspirated member represents a greater magnitude and a greater degree of complexity than the corresponding unaspirated member.*

* If one chooses to suggest in addition that the production of the aspirated stop in each pair requires more energy than the production of its corresponding non-aspirated stop, and that the audibility of the aspirated stop is greater than the audibility of its corresponding non-aspirated stop, the suggestion must be allowed as a surmise which is doubtless correct.

ii. *The Lenes and Fortes Stops* [1]

If we compare the unaspirated phonemic stops *t, p, k* of modern Danish with the unaspirated phonemic stops of modern French we find perceptible differences: the French stops are pronounced with more energy or expiratory force than their corresponding stops in Danish. Because of this difference in energy these voiceless stops of Danish may be called *voiceless lenes* and the voiceless stops of French, for contrast, *voiceless fortes*.[2] For the Frenchman whose language possesses no phonemic lenes stops, the simple term *voiceless stops* would doubtless be an adequate description leading to no ambiguity in his phonemic system. Yet if a Frenchman in speaking Danish pronounced the Danish *voiceless lenes* as French *voiceless fortes*, even though unaspirated, the Dane would very probably imagine that the Frenchman was mispronouncing the Danish aspirates (which are fortes) rather than the Danish voiceless *lenes*.

In the *voiceless fortes* and the *voiceless lenes* we have stops which differ appreciably in magnitude, although their difference in magnitude is far more difficult to indicate by means of sequences of sub-gestures than the difference in magnitude between the aspirates and non-aspirates. All phoneticists will agree, nevertheless, that the voiceless fortes represent the expenditure of more expiratory force in their production than is the case with their corresponding voiceless lenes, and are also presumably more audible. There can therefore be no serious question of the difference in magnitude. According to Bloomfield 'the pressure and action are gentle in the *lenes*, vigorous in the *fortes*.'[3] Hence we may reasonably suppose that, with the *fortes*, the sequence of gestures forming the occlusion is probably much more complex than with the *lenes* because of the greater air pressure to be restrained.

Fortunately for the statistical purposes of Dynamic Philology the problem of representing this difference in complexity by use of symbols need not be immediately solved. For instead of comparing the French *voiceless unaspirated fortes stops* with the Danish *voiceless unaspirated lenes stops*, we can compare the Danish *voiceless unaspirated lenes stops* with their counterparts in Danish, the *voiceless aspirated fortes stops*, where the differences in magnitude of complexity are readily perceptible and easily represented.

Voiceless fortes aspirated stops	t^h	p^h	k^h
Voiceless lenes unaspirated stops	t	p	k

The same general argument which was used on pages 61 ff. to demonstrate the greater magnitude of complexity of Peipingese aspirated stops over corresponding unaspirated stops is valid here for establishing the greater magnitude of complexity of the Danish voiceless fortes aspirated stops over their corresponding voiceless lenes unaspirated stops.

iii. *Voiced Stops and Voiceless Stops*

There is another series of phonemic stops which appear in many languages in corresponding pairs: the voiced and voiceless stops. For example, in English there are the voiced stops *d, b, g* with the corresponding voiceless stops *t, p, k*. The *chief* distinction between these in English is that the former (*d, b, g*) possess a *voicing*[1] which is lacking in the latter (*t, p, k*).

Many, though by no means all, languages possess this voiced-voiceless series of stops as a part of their phonemic system. However, from language to language one often finds slight differences in pronunciation of similar phonemes which are sufficient to give the speaker of one language a foreign accent in speaking a foreign tongue, even in respect to the articulation of common phonemes. For example, in

English the voiceless stops (*t*, *p*, *k*) are slightly aspirated fortes, although other types occur as non-distinctive variants *; in French the voiceless stops (*t*, *p*, *k*) are never aspirated, although they may be accompanied by a simultaneous glottal stop as a non-distinctive variant. In English the voiced stops are lenes, and are not voiced through their entire duration at the beginning and end of a word; likewise in French the voiced stops are lenes, but more fully voiced than in English. As language after language is observed, minor differences in the habitual articulation of similar phonemes are often revealed to close scrutiny, *but not always*. Thus, though the French voiceless stops differ from those in English, nevertheless the voiceless stops *t*, *p*, and *k* in French are practically identical with those, say, in Dutch, Italian, and Czechish.

A striking example of how the articulation of a given phoneme in one language may register as a different phoneme in the ears of speakers of another language is the Latin word *gubernare* doubtless borrowed from the Greek *kubernaō*, 'act as pilot'; both Latin and Greek at the time of this borrowing had the phonemic stops *k* and *g*, but evidently, at least in this one case, the Greek articulation of the initial Greek *k* seemed to the Latin auditor to approximate more nearly the Latin pronunciation of initial *g* than initial *k*. Of course, by and large, the vast majority of borrowings from one language into another, in which similar phonemes are available, is made correctly. Indeed the phoneticist's eagerness for precise statement seems at times to obscure the indisputable fact that in languages which have, say, the voiced-voiceless series of stops as a part of their phonemic systems, the similarities of these like stops *far outweigh* their dissimilarities. Thus if English *t* is not precisely similar to French *t*, it is nevertheless far more similar to French *t* than to French *o*, or *g*, or *m*, or many other French phonemes. However,

---

* E.g. the unaspirated lenes after *s*, as in English *spin*, *stone*, *skin*, see page 57 supra.

the problem of comparing similar phonemes in different languages need not concern us until we have compared similar phonemes in the same language in respect to their magnitudes of complexity.

Taking the pair *t/d* in English as a typical example of a voiceless and voiced stop, we have the question of determining the possible difference in magnitude of complexity between the two. When the stops of this pair are each viewed as a configuration of sequences of sub-gestures, the question of difference in magnitude resolves itself into the following formulation: Is the additional magnitude of complexity represented by *voicing* in the voiced stop *d* sufficient to counterbalance or outweigh a possible greater magnitude of complexity in the voiceless *t* which results from the *fortis* pronunciation and slight *aspiration* in *t*, which are absent in *d*? Thus, if we represent the sequence of basic occluding gestures (cf. page 60) of both *t* and *d* in English as *ace*, which, because of the fortis and aspirated articulation of *t* in English, may be expanded to *abcde* for *t*, and if we represent the concurrent sequence of the gestures of voicing in *d* as *mnlo*, we are confronted by the question of determining whether the total magnitude of complexity of *ace* plus *mnlo* in the configurational pattern of *d* is equal to, greater than, or less than that of *abcde* in the configurational pattern of *t*.[1]

There happens to be some slight direct evidence which clearly though not conclusively suggests that the total magnitude of complexity of a voiced stop *may* be greater than that of the voiceless stop.* The only other course in solving

---

* E.g. Latin *exāctus* developed from the older restored form, **ex-ag-tos*, as reconstructed quite plausibly by Classical philologists. The essential steps in the development are (1) the change of *gt* to *ct* (i.e. *kt*) by the process of assimilation to be discussed later (pages 90 ff.), and (2) the lengthening of *a* to *ā*. The Classical philologists have argued quite convincingly that the voiced *g* in *exagtos*, in changing to its corresponding voiceless stop, *k*, lost its voicing (i.e. our sequence *mnlo* above), and that the lengthening of *a* to *ā* compensated for this loss of magnitude. Since *ā* can be viewed as possessing a greater magnitude of complexity than *a* because of its greater duration, and if the difference in magnitude of *ā* and *a* at that time in Latin

the problem of the difference in magnitude of complexity between voiced and voiceless stops is, it would seem, to approach the matter indirectly, and as follows.   That is, we may and shall first restrict our attention to those pairs of stops, such as the aspirates and non-aspirates in Peipingese Chinese (pages 62 f.) and Danish (pages 63 f.) where differences in magnitude of complexity are determinable.   Then we shall attempt to relate the differences in magnitude of these stops with consistent differences in the relative frequency of their occurrence.   And finally we shall see whether there are any consistent differences in the relative frequency of occurrence of voiced stops on the one hand and voiceless stops on the other in representative languages where these stops are phonemically significant.   Thus, (1) if we find an unmistakable tendency on the part of the Chinese and Danish stops of greater magnitude to be associated on the whole with a lesser or greater relative frequency of occurrence than those of lesser magnitude, and (2) if we find an unmistakable tendency of the voiced stops to be associated on the whole with a lesser or greater relative frequency of occurrence, then (3) we shall presume, until evidence to the contrary is advanced, that, in the pairs of corresponding voiced and voiceless stops, those stops (voiced or voiceless) have the greater magnitude of complexity which possess a relative frequency of occurrence that compares proportionately to that of the stops of greater magnitude in Chinese and Danish.

Our first step, then, in determining whether the voiced or the voiceless stops are on the whole of greater magnitude of complexity, is to present available statistics for aspirates and non-aspirates in Chinese and Danish.

represents the magnitude of voicing in g at that time in Latin, then g possessed a greater magnitude of complexity than k at that time in Latin.   Incidentally, the subsequent behavior of $\bar{a}$ and k (i.e. c) in *exactus* was indistinguishable from that of $\bar{a}$ and k from any other source under similar conditions.

3. THE RELATIVE FREQUENCY OF VOICELESS STOPS OF
COMPARABLE MAGNITUDE

a. Peipingese Chinese

The series of Peipingese stops which consists of pairs of
aspirated and unaspirated fortes have been represented thus:

Aspirated stops	t^h	p^h	k^h	$c\varsigma^h$	$t\int^h$	ts^h
Unaspirated stops	t	p	k	$c\varsigma$	$t\int$	ts

In each of these pairs, as we saw on pages 62 ff., the aspirated
stop represents a greater magnitude of complexity than its
corresponding unaspirated stop. The question arises as to
the relative frequencies of the members of these pairs.

A statistical analysis of the frequency of occurrence of the
phonemes of 20 samplings of modern colloquial Peipingese,
each sampling 1000 syllables long, and totalling 20,000 syllables, or 37,338 phonemes, yields the following percentages
for the above phonemes.[1]

	t^h/t	p^h/p	k^h/k	$c\varsigma^h/c\varsigma$	$t\int^h/t\int$	ts^h/ts
Aspirated stops	2.56	.56	1.02	1.04	1.23	1.40
Unaspirated stops	6.18	2.37	2.58	2.69	2.44	2.63

It is clearly evident from these statistics that the greater
magnitude of complexity of the aspirated member of each
pair is coupled with a smaller relative frequency.

An interesting but not unique feature of this dialect of
Chinese is what may be called the absence of possible disturbing factors. That is, the above stops occur only at the
beginning of a syllable and are always followed by a vowel;
hence the influence of surrounding sounds which might show

a preference for an aspirated or unaspirated phoneme is zero (see pages 97 f.), and all factors involved in the occurrences of each phoneme in the above series of phonemes are constant except for differences in magnitude of complexity and relative frequency.

b. Danish

The series of Danish aspirated fortes and unaspirated lenes were represented thus:

Aspirated fortes stops	t^h	p^h	k^h
Unaspirated lenes stops	t	p	k

In a sample of *phonemically transcribed* [1] modern colloquial Danish totalling 11,604 phonemes in extent (of which 660 were occurrences of the glottal stop) [2] we find the relative frequencies of these phonemes in terms of percentages of the whole to be as follows:

	t^h/t	p^h/p	k^h/k
Aspirated stops	3.47%	1.05%	2.10%
Unaspirated stops	5.42	1.49	3.05

Here again in Danish we find the phoneme of greater magnitude of complexity in each pair clearly in possession of an appreciably smaller relative frequency.

This curious parallel relationship between the aspirates and non-aspirates in Chinese and in Danish, which seems to indicate that the magnitude of complexity of a phoneme tends to bear an inverse * relationship to its relative frequency, is almost too orderly to permit the view that the relationship is but one of chance and coincidence. And surely,

* Not necessarily proportionate.

in view of the differences in history and culture between the Chinese and the Danes, and in view of the great distance between the two, this parallelism cannot conceivably have originated from cross-influence.   Moreover, it cannot easily have its cause in deeply rooted racial traits; for the Chinese and Danes are certainly racially different.   And most surely an English baby growing up in a Danish family in Copenhagen, or a French baby growing up with a Chinese family in Peiping, would each use the language of the adopted country as a mother-tongue which they would speak with an accent indistinguishable from a native, even, in all probability, in respect to the curious frequency distribution of the aspirates and non-aspirates just noted.

This relationship between greater magnitude of complexity and lower relative frequency, and *vice versa*, which is illustrated by the aspirates and non-aspirates of Chinese and Danish [1] indicates probably a basic tendency of language in general rather than the idiosyncrasies of Danish and Peipingese in particular, and should be disclosed in the frequency distribution of comparable phonemes in any other language.

c. Additional Evidence

In addition to the Peipingese and Danish data there are available some admirably accurate phonemic transcriptions of Cantonese Chinese and of Burmese; in the phonemic systems of each of these the aspiration of stops is phonemically significant.   If the texts used as a basis for transcription are in neither case so colloquial as those at the basis of the Peipingese and Danish analyses, the frequency distribution of the aspirates and non-aspirates of Cantonese and Burmese, as revealed by these two studies, confirms our findings from Peipingese and Danish.

i. *Cantonese Chinese*

The material of the Cantonese transcriptions are partly colloquial and partly literary texts.[1] A major portion of the colloquial texts is a discussion between teacher and pupil of the
language and phonetics of Chinese, and of the best method
of learning Chinese. The literary texts include primarily
terse proverbs and poems. In order to obtain a sufficiently
long sampling, the frequency distribution of aspirates and
non-aspirates in both the colloquial and literary texts was
established, and the following relative frequencies (in percentages of the whole) were derived from running texts ag-
gregating 9,400 phonemes in extent.

	t^h/t	p^h/p	k^h/k	ts^h/ts
Aspirated fortes	1.03%	.36%	.50%	1.37%
Unaspirated fortes	6.14	1.97	8.70	3.82

In each of these pairs of stops the phonemes of greater magnitude of complexity are also of lower relative frequency.

ii. *Burmese*

In the Burmese phonemic system there are triplets of similar phonemes instead of pairs as, for example, in Peipingese,
Danish, and Cantonese. That is, the dental stops, for
example, consist not only of the familiar *aspirated fortes*
which we shall represent as t^h, but also of the *unaspirated
fortes* (as in Peipingese) which we shall represent as t, and the
unaspirated lenes (as in Danish) which we may temporarily
represent as t_l. We have, then, two sets of comparisons:
(1) a comparison of the *aspirated fortes* with the *unaspirated
fortes* (e.g. t^h and t) in which the former represent the greater

magnitude of complexity; and (2) a comparison of the *aspirated fortes* and the *unaspirated lenes* (e.g. t^h and t_I) in which the former * again represent the greater magnitude of complexity. The relative frequencies of these phonemes were derived from an aggregate of 6300 phonemes of running text material which consists partly of dialogues in the colloquial style, partly of native fables in a less colloquial style, and partly of literary Burmese.[1]

The statistics for the aspirated and unaspirated fortes are:

	t^h/t	p^h/p	k^h/k	ts^h/ts
Aspirated fortes stops	.81%	.52%	.98%	.38%
Unaspirated fortes stops	1.16	1.92	.91	1.97

It will be noted that only in the case of k^h and k is the non-aspirate less frequent (by .07 per cent) than the aspirate.

The statistics for the aspirated fortes and unaspirated lenes are:

	t^h/t_I	p^h/p_I	k^h/k_I	ts^h/ts_I
Aspirated fortes stops	.81%	.52%	.98%	.38%
Unaspirated lenes stops	3.75	1.84	3.03	.94

It will be noted that in all instances the unaspirated lenes are appreciably more frequent than their corresponding aspirated fortes.

* It is perhaps doubtful that this second comparison (i.e. between the *aspirates* and the *lenes*) is legitimate since the *lenes* have a voiced variant form and hence in part are of indeterminable magnitude (see page 67). The dental lenis, for example, 'is fully voiced only when intervocalic. Initially in a group it is often voiceless, and differs from an unaspirated t in that less effort is used.'[2] The particular problem involved in these voiced-voiceless variant forms will be discussed subsequently in detail (page 106 ff.). Though it is the author's personal belief that these lenes are unquestionably of lesser magnitude of complexity than their corresponding aspirated fortes, these statistics are presented with the understanding that others, in believing differently, may wish to ignore them as being totally irrelevant.

d. *Conclusions*

In all the above data, with the exception of one instance in Burmese, the aspirated stops, which we have presumed to represent the greater magnitude of complexity, are relatively less frequent than their corresponding non-aspirated stops. If we remember that Peipingese offers six opportunities for deviation from this relationship, that Danish offers three, that Cantonese offers four, and that Burmese offers presumably eight, we have a total of twenty-one opportunities for the aspirates to be more frequent than their corresponding non-aspirates, a condition which eventuates, however, only in one instance out of twenty-one. Hence the correlation is 95.2 per cent valid as judged from these statistics, which is a percentage which seems to eliminate completely the possibility of a chance relationship. Until evidence is advanced to the contrary it appears plausible to believe that the magnitude of complexity of a phoneme bears an inverse (not necessarily proportionate) relationship to its relative frequency of occurrence, a belief which is founded, however, only on the evidence of two types of phonemes, the aspirated and un-aspirated voiceless stops.

4. THE RELATIVE FREQUENCY OF

VOICED AND VOICELESS STOPS

In turning to a consideration of the phonemic series of voiced and voiceless stops we have the task of discovering whether in the stream of speech of each of the languages possessing these phonemic series there is any preference for the voiced or voiceless stops in each pair. If we find a clear and unmistakable correlation between high relative frequency on the one hand and voicing or voicelessness on the other, we shall be justified, it seems, in attempting to reduce to a common denominator the phenomenon of voicing with the previously discussed (page 68 ff.) phenomenon of aspiration.

A note of caution must be sounded in respect to using the ensuing tabulation. Strictly speaking, the transcriptions of these different languages fall into three different classes. The percentages for the first three languages (Dutch,[1] Czechish,[2] and French [3]) are derived from *accurate phonemic* transcriptions of these languages; the next three languages (Italian, English, and Hungarian [4]) had their samplings transcribed accurately according to a *phonetic* system of transcription; the remaining six (Bulgarian, Russian, Spanish, Greek, Latin and Vedic Sanskrit [5]) represent transcriptions into the customary *alphabet* of each respective language. Except for Greek, Latin, and Sanskrit, all of these languages are still living and the frequency distribution of any of their phonemes may be analysed again if data in a different form are desired. This note of caution must be sounded because, strictly speaking, the complete results of a phonetic analysis, a phonemic analysis, and an analysis of an alphabetic transcription of a language will by no means be necessarily identical in all respects.*

* At this point, still another note of caution seems to be in order. Dynamic philologists must also beware the often exaggerated statements of phoneticists, especially of professional phonetic transcribers, who generally carry their refinements unnecessarily far from our point of view. For example, the actual number of occurrences of the six different stops in the respective samplings of the twelve languages below would in some cases not be appreciably different whether one selected the phoneme as a unit of transcription, or the variant form, or the alphabetic symbols conventional for each language. Thus, if a given sample of English text were analysed first phonemically and then phonetically and then alphabetically, the differences in actual occurrences of, say, *p*, as adduced by these three methods of transcription, would probably be insignificant. In instances, such as *k*, where the phoneticist would indicate the occurrences of variant forms of a phoneme by the consistent use of different symbols, one need but add these together to obtain the total occurrences of the entire phoneme irrespective of phonetic variant forms, a procedure which has been followed as far as possible in all of the phonetic investigations below. If the conventional alphabet is at times quite inconsistent, as in present-day English and Irish, it is not necessarily inconsistent in respect to all speechelements (e.g. the English alphabet is quite consistent, on the whole, in its use of, say, *b*). Moreover, not all conventional alphabets are of necessity inconsistent; the

Let us now turn to a consideration of the statistics which are given for each language in terms of percentages of the whole of that language. The table is to be read horizontally and not vertically, since we are not yet comparing languages but only the pairs of corresponding stops in each language by itself. The phoneme at the head of each column designates the general phonetic type; we remember that the actual pronunciations may vary from language to language.

	t	*d*	*p*	*b*	*k*	*g*	
Czechish	5.60	3.73	3.52	1.86	3.93	.15	
Dutch	7.83	4.67	1.99	1.20	(3.21)*	(.09)*	phonemic
French	6.28	3.55	3.54	1.39	4.81	.76	
Italian	7.02	4.74	2.78	.89	3.63	.41	
English	7.13	4.31	2.04	1.81	2.71	.74	phonetic
Hungarian	7.18	3.30	1.04	1.71	5.72	2.45	
Bulgarian	7.54	3.55	2.82	1.32	2.98	1.46	
Russian	7.49	3.42	2.19	1.76	3.49	1.10	
Spanish	4.27	5.20	2.64	2.05	3.82	.07	alphabetic
Greek	7.58	2.87	3.38	.49	4.07	1.74	
Latin	7.72	3.41	2.01	1.40	3.71	.96	
Sanskrit	6.65	2.85	2.46	.46	1.99	.82	

conventional Sanskrit alphabet is an amazingly accurate phonetic alphabet, practically *nulli secundum*; on the other hand the conventional Czechish alphabet is practically as accurate a phonemic alphabet as can be devised for Czechish. This note of warning, which was foreshadowed on pages 52 ff., is necessary lest we be persuaded into the erroneous belief that none of our otherwise highly valuable records of past and present speech can ever be utilized by Dynamic Philology for the almost absurd reason that their transcriptions were not made with the use of the most refined phonetic system of symbolization. In approaching these statistics these notes of caution must be borne in mind.

* The absence or presence of voicing in the Dutch speech-element indicated above by *k* and *g* is not phonemically significant in Dutch, the voiced form being but a variant of the voiceless.[1] The fact that these two speech-elements cannot be compared like the others has been indicated by percentages in parentheses.

The first three languages (Czechish, Dutch, and French), which afford the best material, unmistakably show that the voiceless stops are more frequent than their corresponding voiced stops in each language.   The material of the remaining nine languages, though not as accurate as that of the above, points definitely in the same direction with the exception of the Spanish dentals and the Hungarian labials. We shall later find (page 116 f.) that the Spanish dentals, when viewed from the angle of dynamic development in Part II, cease to be an exception.   The exceptional relationship of the Hungarian labials will probably not be found altered in an accurate phonemic transcription.   Save for the Spanish dentals and the Hungarian labials, the unvoiced stops on the whole are appreciably more frequent than their corresponding voiced stops.   Out of thirty-five opportunities for deviation from this general tendency, there are only two actual deviations.   Hence this relationship as evidenced by these data from twelve languages is 94.3 per cent valid.

5. THE RELATIVE FREQUENCY OF OTHER PHONEMES WHOSE MAGNITUDES OF COMPLEXITY ARE IN PART COMPARABLE

The question naturally arises at this time as to the possibility of comparing other phonemes in respect to magnitude of complexity.   For the stops which we have examined, though an important category numerically in the phonemic systems of languages in which they occur, represent neither a majority of available phonemes nor a majority of occurrences of phonemes.

In the case of monophthong-vowels there is frequently the opportunity in many languages of comparing corresponding long and short vowels.   In some cases (e.g. ă and ā in Sanskrit or German) the phonemic difference of sheer length is a

sufficient indication of differences in magnitude of com-
plexity. Thus in the case of German $\bar{a}$ and $\ddot{a}$, e.g. $k\bar{a}n$,
(written *Kahn*) 'boat,' and $k\ddot{a}n$ (written *kann*) 'can,' the $\bar{a}$
may be said to represent a greater magnitude of complexity
than $\ddot{a}$, because $\bar{a}$ represents everything that $\ddot{a}$ represents,
plus added duration. In the case of many other pairs of long
and short vowels in many other languages, however, the difference is more than that of mere duration. For example, in
the English pair $\bar{\imath}$ and $\ddot{\imath}$ (e.g. *machine* and $\ddot{\imath}t$) the position of
the vocal organs is by no means identical and hence the com-
parative magnitudes of the two are not determinable even
though it might be found that the long vowel has a greater
average duration than the short. Though we may and probably correctly do feel that the long vowel represents a
greater magnitude of complexity than the short, the validity
of this subjective feeling would be practically impossible to
prove empirically except by assuming (which is not yet permissible) that relative frequency is indicative of comparative
magnitude, and by showing, as will doubtless be found true,
that the short vowels have on the whole an appreciably higher
relative frequency of occurrence than their corresponding
long vowels. At present there are but few reliable data available on the subject in any language. What we have on the
subject of the phonemes $\bar{a}$ and $\ddot{a}$ is from Vedic Sanskrit,[1]
which show that the phoneme of greater magnitude of complexity is also of lower relative frequency (e.g. $\bar{a} = 8.19\%$,
$\ddot{a} = 19.78\%$).

It is also perhaps possible to compare monophthong-vowels
with diphthongs which contain them, e.g. $\ddot{a}$ with $\ddot{a}i$ and $\ddot{a}u$,
$\breve{o}$ with $\breve{o}i$ and $\breve{o}u$, etc. Whether it can be correctly said that
the magnitude of complexity of the typical vowel $\ddot{a}$ is the
same when occurring in the typical diphthong $\ddot{a}i$ as when occurring alone is doubtful. But on account of our general
subjective feeling that the magnitude of complexity of a
diphthong is greater than that of its component parts when
occurring alone, it may be stated that the few available and

reasonably reliable statistics that exist on the subject indicate clearly that the diphthong, which presumably is of greater magnitude of complexity than that of each of its parts when occurring alone, is also relatively less frequent (e.g. Sanskrit $\breve{a}u = .18\%$, $\breve{a} = 27.97\%$;[1] German diagraph $au = 2.242\%$, German letter $a = 13.147\%$,[2] the German percentages reckoned on the basis of all occurrences of vowels in Kaeding). This new and interesting subject[3] merits the attention of further and more accurate investigation.* The topic does not, however, justify our including in the text here the illuminating statistics for Modern Icelandic vowels and diphthongs.[4]

The problem of comparative magnitudes of complexity of spirants (e.g. f, v, $\flat$, $\eth$, s, z, etc. in English) is truly difficult, even in languages where the presence or absence of voicing is phonemically significant, because of the extremely variable factor of duration. Investigation of these phonemes may, therefore, not be particularly rewarding.

With the *trills* (e.g. the *apical trill* or 'rolled r' of Italian, or the *uvular trill* or 'uvular r' of Danish) as well as with the *laterals* (i.e. the l's) of a language there is not only the variable factor of duration, but also frequently the absence of any other phoneme suitable to serve in comparison.

With the nasals, m and n, it might be taken as some evidence that n is the simpler of the two phonemes because of the observations [5] of comparative philology which indicate that quite often, when m disappears in any of its usages in a given language, it becomes (i.e. 'weakens' to) n before disappearing. Whether we may safely conclude from this fairly frequent phenomenon that n is therefore, on the whole, a phoneme of smaller magnitude of complexity than m is clearly a controversial matter. In any event available statistics [6] reveal that n is, on the whole, appreciably more frequent in occurrence than m (Burmese being the only exception):

---

* The magnitudes of complexity of $\breve{i}$, $\breve{e}$, $\breve{a}$, $\breve{o}$, $\breve{u}$, etc., when compared with one another are at present indeterminable; similarly with $\bar{i}$, $\bar{e}$, $\bar{a}$, $\bar{o}$, $\bar{u}$, etc.

	m	n		m	n
Czechish	3.52	6.42	Latin	5.82	6.47
Dutch	3.18	7.09	Sanskrit	4.34	7.04
French	2.56	3.19	Peipingese	2.18	10.18
Italian	3.11	6.25	Cantonese	4.07	5.70
English	2.78	7.24	Burmese	4.72	4.15
Hungarian	3 35	5.74	Swedish	3.28	7.32
Bulgarian	2.22	7.00	Danish	3.18	5.70
Russian	3.12	5.13	Singhalese	3.12	7.40
Spanish	2.29	6.08	Old English	2.81	8.40
Icelandic	4.37	7.77	Old High German	2.91	10.85
Greek	3.19	8.55			

6. CONCLUSION: EQUILIBRIUM

If we pause now to reflect upon the statistics which have been presented in respect to the relative frequency of occurrence of many different phonemes in many different languages [1] that are but distantly related, if not altogether unrelated, and whose speakers in most cases belong to different quarters of the globe, or to different ages, or to different national cultures, we find two interrelated phenomena. First, it is clearly evident that the frequency distribution of phonemes in the stream of speech is by no means completely a matter of random chance but that the relative frequency of occurrence of a phoneme depends to a considerable extent upon its form. And second, wherever the comparative magnitudes of complexity of phonemes are determinable, the magnitude of complexity bears an inverse (not necessarily proportionate) ratio to the relative frequency of occurrence. Though, in the case of voiced and voiceless stops, the comparative magnitudes of complexity are not determinable, and though we cannot demonstrate *a priori* that the voicing of a voiced stop (however lenis) on the whole more than counterbalances the presence of additional expiratory stress or aspiration or both in the voiceless stop (as computed in terms of differences in magnitude of complexity), nevertheless the evidence of statistics unmistakably reveals that the relative frequency of voiced stops bears the same relationship to the relative frequency of voiceless stops, as the relative frequency of phonemes of determinably greater magnitude to the relative frequency of phonemes of determinably lesser magnitude.

Therefore, in the absence of any significant evidence to the contrary, we seem justified in saying that the magnitude of complexity of a phoneme stands in an inverse (not necessarily proportionate) relationship to its relative frequency of occurrence.   In other words, a condition of equilibrium seems to exist in the phonemic system of a language between the magnitude of complexity of phonemes on the one hand and their relative frequency of occurrence on the other.   Not only does this conclusion follow immediately from our statistics, but it would seem that our statistics admit of no alternate conclusion.

The question, then, arises as to the nature of a possible causal relationship between magnitude of complexity and relative frequency of occurrence.   Is the relative frequency of occurrence dependent upon the magnitude of complexity, or the magnitude of complexity upon the relative frequency of occurrence?   Since, in speaking, we obviously select our words according to their meanings and rarely if ever according to the magnitude of complexity of their component phonemes, and since comparatively few persons are aware of the fact that an equilibrium presumably exists between the magnitude of complexity and relative frequency of occurrence of their phonemes, it seems highly unlikely that the magnitude of complexity is the cause of the relative frequency of occurrence. It can, however, be demonstrated that the reverse is true, and in a manner which incidentally sheds light on many complex problems in the dynamics of the form and behavior of phonemes in the stream of speech.

PART II

THE DYNAMICS OF CHANGE IN THE DEVELOPMENT OF A PHONEMIC SYSTEM

I. THE PHENOMENA DESCRIBED UNDER GRASSMANN'S LAW; HAPLOLOGY

The nature of the causal relationship between the magnitude of complexity of a phoneme and its relative frequency of occurrence can be established from examples of *change in magnitude* connected with *change in frequency* in which the motivating factor is observable. There are two especially clear examples of this process,[1] one in Sanskrit and one in ancient Greek, which are closely similar and are designated after their discoverer Grassmann's Law.* In either example we find (1) changes in form resulting from what amounts to changes in frequency of occurrence, which are (2) changes toward a lesser magnitude of complexity resulting from what may be considered a change toward a greater frequency of occurrence. As we view in turn the conditions under which Grassmann's Law operated in Sanskrit and Greek, it will become increasingly more evident not only that the magnitude of complexity depends upon relative frequency of occurrence, but how this dependence is possible.

* That the reader who is unfamiliar with the terminology of comparative philology may not be confused, it should be pointed out that the term *law* as used by comparative philologists generally designates formulae of correspondences (e.g. Grimm's Law, see page 121 ff.) and not causal relations.[2]

a. *Grassmann's Law in Sanskrit*

Grassmann's Law in Sanskrit describes the behavior of voiced aspirated stops under certain specific conditions. These voiced aspirated stops (henceforth referred to as *mediae aspiratae* for convenience) were phonemes composed of the voiced stops *b*, *d*, *g*, etc., plus a following aspiration, *h*. Though generally transcribed today into the Latin alphabet with the digraph *bh*, *dh*, *gh*, etc., these *mediae aspiratae* were felt as simple phonemes by the native speakers, and hence were represented in the native alphabet by single speech-symbols.

Grassmann discovered that if two mediae aspiratae occurred in the same stem in Sanskrit, the one lost its aspiration. For example, Sanskrit *dahati* 'it burns' represents an older **dhaghati*, from the root **dhagh* 'to burn' which is also the root of our word *day* (Gothic *dags*, German *Tag*). There are other similar examples of roots with two mediae aspiratae of which one has lost its aspiration in Sanskrit. But Grassmann's Law is especially important in reduplication, that is, in those instances where certain tenses or tense stems of verbs are made by a repetition, generally of the initial phonemes of the root; for example, the present stem of the root *dā* 'to give' is *dadāmi*, the perfect stem is *dadau*. Of course whenever the initial phoneme of a root was a media aspirata, as was the case with many roots (such as *dhā* 'to put,' *bhṛ* 'to carry'), the conditions were correct for the operation of Grassmann's Law whenever the root was reduplicated. Hence the perfect of *dhā* was *dadhau* instead of **dhadhau*; the present of *bhṛ* was *bibharmi* instead of **bhibharmi*. Moreover, the voiced stops *b*, *d*, *g*, etc., which arose from an older *bh*, *dh*, *gh*, etc., through the operation of Grassmann's Law, behaved subsequently indistinguishably from the voiced stops *b*, *d*, *g* which had been members of the phonemic system prior to the operation of Grassmann's Law.

That Grassmann's Law was as powerful as it was precise in its operation is illustrated by the astonishing irregularities which it introduced into an inflection — irregularities which the language preferred to tolerate rather than to disobey Grassmann's Law by allowing two mediae aspiratae to occur too closely together. For example, serious irregularities arose in an inflection whenever a suffix or ending was added to the stem in such a fashion that the second media aspirata lost its aspiration because of assimilation. Once the second media aspirata lost its aspiration, Grassmann's Law became inoperative with the result that the first media aspirata retained its aspiration. That the extent of the inflectional irregularities described above may be apparent even to one not familiar with Sanskrit, let us present as illustration the present tense middle voice indicative of the root *dha* 'to place' in which assimilations of the second media aspirata had taken place (2. and 3. person singular and 2. person plural):

	Singular	*Plural*
1. Person	*dadhe*	*dadhmahe*
2. Person	*dhatse*	*dhaddhve*
3. Person	*dhante*	*dadhante*

Since we have no phonemic mediae aspiratae in English, a hypothetical parallel in English will enable one to appreciate the enormity of the inflectional irregularity occasioned by the operation of this law:

	Singular	*Plural*
1. Person	I tell	we tell
2. Person	you dell	you dell
3. Person	he dells	they tell

b. *Grassmann's Law in Greek*

Fortunately Grassmann's Law applies similarly to Greek, thereby proving that the Law was in no way the effect of random chance in the Sanskrit language, nor the result of any peculiar environmental conditions in India, or of any peculiar

Indian habits.   In Greek, however, the phonemes which appeared in Sanskrit as voiced aspirated stops had lost the
voicing, and had become unvoiced aspirated stops in prehistoric Greek well before the time when Grassmann's Law
began to be effective in Greek [i.e. *dh* had become *t^h*; *bh* had
become *p^h*; *gh* had become *k^h*, written in the Attic alphabet
as θ, φ, and χ, respectively].

Now, in Greek, as correspondingly in Sanskrit, whenever
an aspirate (from whatever source) was followed in the first
or second succeeding syllable by another aspirate, the aspiration of the first aspirate was lost, even though the first aspirate was only an *h* (*spiritus asper*), that is, a phoneme which
consisted exclusively of the aspiration.

In Greek, too, the assimilation of the second aspirate ren-
dered Grassmann's Law inoperative.   When the root occurred, for example, in a different tense or case or degree
and thereby received a suffix which through assimilation
changed the unvoiced aspirated stop, for example, to an unvoiced unaspirated stop (e.g. *t^h* to *t*), the initial aspirate, as in
Sanskrit, retained its aspiration.   To illustrate this point, let
us present a few of the numerous available examples:

> present *tít^hēmi* from **t^hít^hēmi*
> equivalent to Sanskrit *dadhāmi*
> nominative *t^hríks*, but genitive *trik^hós*
> present *trép^hō*, but future *t^hrépsō*
> positive *tak^hús*, but comparative *t^háttōn*
> present *ek^hō* from earlier **hek^hō* from
> either **sek^hō* or **wek^hō*

c. *Interpretation of the Phenomena Described by Grassmann's Law; Haplology*

If one asks what actually took place in Greek and Sanskrit
under Grassmann's Law, it can only be answered that, of two
similar phonemes each of a high magnitude of complexity,

one phoneme changed its form by a *truncation* of its aspiration, thereby reducing the magnitude of its complexity. If, however, one asks why this diminution in magnitude of complexity occurred, it can only be answered, as it has always been answered, namely, that the two aspirated stops stood in too close proximity. That in the phenomenon under consideration it was a question of a great magnitude of complexity on the one hand and too close a proximity on the other can be established from the behavior of the same and other phonemes in Sanskrit and Greek. Phonemes of lower magnitude of complexity could tolerate an equally close proximity without undergoing dissimilation *; for example, the unaspirated voiced stops of Sanskrit or the unaspirated voiceless stops of Greek were not regularly dissimilated, regardless of how closely they were juxtaposed. Furthermore, the phonemes which were dissimilated under Grassmann's Law in Sanskrit and Greek remained stable when far enough separated.

This tendency, illustrated by Grassmann's Law, of complex phonemes or phoneme-groups to become dissimilated under too great proximity is, moreover, fairly frequent in language. Witness the phenomenon called haplology;[1] when two similar syllables — they need not be identical — are adjacent, one may become permanently truncated. E.g. the classical Greek *didáskalos* (διδάσκαλος) appears in modern Greek as *dáskalos* (δάσκαλος); the initial syllable *di*, because it was similar to the following syllable, was dropped without leaving a trace behind. Similarly the colloquial New England form *calate* for *calculate* is an instance of haplology. It is unnecessary to remind the linguist that haplology has influenced to a greater or less degree all spoken languages, not least of all the Germanic from which our own English is descended.

* The phenomena described by Grassmann's Law belong to the general type of sound-change technically known as *dissimilation*: 'When a phoneme or type of phoneme recurs within a form, one of the occurrences is sometimes replaced by a different sound.' — *Bloomfield*.[1]

Now the changes in the form of phonemes under Grassmann's Law represent in all cases a diminution in the total magnitude of complexity of the changed phonemes resulting from the truncation of the aspiration.   In the case of haplology, the changed form is entirely truncated and its magnitude of complexity reduced to zero.   These changes in magnitude of complexity result from an excessive, though sporadic, increase in the relative frequency of occurrence of these affected forms in the stream of speech.   That is, the average intervals of occurrence between the same or similar phonemes (or phoneme combinations in examples of haplology) have become much shortened in some words, and this shortening has caused truncation of at least a part of the form, which in the case of Grassmann's Law in Sanskrit and Greek has always resulted at least * in different and simpler phonemes (e.g. *dh* i.e. d^h, becoming *d*, t^h becoming *t*).

The question now arises as to the relationship between these phenomena described under Grassmann's Law to (1) the general phenomena of equilibrium discussed in Part I of this chapter, and (2) the general phenomena of phonetic change of which the dissimilations of Grassmann's Law are but one typical example.

2. PHONETIC CHANGE AND THE
QUESTION OF EQUILIBRIUM

We have seen, on the one hand, that the phonemic system of a language when viewed in a steady state is in a condition of equilibrium between the magnitude of complexity of the forms of phonemes and the relative frequency of their occurrence.   We are, on the other hand, assured by comparative philologists that in the history of any language the phonemic

---

† * At times not even that; for, in the event that the preceding phoneme in Greek was a simple aspiration (i.e. an *h*) and not a stop, this entire phoneme consisting solely of aspiration was annihilated; see example $ek^h\bar{o}$, page 84).

system undergoes extensive changes [1] which may seriously affect both the magnitude of complexity of phonemes and their relative frequency of occurrence. Thus, in the histories of the eleven * languages of common ancestry for which the percentages of relative frequency of occurrences of voiced and voiceless stops have been presented (page 75), numerous changes in the form of phonemes have taken place which have greatly modified their form and frequency of occurrence (even to the point, at times, of temporary or permanent obliteration), and which have in turn given rise to languages as widely different as Russian and English, French and Bulgarian. These changes, as we shall see, affected the form and frequency of voiced and voiceless stops as well as of other phonemes, so that in many if not most cases the occurrences of given stops in specific words in one language have no counterparts in comparable occurrences of cognate words in another or other languages. We find, nevertheless, that the relationship between the magnitude of complexity and relative frequency of comparable stops in these now completely different languages has remained on the whole quite similar. Hence it seems by no means rash to suppose what we shall now attempt to demonstrate in detail that this condition of equilibrium in the phonemic system is preserved or restored from disturbance by acts of phonetic change exemplified in part by the phenomena described under Grassmann's Law and haplology.

a. Phonetic Change as an Orderly though Apparently Capriciously Occurring Phenomenon

It has been quite generally observed, though perhaps at times differently expressed, that the emergence of a phonetic change in the phonemic system of a language is almost in-

---

* The twelfth language, Hungarian, is not of common ancestry with the others as far as has yet been determined.

variably so incalculable as to appear capricious, yet, that the change itself, once begun, is of a high degree of orderliness. To be more explicit, it may be said unqualifiedly on the basis of past performance that at seemingly any time in any language any particular phoneme or phonemes may without warning become unstable and undergo a change in form either in all occurrences of the phoneme or phonemes, or in occurrences in certain specific positions.   Yet, once the change has commenced, it runs its course like a self-limiting disease with the general result that the affected phonemes which survive are again stable though changed. These changed phonemes may remain stable or they may not. A language may be spared from change and remain remarkably conservative for years, or it may undergo many changes simultaneously which are followed by other changes extending over centuries. The fact that phonetic change may at times lead to highly inconvenient homonyms (witness *let* 'to allow' from Old-English *lætan* 'to allow,' and *let* 'to hinder' from Old-English *lettan* 'to hinder'; see page 33) does not seem on the whole to restrain the emergence of change or seriously to modify its course.

Though the emergence of phonetic change is apparently capricious, actual phonetic changes seem to fall into four main and orderly types: (1) the so-called '*spontaneous*' *changes*,* (2) the *accentual changes*, (3) the *assimilatory changes*, and (4) the *dissimilatory changes*.

i. '*Spontaneous*' *Phonetic Change*

'Spontaneous' phonetic changes are particularly interesting because they apparently occur independently of any other perceptible contextual factor.   Without warning a phoneme

---

* So-called formerly because they could be ascribed to no perceptible cause; evidence will be adduced to show that they are neither more nor less spontaneous in this sense than any other type of phonetic change.

may become transformed into a different phoneme which may or may not have been present in the original language. In many dialects of Middle English, for example, $\bar{a}$ shifted to $\bar{\varrho}$, wherever it occurred, e.g. *stān* becoming *stǭn* (stone), *rāp* becoming *rǭp* (rope). The original Indo-European $\breve{e}$ and $\breve{o}$ changed to $\breve{a}$ in prehistoric Sanskrit; the three originally different phonemes $\breve{e}$, $\breve{a}$, $\breve{o}$ became thereby completely indistinguishable in their pronunciation, while $\breve{e}$ and $\breve{o}$ ceased to exist in the language. Phonemes which are not vowels may undergo similar change; thus, the original *d* of Indo-European shifted everywhere to *t* in prehistoric Germanic, e.g. the *d* of Latin *duo* 'two' appearing as *t* even today in English *two*.

It must not, however, be inferred that the original form of the shifted phoneme remains forever lost to the language; on the contrary, no sooner may a phoneme with form *x* shift to form *y* than some other hitherto stable phoneme with a form *z* may change and adopt the abandoned form *x*. Thus, after Indo-European *t* had shifted in most positions to Germanic *þ* (as *th* in English *three*, Latin *tres*) the Indo-European *d* subsequently shifted everywhere to *t*, a form which has remained stable for the most part until today (see above). Consistent changes of this general type may at times disturb the meanings of words as little as the consistent substitutions of an alternate set of symbols may modify the applicability of an algebraic formula.[1] Incidentally, changes of this type have years ago provided comparative philology with negative proofs[2] on the subject of the causation of sound-changes; whatever the ultimate cause of 'spontaneous' phonetic changes may be, it cannot reside in physiological changes in the vocal apparatus, or in permanent changes in climate, or in the inability of children to pronounce a given phoneme, or in a linguistic 'substratum,' since frequently the seemingly tabu phonemic form later reappears in the phonemic system as the result of a subsequent change. This same negative information is similarly derivable from the phenomena of accentual and assimilatory changes and, circuitously, from dissimilatory changes.

ii. *Accentual Phonetic Change*

Phonetic changes may also result from the position of accent. For example, a vowel,* when in an unaccented syllable, may become "weakened," a "weakening" which frequently results either in the complete annihilation of the vowel (e.g. loss of final *e* in English *I sing* from Old-English *ic singe*), or, in a change of membership in the inclusive phonemic type. As example of the latter, prehistoric Latin *ă* changed in an unaccented closed syllable to *ě* (e.g. *cónfăctus* became *cónfěctus*), and in an open syllable to *ĭ* (e.g. *cónfăcere* became *cónfĭcere*). Since both *ě* and *ĭ* had been distinctive phonemes in Latin before this accentual change of *ă* to *ě* and *ĭ* respectively, the change was one in membership in a phonemic type; subsequent to the accentual change, the *ě* and *ĭ* from *ă* behaved indistinguishably from *ě* and *ĭ* from any other source in like positions. Though these accentual changes in English and Latin were typically orderly their appearance was also typically capricious, as defined on pages 87 f. On the other hand, the form *ich sínge*, 'I sing,' in present-day German is reasonably stable; all unaccented vowels of Latin in the same period were by no means changed (e.g. *ā*, *ē*, *ō* were stable), nor is *ă* invariably changed in languages throughout the world whenever unaccented (see pages 177 f.).

iii. *Assimilatory Phonetic Change*

A very frequent type of phonetic change is the change in position or manner of articulation of a phoneme in certain positions so that it will approximate the position or manner

---

* Consonants may also change because of the position of accent, e.g. the changes of Germanic *f* to *v*, etc., described under Verner's Law.[1]

of articulation of a near or contiguous phoneme. This type of change is termed *assimilatory*,[1] and an example has already been tendered in our discussion of the change of *g* to *k* when Latin **exagtos* became *exaktus* (written *exactus*); see page 66, footnote. Sometimes two contiguous phonemes are assimilated to one another and combine to make a third phoneme, e.g. English *would* and *you* becoming what might be conventionally written *wouldjew* [phonetically, *wujū*], the *t* and *y* of *courtyard* coalescing into the combination frequently transcribed by *ch* as in *child*. Copious examples of assimilatory changes affecting almost every known phonemic type are readily available in the historical and comparative handbooks of the different languages. Assimilatory changes are no exception to the prevailing rule that phonetic changes are orderly though seemingly capricious.

iv. *Dissimilatory Phonetic Change*

Since we have already described and illustrated *dissimilatory phonetic changes* in our discussion of the phenomena covered by Grassmann's Law (pages 81 ff.) it need now only be mentioned that dissimilatory phonetic changes, like the others, are orderly though apparently capricious.

3. THE EFFECT OF PHONETIC CHANGE
ON MAGNITUDES OF COMPLEXITY

Since a phonetic change generally influences in some way the form of a phoneme, it therefore influences, at least often, the phoneme's magnitude of complexity. Of course when the comparative magnitude of complexity of a phoneme is indeterminable,* the changes which it may undergo are in-

---

* E.g. the change of *ā* to *ǭ* in Middle English (see page 89), or of *ĕ* and *ŏ* to *ă* in Sanskrit (see page 89).

determinable in respect to magnitude of complexity. Hence, as long as a given phonetic change must be viewed as indeterminable because of the shortcomings of our knowledge, it rests with every individual to decide for himself whether indeterminable phonetic changes presumably obey the observable laws of determinable phonetic changes in whole or in part, or possess independent laws of their own, or behave according to no law and are random. Since the present investigation is empirical, we shall devote our attention only to phonetic changes in which are involved comparative magnitudes of complexity which are determinable. These, as we shall now see in detail, fall into two mutually exclusive classes: (1) the abbreviatory changes, and (2) the augmentative changes, according to the effect of phonetic change on the comparative magnitudes of complexity of the phonemes involved. Our interest, however, is in the total effect of change — not only on magnitude of complexity but also on the relative frequency of occurrence of the phoneme — in restoring balance between magnitude and frequency.

a. Abbreviatory Phonetic Changes

Abbreviatory phonetic changes are changes in which the comparative magnitude of complexity of the changing phoneme is abbreviated either completely or only partly. Since a description of the dynamics involved in the latter is quite complex and at times inferential, we shall commence our discussion with a consideration of the former, that is, the completely abbreviatory changes.

Complete abbreviatory changes are those in which the form and magnitude of complexity of a phoneme are reduced to nothing, with or without compensation elsewhere for the loss. Examples of this are the loss in late vulgar Old English of initial *h* in the consonantal groups *hr, hl, hn* (e.g. *hring > ring; hlēapan > leap; hnecca > neck*), or of initial *k, g,* and *w* in the combinations *kn*, *gn*, *wr* (e.g. *cnēow* > *knee*; *gnagan* > *gnaw*; *wringan* > *wring*). There is no trace of these lost consonants in present-day spoken English. Examples of complete abbreviatory change might be multiplied indefinitely in practically any language. Changes of this type are in substance complete truncations of the phoneme involved. The effect of the change is a diminution in the phoneme's total relative frequency by an amount equal to the total occurrences of the phoneme in all positions where truncation occurs.

The partial abbreviatory phonemic changes have precisely the same effect in diminishing the total relative frequency of occurrence of the phoneme-types in which change occurs, together with a corresponding increase in the relative frequency of the phoneme-types whose forms are adopted. Thus, when *ĕ* and *ŏ* became *ă* in all positions in Sanskrit, the relative frequency of *ĕ* and *ŏ* became zero, and that of *ă* increased enormously; when *dh*, for example, was dissimilated in certain positions in Sanskrit to *d*, the loss in frequency of occurrence to *dh* was added to *d*. However, in partial abbreviatory changes, the decrease in magnitude of complexity is only partial; instead of a truncation of the entire phoneme, the truncation is only of one or more of the subsidiary sequences of articulatory sub-gestures. Thus, if all else is equal, the change of *dh* to *d* truncates the sequence of aspiration; the change of *d* to *t* truncates the sequence of voicing; the change of *ā* to *ă* truncates a section of the duration of the phoneme.

These abbreviatory phonetic changes, whether complete or partial, may be 'spontaneous,' or accentual, or assimilatory, or dissimilatory, and their effect upon the equilibrium of the entire phonemic system of a language is in each case similar, though perhaps different in degree. That is, the product of magnitude of complexity and relative frequency of occurrence is diminished by any abbreviatory phonetic change. Hence, when at any time the product of magnitude and frequency for any phoneme is excessive, an abbreviatory phonetic change of that phoneme, whether 'spontaneous,' accentual, assimilatory or dissimilatory, will tend to diminish this excessive product in the direction of a more perfect condition of equilibrium.   Be the ultimate purpose of phonetic change what it may, one possible effect of phonetic change, at least when abbreviatory, is clearly to restore equilibrium.

Of course, if carried sufficiently far, an abbreviatory change could in itself upset equilibrium in the other direction by making the product of magnitude and frequency too small. Though this risk is, as we shall see, not entirely absent, it is minimized nevertheless by neat checks and counterbalances, which indicate (as is observable statistically) the two limits of toleration in the relative frequency of each phoneme of determinable magnitude beyond which both the necessity for, and the likelihood of, occurrence of abbreviatory or augmentative changes to restore equilibrium increase.   In other words, these phonetic changes which have been found so orderly in their course are also not less orderly in their emergence, though they give the impression of capriciousness in the unexpectedness with which they beset the phonemes of a tongue.   That is (as can and will be demonstrated *a priori* and as can and will be established statistically with a high degree of probability of truth), as the equilibrium between magnitude and frequency of a phoneme or phonemes becomes more and more disturbed, the likelihood of phonetic change becomes greater and greater.   The change may be rapid, occurring almost literally overnight, or it may be slow, extending over considerable time; in either case, its course seems to be run, once equilibrium is restored.   If phonetic change is viewed as a restorative of balance, then the various types of phonetic change become but different manifestations of a single basic force which assumes one manifestation rather than another because of what may be termed the 'accidents' of arrangement of the vocal apparatus.

Once it is made clear in what respect the arrangements of the vocal apparatus are 'accidental,' it becomes clear (1) why phonemes are more stable in one position than in another, and (2) why this difference in stability introduces variant forms (see *skewness*, pages 101 ff.) of the phoneme, which in turn shunts phonetic change in the direction of assimilation or of dissimilation, etc., the moment the threshold of tolerable frequency has been significantly overstepped. Since each of these two points represent an essential factor in the total dynamics of the form and behavior of phonemes in the phenomenon of equilibrium, let us view each in turn.*

b. The 'Accidents' of Arrangement of Vocal Apparatus

From one point of view the entire vocal apparatus, including its physiological arrangement and the gestures of which it is capable, belongs to the most fundamental realities involved in the production of speech; but from another point of view this entire inclusive vocal apparatus belongs to the accidents of speech-production. The situation is analogous to the course of a river. The various topographical features of the terrain, such as its contours and the like, through which the river flows, are from one viewpoint highly important features in determining the course of the river; yet from another viewpoint these features are but fortuitous to the fundamental and universal forces of gravitation. That is, the tendency of the parts of a phonemic system to preserve equilibrium is presumably a biological force valid for all language; the actual course of behavior of speech in preserving equilibrium is contingent upon the organization of speech-apparatus. If there are striking similarities in the form and development of individual phonemes among the various languages of the earth, that is because there exists a fundamental similarity of vocal apparatus so close indeed that a

* For the discussion of augmentative changes see pages 113 ff.

phoneme type of any one language may conceivably develop in the system of any other.   If the vocal apparatus were different among different races, the form and development of their phonemes would be different; yet, for all we can see to the contrary, the urge to preserve a condition of equilibrium among the different phonemes of these hypothetically different races would still be present.   From the viewpoint of this primal urge, the highly important work of the experimental phoneticist (not to be confused with the numerous professional phonetic transcribers who are but animate and not very accurate phonographs) is in the field of linguistic 'accidents.'   If the dynamic philologist attempts to discover when the basic conditions are ripe for change in the form of a given phoneme, toward augmentation * or diminution in magnitude of complexity in a given language, the experimental phoneticist, on the other hand, attempts to determine by his laboratory study of speech-physiology what changes are possible.   By working together, the two fields may some day be able to determine which changes are probable in any given instance of this peculiar form of biological mutation.

In commencing our analysis of the accidental nature of vocal apparatus in the sense defined, we may profitably mention a fact which has long been familiar to comparative philology: the articulation of many given phonemes is more favored in some positions than in others, depending primarily upon the nature of near-by or contiguous sounds.   That is, because of the physiology of the mouth, it is easier to pronounce for example a *d* after *n* than after *m*, yet it is easier to pronounce a *b* after *m* than after *n*.   Similarly *t* is easier to pronounce in the combinations *st* or *ts* than in *tk* or *tm*.   In each case the reason for the greater ease is that the vocal apparatus when arranged for pronunciation of the preceding sound is already to a considerable extent arranged for the following sound.   Thus, in *nd*, much of the vocal apparatus

---

* See pages 113 ff.

in being arranged for *n* is also arranged for *d*; in *st* or *ts* the difference in arrangement is almost exclusively a question of a slight difference in the movement of the tip of the tongue. On the other hand, in the articulation of *md* or *tk* an extensive rearrangement of the vocal apparatus is necessary after the first phoneme has been articulated. Naturally the sound following the phoneme is quite as important in determining the ease of pronunciation of the combination as the sound preceding it; the combination *tn* is difficult not only for *n* but also for *t*. For the rearrangement of the vocal apparatus, which is necessary when two phonemes are uttered, generally [1] takes place during both the end of the first phoneme and the beginning of the second.

Hence, because of the so-called accidents of the organization of the vocal apparatus, any given phoneme in any given language is more easily pronounceable in some of its various occurrences than in others, depending upon the nature of the combinations in which it occurs. We should then be quite justified, it seems, in arranging in our mind the different combinations in which any phoneme occurs according to the comparative ease or difficulty of its utterance when combined with them. And the positions of a phoneme in combinations where pronunciation is comparatively easiest, are the most favorable positions of the phoneme, though favorable position is of course a matter of degree.

c. *The Effect of Position upon the Pronunciation of a Phoneme*

The effect of the varying degrees of ease or difficulty in the pronunciation of a phoneme which results from its position in combination with other sounds is largely upon its range of variability. That is, the more difficult a phoneme is to utter, in the sense that its complete utterance from beginning to end necessitates more complex and hence difficult rearrangement, the greater is the possibility of error in approximating the phonemic norm.   To use the analogy of the target (page 53), we may say that the greater the difficulty is in shooting, the more likely is deviation from the bull's eye.   It is as if the linguistic target were moved to within a few feet of the marksman when the utterance of a phoneme is in a favorable position and moved appreciably farther away when the utterance is appreciably less favored.   If a given phoneme, a, occurs predominantly in favorable positions, and another, b, in predominantly unfavorable positions, the cluster of bullet holes of a will be smaller and denser than of b, and hence the range of variability will be smaller for a than for b.

However, if we take into consideration the relative frequency of occurrence of the phoneme in each of its various combinations, we find that range of variability is not the only factor in the distribution, as can be shown from our example of the target.   We have seen that the range of variability increases presumably with distance from the target; so, too, probably with decreasing visibility.   This greater deviation is presumably equally great in all directions from the bull's eye.   If the successive deviations to the East (i.e. right) and to the West (i.e. left) of a medial vertical line through the bull's eye were plotted on a line, the curve would represent the outline of a hill; the greater the range of variation is, the flatter will be the contour of this hill if all else is equal.   However, if a wind is blowing, say, from the East while the marksman is shooting, and if he does not allow for this wind, the mode of the distribution (i.e. the apex of the hill) will be to the west of the medial vertical line and the curve of distribution (i.e. the contour of the hill) will be askew (to use the technical statistical term).

Now the varying degrees of difficulty in the articulation of a phoneme resulting from the different combinations in which it occurs, together with the various relative frequencies of occurrences of the phoneme in its different combinations, may introduce a modification in the normal distribution of speech-sounds about the phonemic norm which, it seems, may well be termed *skewness*.*

Although it is practically impossible to visualize in merely two dimensions a speech-sound which may vary in duration, amplitude, pitch, and the like, nevertheless for the sake of illustration we can represent in two dimensions the individual attributes of a phoneme. Thus our target may represent deviations to the East and West according to duration: we can draw a medial vertical line through the bull's eye representing the phoneme *a* in English and consider that shots falling to the East represent abnormally long duration while shots to the West represent abnormally short duration; that is, as we proceed from the medial line toward the East, the articulations become increasingly longer than that at the norm of the bull's eye, while as we proceed from the medial line toward the West, the articulations become increasingly shorter than that at the norm of the bull's eye. Similarly, we may select the amplitude or loudness of *a*, with increasing loudness at the East and diminishing loudness at the West. A similar arrangement may also be imagined for a consonant. For example, we may take the voicing of a voiced consonant, say *d*, in a language, or rather the percentage of voicing to the entire duration of a phoneme; thus the speech-sounds of increasingly high percentage of voicing above the norm would be at the East, and increasingly low percentage of voicing below the norm at the West. Naturally as one goes

---

* There is no known way of proving that the normal distribution of speech-sounds about a phonemic norm will follow the Gaussian curve if plotted according to success and failure in approximating the norm. It is, however, a reasonably certain inference that they would conform to this curve; for, insofar as measurable human activity is an approximation of a norm, it is found to follow the familiar Gaussian distribution. If it should subsequently be found that the entire magnitudes of speech-sounds can be measured, and that their distribution is not according to the Gaussian curve as we shall henceforth assume for convenience in demonstration, the modifications to the normal distribution which we shall investigate under the heading of *skewness* will still be of the same nature, whatever the normal curve may be. For an example of a Gaussian curve of normal distribution see the curve *AB'C* of Plate V.

to the West on this *voicing*-target of *d* the speech-sounds are increasingly more voiceless until they might perhaps equally well be considered *per se* as approximations of the *t* norm (see page 60 f). Or, as a final example we might consider merely the variations in the degree of aspiration (page 56 f.), indicating excessive aspiration at the East and insufficient aspiration at the West.

But though it is difficult to visualize in two dimensions the total phenomenon of any one phoneme, still we may suppose for the sake of demonstration that a device exists whereby the total magnitude of complexity of a speech-sound may be represented on a plane. That is, we shall imagine that the medial vertical line represents the norm of total complexity, and that to the East are increasing magnitudes, while to the West are decreasing magnitudes. If there is no modifying factor involved, the distribution of these speech-sounds around the norm will in all probability follow the Gaussian curve (see footnote, page 99).

Now, since the varying degrees of difficulty in articulating a speech-sound as described above (page 97 f.) modifies, in one way or another, the action of blind chance in the successes and errors of approximation, the curve of distribution of speech-sounds about a phonemic norm may in some cases be askew. That is, the proportionately more frequent the occurrences are in any particular abnormal position, the more likely it is that the curve of distribution will be askew at that portion which represents the occurrences of this proportionately very frequently occurring position. To illustrate more graphically this matter of skewness let us present (Plate V) a target with a hypothetical curve of distribution for the phoneme *t* in English.

We recall that just above it was said that variations in the aspiration of a phoneme might be represented on a plane. We also recall (page 57) that the phoneme *t* in English is perceptibly aspirated in most of its occurrences, though not in the combination *st*, where the aspiration is much diminished,

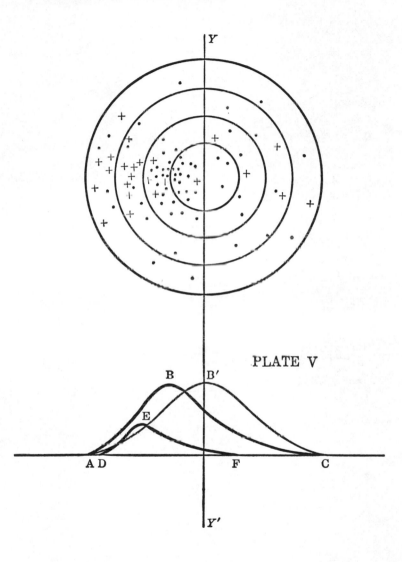

PLATE V

if not absent. Now, in the figure (Plate V) is given a target for the *t* phoneme in English together with a curve which plots its imaginary occurrences. All the marks on the target (the dots and the crosses) represent the articulations of *t* speech-sounds during a given period of speech; the dots and crosses at the East (*right*) of the medial line *YY'* are speech-sounds of abnormally great aspiration, those to the West (*left*) are of abnormally low aspiration. The heavy curve *ABC* represents the distribution of these shots. The light curve *AB'C* is a typical Gaussian normal curve of distribution, presented for comparison. The curve *DEF* is the curve for the shots on the target marked by crosses which represent *t* in the combination *st*. It will be noticed that the distance on the abscissa from *D* to *F* which represents the range of variability of *t* in *st* is less than the distance *AC* which is the range of variability for the entire phoneme *t*. Furthermore, the position of the points on the curve is different; since the *t* of *st* is consistently less aspirated from the average, its mean is to the left of the medial line.

Now the difference between the curve *DEF* and the curve *AB'C*, that is, its difference from a Gaussian normal curve of distribution, is, by present definition, the *st* skewness of *t*. Similarly there is a *ts* skewness of *t*, a *ts* and *st* skewness of *s*, an *nd* skewness of *d* and *n*, etc. In every such combination of two speech-sounds, there is a possible skewness of the first element (*anterior skewness*) and of the second element (*posterior skewness*).

d. The Effect of Skewness on the Development of a Phoneme

We have discussed the skewness of a phoneme from the point of view of experimental phonetics (pages 95 ff.) and of statistical representation (pages 97 ff.); let us now investigate it from the point of view of its influence on the evolutionary development of the phoneme. The justification of this detailed consideration of skewness is that skewness is doubtless the factor which determines which phonemes are to be selected for assimilatory changes, and which spared by 'spontaneous' changes.

As illustration let us take the combination *ts* as it occurs in English and view it as a sequence of articulatory sub-gestures (as explained pages 59 ff.). In pronouncing *t* and *s* to oneself, one perceives, as we remember, that the two phonemes have similar elements in common (e.g. the position of the tongue, voicelessness, etc.), though the significant elements, which we shall represent arbitrarily as ψ and ϕ, are different to such a degree that the two are not identical. For convenience in illustration and without pretense to accuracy, let us represent *t* as a whole by the arbitrary sequence $m\,\psi\,n$, and *s* as a whole by $n\,\phi\,o$. In a stream of speech where each phoneme is distinctly and, as far as possible, independently articulated, *ts* appears as $m\,\psi\,n\,n\,\phi\,o$, — that is, the juxtaposition of *t* $(m\,\psi\,n)$ and *s* $(n\,\phi\,o)$. In rapid speech, with the abbreviation by haplology (see page 85) of superfluous elements, we may have $m\,\psi\,n\,\phi\,o$, in which *n* does double duty, as the end of *t* and as the beginning of *s*. Although one cannot determine whether the *n* of $m\,\psi\,n\,\phi\,o$ belongs primarily to ψ or to ϕ, we cannot for that reason maintain that there is not a full-fledged *t* and *s* in the sequence $m\,\psi\,n\,\phi\,o$, even though the sequence does not represent the sum of its two parts. The *t* and *s* agglutinated in $m\,\psi\,n\,\phi\,o$ will doubtless cause a skewness in the total distribution of either *t* or *s* and may be termed the anterior *t* skewness of *s* or the posterior *s* skewness of *t*. This formula $(m\,\psi\,n\,\phi\,o)$ is equally descriptive of many other phonemes in skewed position.

Let us now ask what will happen to a phoneme, skewed in some of its positions, when the phoneme undergoes an increase in relative frequency. In attempting to answer this question we shall retain our previous example of the phoneme *t* and its *ts* skewness in English. Referring to our target and graph (Plate V), we shall say that East represents an increase in total magnitude of complexity, and West a decrease in the same, and that the curve ABC represents the total distribution of all occurrences of t (dots and crosses), whereas the curve DEF represents the occurrences of t in the skewed combination ts (marked by crosses on the target).

Now, if the relative frequency of t is doubled, the total number of shots (dots plus crosses) will be doubled, and the area described by the new curve ABC' representing this increase will also be doubled. But will the shape of the new curve, representing the distribution of doubled relative frequency, remain the same? The answer to this question, if all other factors are constant, may be in three different ways depending upon whether the occurrences of t in ts were (1) likewise doubled, or (2) more than doubled, or (3) less than doubled, in the general twofold increase in the relative frequency of all occurrences of t. In other words, the answer will depend upon whether the area enclosed in the curve DEF is (1) doubled, or (2) more than doubled, or (3) less than doubled.

Let us first suppose that the occurrence of t in ts increased more than proportionately, and that the area DEF was more than doubled, resulting, say, from the increased usage of certain affixes in the language which contains ts. Indeed, for clarity of demonstration, let us assume that the increase in ts alone accounted for the doubled relative frequency of t. Now, when the time for abbreviation of articulatory sub-gestures arrives, we can say that the t of ts is more likely to undergo abbreviation than t in any other position, if for no other reason than that of favoring chance, since the articulation of t in the combination ts is now (with increased relative frequency) the most frequent articulation of t in any one position.

But, as the full form of ts, represented as $m\ \psi\ n\ n\ \phi\ o$, undergoes abbreviation, the t becomes less and the s increasingly more important in the combination. Proceeding from the full form *m ψ n n φ o* to *m ψ n φ o* to, say, *ψ n φ o*, by abbreviations, we have in *ψ n φ o* a highly frequent sequence which is neither a *t* (*m ψ n*), nor an *s* (*n φ o*), nor a combination of the two, but rather almost a new phoneme, more like an *s* than a *t*. And this *quasi* new phoneme would have a high relative frequency. If there were further need for abbreviation in this sequence, *ψ* would be deleted; for though *ψ* was by definition the distinctive element of the phoneme *t*, it is but a fortuitous element from the viewpoint of *s*. The hypothetical steps in the change from *m ψ n n φ o* to *n φ o*, as presented above, illustrate the assimilatory phonetic change of *t + s* to *ts* to *ss* to *s*, of which there are copious examples in the histories of many languages (for example, the Indo-European *t* remained generally constant in Latin, e.g. *tres, pater, factus*, though it showed a marked tendency to shift in skewed positions, including the shift *ts* to *s*, e.g. pre-Latin *mitsi > misi*). Similarly *s* in the skewed combination *ts* may become *tt* and then *t*; or, in the skewed combination *nd*, we might find a development, by assimilatory abbreviatory change, to either *n* (by way of *nn*) or *d* (by way of *dd*).

And, we may say (reverting again to the target, Plate V, with the example *ts*) that as *ts* becomes *s*, the crosses on the target vanish, and the total relative frequency of *t* diminishes correspondingly towards its norm of frequency distribution. Hence, the effect of assimilatory change is to restore equilibrium by a change of only part of the occurrences.

But now let us suppose that the double relative frequency of *t* (see Plate V) is the result of a general increase in the occurrences of *t*, *except t in the skewed position ts*. Indeed, for ease of illustration, let us assume that the occurrences of *t* in *ts* actually decrease so that the area *DEF* (see Plate V) becomes proportionately a smaller part of the whole. By a reversal of the preceding demonstration, we may say that as the relative frequency of *ts* decreases, the combination is felt more and more to be the sum of its parts, that is, as a *t* plus a following *s*. A 'spontaneous' change (say of *t* to *þ*) would then have no cause to spare the *t* of *ts*; *ts* would become *þs*.

Somewhere between the point where *ts* would become *s* by assimilation (see page 90) and the point where *ts* would become *þs* by general 'spontaneous' change (see page 88), is a range of frequency where the skewed phoneme *t* in *ts* would be most stable, resisting both assimilatory and 'spontaneous' change. This condition is perhaps represented by the sequence *m ψ n φ o* (see page 104) where the articulatory sub-gesture *n* does double duty for *m ψ n* and *n φ o;* in *m ψ n φ o* the two phonemes are sufficiently agglutinized to keep each other from following a spontaneous change, though not sufficiently agglutinized to undergo an assimilatory change of their own.

As a typical example of the many ways in which a phoneme may behave in a given combination let us take the posterior *s* skewness of *k* and observe its past behavior in several different languages. In one language it may remain in its skewed position as the *ks* (written *x*) in English *ox*, so agglutinized that many would feel that English *x* is a single phoneme. In another language *k* in combination with *s* may join with other occurrences of *k* in a general 'spontaneous' change, e.g. the change of *k* to the spirant (written *ch*) in present-day German,* exemplified by *Ochse* 'ox.' Or the *ks* may remain as two distinct phonemes, e.g. Sanskrit *ákṣas* 'ox.' [1] Or the *k* may become assimilated to the following *s* as in Oscan *destrst* (the nature of whose older form is indicated by Latin *dextra est*) or Oscan *meddiss* from older **meddix*.†

There are instances where a phoneme in skewed position may escape a 'spontaneous' change only to undergo an assimilatory change. For example, the *k* in primitive Germanic

---

* Though present-day German *Ochse* is generally pronounced as if it contained a *ks*, both the modern orthography and that of Old High German (e.g. *ahse*) lead us to believe that this was not originally the case.

† It is uncertain whether the *ks* of Oscan *eksuk* is original or secondary.

shifted 'spontaneously' to a spirant (cf. Grimm's Law, page 121) in the vast majority of its occurrences, yet was regularly stable when preceded by *s*, i.e. the anterior *s* skewness of *k*. Subsequently in both English and German (but not in Icelandic) this *sk* [1] became assimilated by coalescing into the single phoneme (pronounced as the *sh* in English *she*): e.g. early Old-English *scip*, Icelandic *skip*, versus present-day English *ship* and German *Schiff*; or English *fish*, German *Fisch*, present-day Icelandic *fiskur*, cognate with Latin *piscis*.

Examples of this sort could be multiplied almost indefinitely from the material of handbooks on the different languages. It is unfortunate that in no case of changes of these various sorts are there conclusive available statistical data on the phonemic system before and after the change. Until supporting data are available, our discussion therefore remains speculative. The speculation is, however, useful as a working hypothesis in illustrating the various ways with which the disturbed equilibrium between magnitude of complexity and relative frequency in a phoneme may be restored.

e. *The Voicing of Intervocalic Voiceless Stops*

There is one particular type of phonetic change which merits mention because it illustrates the presumable manner in which two distinct phoneme types may under certain circumstances fall together: the voicing of a voiceless stop as an act of assimilatory change to surrounding vowels. For example, Latin *ripa* 'river bank' later became *riba* in Old Provençal. Comparative philologists have argued convincingly that in an intervocalic position (e.g. the *p* of *ripa* or *b* of *riba*) the *b*, which differs from *p* chiefly in respect to voicing, is easier to pronounce because it is less difficult to vibrate the vocal cords uninterruptedly through the word *riba* than to interrupt them momentarily in order to pronounce the voiceless *p* in *ripa*. However, when an intervocalic *p* becomes voiced in a given language, it is an indication rather of the instability of *p* in that given language than of a universal instability of intervocalic *p*; for example, we have for centuries been pronouncing intervocalic *p* in English *rapid*, *tepid*, *paper* without the shifting of *p* to *b*.

In some dialects of American English [1] there is a similar tendency toward voicing the intervocalic explosive *t*. In these dialects the differences between *latter* and *ladder*, *kitty* and *kiddy*, *metal* and *medal* are practically subliminal; the couplets are distinguished more by the usages of the words than by perceptible differences in the phonemes. Informal experiments performed on native speakers of these American English dialects reveal that without a context the couplets are really indistinguishable. The professional phonetic transcriber who, trusting his own ear,[2] puts the *t* of *latter* in these dialects under the heading of either the *t* or *d* phoneme, merely expresses his opinion in the matter. As we shall presently see, there is no positive empirical method of determining whether the dental of *latter*, *kitty*, and *metal* in these dialects should be considered as a *t* or a *d*. When the variant forms of two different phonemes (say *t* and *d*) are for all intents and purposes identical, one may classify a given occurrence as a variant of *d* or of *t* only by referring it, if possible, to the norm of which it is a variant; this reference to a phonemic norm is not always possible. To illustrate this point and make clearer the difficulties of the problem, let us again adopt the simile of the target, with the bull's eye as the phonemic norm and the speech-sounds as the shots.

Let us, for the sake of illustration, imagine two targets, immediately juxtaposed to one another, one marked *t*, the other, *d*. Let us ask a marksman to fire a thousand shots at *t* and a thousand at *d*, passing from one target to the other at random. If we did not know at the time which target was being aimed at, we could not determine, whenever he hit the bull's eye *d*, whether the shot were an excellent aim at *d* or a poor aim at *t*. Either inference is possible. If the marksman will not reveal his intention, our only other recourse, after he is finished, is to try to fit the shot into the normal distribution of shots around one bull's eye or the other.   If this cannot be done, then it is impossible ever to deduce his aim in this instance from his achievement.

In the phonemic system of any language, the norm of many a phoneme is so close to that of many another, that an occasional deviation from the one into the significant domain of another is by no means an extremely rare event in the stream of speech.   Since the difference in pronunciation between the *t* and *d* in *latter* and *ladder* respectively is frequently not perceptible, the difficulty of categorizing the doubtful phoneme is considerable.   As long as the dental of *latter* is now voiced and now unvoiced, it may perhaps still be considered an approximation of the *t* norm.   But once the voicing is habitual, there is only one way of deciding empirically whether the sound belongs to the *t* phoneme or the *d*: if in the future development of the doubtful dental of *latter*, in those dialects which habitually voice it, the doubtful dental subsequently behaves as a *d* in like position, then the doubtful sound *was* a *d*.   If the doubtful dental of *latter* does not behave as a genuine *d* in like position, then the doubtful dental *was not* a *d* but merely a variant of *t*.   In other words, in instances of the above sort in linguistic patterns, the state of present conditions can be decided empirically only by future behavior.   The *p* of Latin *ripa* (see page 106) did become a *b* at some time in its later development, or at least became a phoneme identical with intervocalic *b* under the same conditions, because intervocalic *b* and *p* in Latin both merged in later times into the voiced spirant written *v*.   For example, Latin *ripa* became (by way of *riba*) French *rive*, and Latin *faba* became French *fève*.   In other words, the intervocalic *p* of Latin began to approximate the norm of *b* to such an extent that in intervocalic positions the two behaved indistinguishably, and subsequently, in losing their explosiveness in this position, both began to approximate the norm of *v*.

The average Frenchman today in pronouncing *rive* (from Latin *ripa*) and *fève* (from Latin *faba*) and *vie* (from Latin *uita*) does not in any way reveal in the articulation of the three *v*'s the different consonants from which they originated. The shift of a phoneme from one form to another in the phonemic pattern is such a slow process of approximation, often extending over considerable time, that there is often likely to be an interval in the metamorphosis where classification is impossible.* Between the norm for *t* and the norm for *d* in English there is an interval in which a speech articulation may occur as a deviation from either norm. Historical study can often indicate the origin of the phoneme in question, yet only its future behavior can determine the category to which it pertains.

Although it is at times difficult to categorize a given speech articulation at the time of its occurrence, nevertheless the dynamic forces behind the phenomenon are not difficult to detect, if the present theory of relative frequency and equilibrium be true. For, in the terms of our theory, every *assimilation points to a weakening or instability of the assimilated sound, and this weakening or instability is caused primarily by the excessive relative frequency of the assimilated sound.*

f. Frequency Thresholds of Toleration of Phonemes

Until this point in our investigation of the phoneme our method of analysis has been primarily inductive rather than deductive, and by this method we have found a state of equilibrium in the phonemic system of languages which seems to be maintained by various types of phonetic change. These same conclusions, as we shall now see, may be ob-

* Hence, a dynamic philologist who is making a frequency count of phonemes in a living language like modern English must be careful to indicate the doubtful phonemic norm of phonemes which seem to be in the process of gradual metamorphosis. It should be borne in mind, however, that doubtful phonemes of this type may be statistically insignificant.

tained by an *a priori* approach, which has the virtue of shedding additional light on the nature of the phoneme, by establishing the probable existence of *thresholds of toleration* of phonemes.   These thresholds of toleration are nothing more than limits to the relative frequency of a phoneme, above which a phoneme will tend to weaken (abbreviatory change, page 92 f.) and below which it will tend to strengthen (augmentative change, see page 113 f.).

In commencing an analysis of these thresholds, we must remember a very obvious fact: every language must possess a sufficient variety of discernibly different vowels, consonants, and other phonemic units, so that permutations of the same, together with other resources (such as accent, tones, syntax), can adequately express its body of concepts.   Upon this statement, which is axiomatic, follows a corollary equally self-evident: no one phoneme in a phonemic system can have an unlimited relative frequency up to 100 per cent, for the simple reason that a 100 per cent relative frequency of any phoneme would preclude the existence of any other phoneme in the phonemic system.   Since there is clearly an ultimate limit to the relative frequency of any one phoneme, the question arises whether this ultimate limit is the same as the presumed threshold of tolerable frequency for a phoneme.   To make the discussion of this problem more tangible, let us refer it to some hypothetical language.

For instance, let us assume for the sake of argument that a language existed in which every word began with a *d*. Is it not difficult to believe that an idiosyncrasy of this sort could persist indefinitely?   The ever-present initial *d* of this hypothetical language would cease to be a signally characteristic part of any word, inasmuch as every word possessed it. The *d*, being in no way peculiarly characteristic of any one word, would be completely unessential to a perfectly adequate conveyance of the meaning of any word.   In short it would have no cogent reason for persisting as a symbol.   The speaker might pronounce it out of sheer habit, but not from the exi-

gency of distinguishing different meanings.   Similarly the
auditor would have no cogent reason for insisting urgently
upon normal care in articulating this initial d.   The particular
permutation of phonemes which distinguished one word from
another, would not include the initial d as an essential, or indeed even as an unsuperfluous element.   It would be quite
comprehensible if the articulation of this d were constantly
neglected in the stream of speech and became weakened (an
abbreviatory change, partial or complete, see page 92 f.).
But would not the same neglect and weakening of d occur if,
instead of being everywhere in the initial position, it were
everywhere in the final position, or in the middle position in
every word?   Indeed, it would scarcely be necessary that
every spoken word in the stream of speech had a d initially,
medially, or finally before it began to be sufficiently superfluous to suffer neglect.   The phoneme d would seem superfluous if every word contained it somewhere.   Such a frequent
phoneme would be a far less important characteristic of a
word than, say, a phoneme which occurred only once in ten
thousand words.   In the short and frequently occurring words
especially, the ever-present d would seem much less significant than any of the remaining phonemes.   However, let us
go further and assume that one half or three fourths or some
other equally large fraction of the consonants in use were
d's, scattered initially, medially, and finally.   Or suppose that
the three hundred most frequently used words contained at
least one d.   Surely with the proportion of d's so high, the d
would tend to weaken.

Hence, there must presumably be some percentage of relative frequency, or *upper threshold of toleration* in a language
above which the d will tend to weaken.   Although we do not
know what this threshold is, its existence is quite probable.
Furthermore, the above discussion of d applies correspondingly to every other phoneme in the phonemic system of a
given language: every phoneme must presumably have an
upper threshold of frequency above which it cannot pass
without tending to weaken.

But when we say that any phoneme, for example *d*, will tend to weaken in a dialect when its relative frequency passes a certain upper threshold of toleration, the question arises as to the possible effect of this weakening on the subsequent form of the phoneme. The answer is again the abbreviation of articulatory sub-gestures. If the *d*, for example, is pro-portionately too frequent in the beginning of words, weaken-ing may occur by a tardiness in voicing it. The initial voiced stops of many languages [1] exemplify this tendency toward tardiness in voicing, which is absent in other occurrences of the voiced stops. This tendency may reach such a point that the voicing is entirely deleted. For example, the German dialectal word *teutsch* 'German' resulted from excessive tardi-ness in voicing the initial *d* of *deutsch*. Similarly if the *d* is proportionately too frequent at the end of words, weakening may be shown in ceasing the voicing before articulation is completed. This neglect of voicing of final voiced stops may again reach such a point that it is deleted. Thus, in German, final *d* is always voiceless; the historical *d* of *Tod* 'death' and final *t* of *tot* 'dead' are today indistinguishable in standard German pronunciation. Naturally the positions and manner of weakening of a phoneme are numerous; by the abbrevia-tion of respective articulatory sub-gestures, a *d* may assume a form which may be described as an *n*, an *ð*, a *t*. And these forms (e.g. *n*, *ð*, *t*), resulting from partial abbreviation, may rightly be viewed as weaker, less complex, and even more economical than the *d* from which they weakened.

It follows from the above that all phonemes need not, in-deed cannot, have the same actual percentage-thresholds of toleration; for if a phoneme *x* weakens because of excessive relative frequency to *y*, then the new phoneme *y* must *ipso facto* be capable of sustaining a higher relative frequency than *x*. In other words, if *d* weakens to the voiceless stop *t* because of excessive relative frequency, then this *t* can toler-ate a higher threshold of relative frequency than *d*. Although this particular *t* which has weakened from a *d* can tolerate a

greater relative frequency than a d, yet the t too must presumably have an upper threshold of frequency, and for precisely the same reason that d must have an upper threshold
of frequency. If t surpassed its upper threshold, it too would
tend to weaken, that is, tend to abbreviate one or more of its
articulatory sub-gestures. For example, the occlusive gestures might be abbreviated in such a way that there would
be no explosion; in this case the tongue would, say, not move
so far, and the loss of explosion would represent a true weakening. The resultant weakened form would then be a spirant,
probably similar to the English $þ$ (written _th_ in English
think). By the same reasoning, there must also be an upper
threshold of frequency for $þ$, which, like a vowel, may vary
in duration. Indeed, if the frequency of any phoneme increases too much, it may weaken so far as to be completely
dropped (i.e. deleted) from the stream of speech.*

We are led by the same manner of analysis to another conclusion: every phoneme must also have a lower threshold below which it cannot pass without strengthening. For we can
reverse the argument and suppose that the relative frequency
of a phoneme, say t, is abnormally low, so low that there are
only a few t's appearing in the stream of speech, so few indeed
that t occurs only very rarely. The phoneme t would then
become a distinctive and very characteristic part of every
word in which it occurred, pronounced carefully by the
speaker, heard distinctly by the auditor. It is quite conceivable that the speaker, in taking care to pronounce the t distinctly, would unconsciously add a following aspiration, or
spirant, or some other element. Of course the speaker would
not intentionally add an h or an s or some other element to
the t. The speaker would merely unconsciously tend to
articulate the t more carefully; the additional s, h, or other appended element would be a fortuitous excrescence, a kind of

---

* Especially weak phonemes, like h, are therefore especially susceptible to loss;
e.g. the loss of h in Latin in developing into Romance, Latin _habēre_ but French
avoir.

accidental epenthesis — the result of an over-careful articulation. Since any tendency in this direction might easily become a consistent tendency, the infrequent *t* might develop into an aspirate *t*^{h}, or an affricate *ts*. Surely a *t* which has developed into a *ts* or *t*^{h} gives every indication that it was by no means neglected in the stream of speech.*

Hence a phoneme has not only an upper threshold but also a lower threshold. If its frequency surpasses the upper, the phoneme 'weakens'; if the lower, it 'strengthens.' It seems permissible, therefore, to infer likewise from the existence of lower thresholds that many phonemes may be viewed as potential strengthenings and weakenings of other phonemes.

Seemingly quite conclusive proof of the existence of these upper and lower frequency thresholds of toleration is offered by the percentages of voiced and voiceless stops for the twelve languages presented in the table on page 75. In each pair of corresponding voiced and voiceless stops, with the exception of the Spanish *d* and *t* and the Hungarian *b* and *p*, we find not only that each voiceless stop much outnumbers its voiced stop, but that the percentages of similar stops throughout the twelve languages are on the whole amazingly similar. For instance *t* is approximately 7 per cent, *d* approximately 3.5 per cent; the percentages for English and Bulgarian are especially close. Furthermore, a similar correspondence is evinced by the percentages for *m* and *n* on page 79. Of course, more extensive and refined phonemic analyses of many of these languages might well reveal an even closer correspondence. However, we must be prepared to expect minor differences among the percentages of similar stops in

---

* An example of a general strengthening of *t* to *ts* is tendered by the Old-High-German sound-shift in which a Germanic *t* shifted to a *ts* in the majority of positions (though in many cases it went even further into *ss*, see page 119 infra). E.g. primitive Germanic *t*, still preserved in English, *two*, became *ts* (written z) in German *zwei*. Examples can be multiplied indefinitely, *ten, zehn; tug, zug; tooth, zahn*. That the probable cause of this was a decrease in relative frequency below the lower threshold, see page 120.

different languages if only because the phonemes in the different languages may vary slightly in their normal magnitudes of complexity. Furthermore, in remembering that this is but a statistical law which merely states probabilities of behavior we must, it appears, be prepared to find that an occasional phoneme continues to exist though its relative frequency be appreciably above its upper or below its lower frequency threshold of toleration. For no matter how very convenient it would be if we had absolute percentage-thresholds for every phoneme, above which or below which a phoneme would instantly change in form, the simple fact remains that at least so far as our present findings are concerned there is no absolute threshold.[1] On the basis of our findings we are justified in saying only this: as a given phoneme approaches a threshold, the chances favor the appearance of an instability in the form of the phoneme which will lead to change; and as the relative frequency of the phoneme surpasses a threshold by ever more and more, the chances of its change become ever greater and greater. Though the chances may be a hundred to one in favor of change, the eventuation of no change in one case out of a hundred is no disproof of our statistical law. And finally we must not be misled by a very striking and probably deeply significant relationship among our percentages. For instance, in the Peipingese aspirated and unaspirated stops, the ratio of the percentages of frequency of aspirated to unaspirated is on the whole approximately 1 to 3; with the Danish aspirated fortes and unaspirated lenes the ratio is on the whole approximately 2 to 3; with the voiced and voiceless stops of the twelve languages the ratio is on the whole approximately 1 to 2. These ratios are strikingly simple and seem in accord with Nature's frequent fondness for simple relationships. Nevertheless the simplicity of these ratios has not been accounted for in any way in our investigation.[2] We have shown only that the total magnitude of complexity of a phoneme bears some inverse relationship to the relative frequency of occurrence; this inverse relationship may of course be directly proportionate or it may be some non-linear mathematical function — the present investigation remains noncommittal on that point; whoever succeeds in measuring quantitatively the magnitude of complexity of phonemes without respect to the relative frequency of their occurrences will be able to give us more precise information on that point (see pages 58 ff.). In short, our thresholds of frequency are only approximate and indicate only probabilities of behavior.

Yet even approximate thresholds which indicate only probabilities of behavior may be highly useful [1] and we shall now see that with the help of our thresholds of toleration many apparent exceptions to the rule of relative frequency may be explained.

g. *The Apparent Exception of Spanish Dentals and Other Phonemes*

In the table of percentages for the relative frequencies of occurrence of the voiced and voiceless stops in twelve languages (page 75) there were only two pairs in which the relative frequency of the voiced stop was greater than that of its corresponding voiceless stop, i.e. the Spanish dentals and the Hungarian labials. Evidence will now be advanced to show that the Spanish dentals, though apparently exceptional, conform in all probability to what we may term the principle of relative frequency. Whether the Hungarian labials also substantiate this principle, or whether they are to remain the sole exception in the entire tabulation cannot be decided by one who is as unfamiliar with the historical development of Hungarian as is the present writer. Hence we shall restrict our immediate attention to the Spanish dentals.

When the statistics were first discussed (page 76), Spanish *d* with a percentage of relative frequency of 5.20 per cent and

Spanish *t* with a percentage of 4.27 per cent seemed to offer
an exception to our general findings and evidence against our
rule. Now we shall see that the excessive frequency of Spanish *d* offers in all probability a confirmation. If 5.20 per cent
represents the frequency of *d* in Spanish, we may plausibly
assume that it has crossed the upper threshold,[1] either because it is the most frequent *d* in the column, or because it is
almost 25 per cent more frequent than the Spanish *t*. We
should, therefore, expect that in Spanish the *d* would tend to
lose some of its articulatory sub-gestures, as happens to be
actually the case. According to the Spanish phoneticist
T. Navarro Tomás,[2] only in the absolutely initial position, or
when preceded by *n* or *l* is the written *d* pronounced as a
voiced stop, and then only with weak articulation. Elsewhere
it has lost its explosiveness, becoming a spirant (ð or þ). In
many cases the spirant is so weak as to be neglected entirely
in the vulgar pronunciation current in the greater part of
Spain (see footnote, page 113). Hence the weakening of an
excessively frequent phoneme seems to be illustrated by
Spanish *d*.

The frequency of Latin *m* with 5.82 per cent (see page 79)
is another point in question. Not only does it have the highest relative frequency for *m* of any of the languages, but it is
over twice as frequent as the least frequent, and nearly one
third more frequent than the next most frequent (i.e. Burmese *m*, 4.72 per cent). Faithful to our expectations, Latin
m subsequently weakened, particularly in the final position
where it eventually vanished. The extent to which the total
relative frequency of *m* in Latin was reduced by the loss of
final *m* in all occurrences is indicated by the fact that 56 per
cent of the total occurrences of *m* in the Latin analysis were
final; * from this one change alone, all else being equal, the
total relative frequency of Latin *m* would decline from 5.82
per cent to 2.55 per cent, coming well below any upper

---

* It is to be remembered that the maintenance of final *m* in Latin was often merely
orthographic.

threshold. The case of *m* in Latin not only illustrates a weakening attendant upon crossing an upper threshold, but it offers a valuable example of the weakening of a phoneme in one position made especially vulnerable by a concentration of occurrences in that position. It need scarcely be pointed out that initially and medially Latin *m* remains remarkably stable (witness present-day French *me* from Latin *me*, French *ami* from Latin *amicus*).

The Cantonese velars (page 71) are another point in question, especially the unaspirated voiceless stop which with a percentage of 8.7 per cent is more frequent than the corresponding dental (cerebral) stops of that dialect (*t* is 6.14 per cent). It may be remarked that in final position in Cantonese, *k* is often replaced by the glottal stop.[1]

These three typical examples of weakening suffice to illustrate the effect upon the form of a phoneme when it transgresses the upper threshold. The general phenomenon of these three examples is clearly the same as the general phenomenon discussed from the point of view of abbreviatory phonetic changes (pages 92 ff.).

h. Lower Thresholds and Augmentative Phonetic Changes

On page 92 we classified determinable phonetic changes into abbreviatory and augmentative phonetic changes, depending upon whether the total magnitude of complexity was abbreviated or augmented by the change. The determinable changes discussed until now have all been examples of abbreviatory changes, a class which appears to be far more frequent in occurrence than the augmentative. Indeed, abbreviatory changes are so predominant in the histories of languages that some early scholars were again and again tempted to explain phonetic change solely on the basis of simplification or attrition. However, to the minds of later scholars, the instances of augmentative change were sufficiently abundant to lead to the belief that the abbreviatory changes were the exceptions and that the probable cause of phonetic change was the desire for increased complexity. And so convincingly has each side argued that the comparative philologists of today, insofar as they are concerned with the dynamic problems of the phoneme, may perhaps be said to be divided into three camps:[1] (1) the proponents of greater simplification, (2) the proponents of greater complexity, and (3) those who reserve judgment.

Augmentative phonetic changes may be expected, according to our theory of relative frequency and equilibrium, whenever a phoneme becomes so rare as to cross its lower threshold. The Slavic languages are said to provide many examples of augmentative changes. But since our immediate interest is more in illustration of principle than in marshalling examples, the single instance of the shift of voiceless stops to voiceless affricates in many of the dialects of Old High German will perhaps suffice.

In Old High German the Germanic *d* changed in form * until it became a phoneme similar to *t*; thus the Germanic *d* preserved in English *do* appears in High German as *t* in *tun* because of this change. Similarly the Germanic interdental spirant preserved and written today in English as *th* (e.g. *that* or *think*) became a *d* in Old High German, appearing in present-day German as *d* in the words *das* and *denken*. The Germanic *t* of English *to, eat, heat* changed according to its position in Old High German words and according to the particular Old High German dialect either to the affricate *ts*

---

* While it is convenient in exposition to say that Germanic *d* changed to *t* in Old High German, it is more accurate to say that Germanic *d* changed until its form was one of *t*. Though this qualification may perhaps seem pedantic, it is nevertheless a more accurate description of the phenomena involved in this, or any other phonetic change. For convenience only do we speak of 'phonemic types'; actually there is in a phonemic system a gradation of countless steps in the matter of magnitude of complexity, and hence of form. In strengthening or weakening to restore balance, a phoneme passes up or down this scale until it attains a point where equilibrium is restored, regardless of whether or not this point of equilibrium falls within a well-recognized 'phonemic type.'

(often written as *z* in present-day German), or *s*, *ss* (generally written *ss* today); e.g. German *zu* 'to,' *essen* 'to eat,' *Hitze* 'heat.' Because of similar changes in Old High German, the English voiceless stops *p* and *k* appear in German as *pf*, *ff*, and *k*, *ch*, respectively (e.g. English *pipe*, German *Pfeife*, Old English *cirice* 'church' and German *Kirche* 'church,' borrowed from the Greek *kuriakon*). These changes differed slightly in different Old High German dialects, and were more stable in some dialects than others. Our chief interest in them at present, however, is not one of dialect geography, but rather that they were all 'spontaneous' phonetic changes (see page 88), and all augmentative changes (see page 92) except the change of *d* to *t*.

Before turning to a statistical analysis of a sample of Old High German prose, let us formulate what we may theoretically expect to find statistically. In the first place, the new *t* from older *d* should have a percentage approximating 7 per cent, or roughly 3 per cent more than the upper threshold of *d* which we maintain was crossed in the change. The new *d* from older *þ* and *ð* should have a percentage approximating 4 per cent (the Spanish *d* which has crossed its upper threshold and is weakening to *þ* and *ð* has 5.20 per cent, see page 116). The affricates which developed from *t*, *p*, and *k* respectively should have only minimal percentages to justify such a severe augmentative change.

In an analysis of samplings from Tatian's *Gospel Harmony* (*Evangelienharmonie*),[1] totalling 50,000 phonemes in extent and reduced to a uniform orthography consistent with the phonemic data derived from our knowledge of the origin and subsequent development of Old High German, we find that the new *t* has an occurrence of 7.77 per cent; the new *d* has an occurrence of 5.38 per cent, the affricates from *t*, *p*, and *k* having the low frequencies of 1.87 per cent, .11 per cent, and .39 per cent respectively. In other words, we find actually what we have anticipated theoretically.

Expressed differently, it may be said that if the original
Germanic *d* had undergone no change in Old High German,
its percentage of 7.77 per cent would have been excessively
above what appears to be approximately the usual upper
threshold of *d*. On the other hand, the Germanic voiceless
stops, had they remained unchanged, would have been well
below their lower thresholds. In view of these considerations, which do not seem to be the results of random chance,
the inference appears quite plausible that the abbreviatory
and augmentative changes which occurred in Old High
German were to restore equilibrium, in whatever way that
equilibrium may have been originally disturbed.

i. Analogy as a Coercive and Restraining Factor in Phonetic Change; the First Germanic Sound-Shift

There is, however, another factor which may operate in
phonetic change: analogy. Since analogy is often important in accentual changes where the peculiar nature of its
behavior is perhaps most readily apparent (pages 159 ff.),
we shall at present merely illustrate the manner in which
analogy may coerce or restrain the behavior of a phoneme
in respect to a phonetic change, thereby in itself disturbing
what the normal course in preserving or restoring equilibrium would otherwise be. Since the influence of analogy
upon phonetic change has never received, even from comparative philologists, the attention which it deserves, the
territory is therefore practically virgin, and this brief discussion of it may be viewed merely as a beginning in the
direction of exploration.

The clearest example of analogic phonetic change is the
familiar First Germanic sound-shift (i.e. phonetic change),
described under Grimm's Law, in which all the voiced,
voiceless and aspirated stops of Indo-European were
changed.

The Indo-European stops which changed in pre-Germanic *
are generally listed thus:

	Voiceless	Voiceless Aspirates	Voiced	Voiced Aspirates †
dental	t	th	d	dh
labial	p	ph	b	bh
guttural (velar or palatal)	k	kh	g	gh

These stops are arranged horizontally according to their
position of articulation, and vertically according to their
manner of articulation.   That is, the dentals taken as a
typical example, *t*, *th*, *d*, and *dh* have the dental position of
articulation in common.   Furthermore, the voiceless aspirates (*th*, *ph*, *kh*) have aspiration in common; the voiced
stops (*d*, *b*, *g*) have voicing in common; the voiced aspirates
(*dh*, *bh*, *gh*) have both voicing and aspiration in common;
and all are stops.   If the three voiceless unaspirated stops
(*t*, *p*, and *k*) have nothing actual in common except the negative factor of *voicelessness*, nevertheless they are similar in
respect to their relationship to their respective voiceless
aspirates on the one hand and to their respective aspirated
and unaspirated voiced stops on the other.   That is, *t* is to *p*
and to *k*, as *th* is to *ph* and *kh*, and as *d* is to *b* and to *g*, and
as *dh* is to *bh* and to *gh*.   That is, though *t*, *p*, and *k* have no
immediately perceptible element in common, they have
what we may term the element of *analogical arrangement*
in common.

Although analogical arrangement is not perceptible, its
existence and its strength can be demonstrated by the
influence it exerts on the behavior of stops thus arranged.

* The term *pre-Germanic* designates the period of time during which a branch of
the parent Indo-European language was developing into *Germanic*. The pre-Germanic period was marked by many changes; for convenience we shall assume that
the First Germanic sound-shift closed the pre-Germanic period and commenced the
Germanic period which later (prehistorically) broke into the Germanic dialects.

† The *mediae aspiratae* of Grassmann's Law; see page 82 above.

For example, if the voiced aspirated stops (*dh*, *bh*, and *gh*) all changed in a given language to their corresponding voiced unaspirated stops (*d*, *b*, *g*), one would be justified in presuming in the absence of data to the contrary that the voiced aspirated stops, as a category, had become too frequent; so, to, correspondingly with similar abbreviatory changes of the voiced stops and the voiceless aspirates. But if the voiceless stops *t*, *p*, and *k*, all underwent abbreviatory changes (say to the weak spirants *þ*, *f*, and χ* respectively), and if we could not find that *t*, *p*, and *k* had each crossed its respective upper threshold of frequency, but that only one or two of the voiceless stops (*t*, *p*, and *k*) had crossed the upper threshold, we should be justified in presuming that the remaining voiceless stops or stop had changed analogically, or had undergone *analogic change*.

An apparently excellent example of *analogic change* for which suitable statistics are available is provided by the First Germanic sound-shift. In prehistoric times in the Germanic dialect, the Indo-European voiceless unaspirated and aspirated stops, *t*, *th*, and *p*, *ph*, and *k*, *kh* changed in most positions to their respective voiceless spirants, *þ*, *f*, and χ; subsequently, the voiced stops *d*, *b*, and *g* changed to their respective voiceless stops, *t*, *p*, and *k*; subsequently, the voiced aspirated stops, *dh*, *bh*, and *gh*, changed to their corresponding non-aspirated voiced stops (*d*, *b*, *g* respectively) in some certain positions, and to their corresponding unaspirated voiced spirants (ð, *v*, ʒ) in the remaining positions. Thus:

t, tʰ > *þ*	*d* > *t*	*dh* > *d*, ð
p, pʰ > *f*	*b* > *p*	*bh* > *b*, *v*
k, kʰ > χ	*g* > *k*	*gh* > *g*, ʒ

The explanation which has been previously advanced by the author for this wholesale 'spontaneous' change of stops

---

* Pronounced in the manner of present-day German *ch* either in *ich* or in *Buch*. See page 54.

is that the stops as a whole had acquired an excessive relative frequency, because of the weakening and loss of many vowels and endings in pre-Germanic [1] (illustrative material available in current handbooks). However, it seems improbable that each stop had also independently crossed its upper threshold. Indeed, when entire categories of stops are involved, one seems justified in suspecting that analogical change is involved, as was indeed the case with the pre-Germanic stops; this can be shown by the findings of statistical analyses.

For though the 'spontaneous' change just described occurred in prehistoric times, we can investigate this change by analyzing the early records of some dialect of Germanic. Having established percentages for the phonemes resulting from phonetic changes of Grimm's Law, we can determine whether, had each phoneme remained unchanged, it would have possessed a percentage clearly above the upper threshold for the phoneme which was abbreviated. For example, if we find in, say, Old English, that k has a relative frequency suitable for k but decidedly above the upper threshold of the g from which it changed, we may assume that had Indo-European (i.e. pre-Germanic) g not shifted to k under Grimm's Law, the g would have been far too frequent.

King Alfred's Old English translation of Boethius' *De Consolatione Philosophiae* [2] has been selected as the most suitable available material for statistical analysis. Two samplings were made of this material, each 25,000 phonemes in extent, and totalling 50,000 phonemes; analysis of these disclosed the following percentages, which, for the reader's convenience are presented as of the stops *before they changed under Grimm's Law:*

$t = 9.12\%$	$[p = 2.52\%]$	$k = 4.14\%$
$d = 4.08$	$b = .144$	$g = 2.64$
$dh = 3.83$	$[bh = 1.11]$	$[gh = 2.98]$

The percentages for *p, bh,* and *gh,* which are enclosed in brackets, are doubtful because they include occurrences of phonemes of doubtful form in pre-Germanic. That is, the phoneme f in Old English which is presented above as pre-Germanic p with a percentage of 2.52 per cent represents not only the form resulting from pre-Germanic p but also in many instances from pre-Germanic bh; similarly, gh above, with 2.98 per cent, which is the percentage of Old English g, represents many instances of original j (pronounced as y in English yet). Nevertheless, the remaining six stops are reasonably trustworthy in view of both their history and their orthography.

Using the thresholds of frequency as approximately deduced in the table on page 75 as standards for comparison, we can examine the above frequencies, phoneme by phoneme:

The t at 9.12 per cent and the k at 4.14 per cent are each above the average frequency for these phonemes, and had cause to undergo an extensive abbreviatory 'spontaneous' change to $þ$ and x respectively; the doubtful percentage of p with 2.52 per cent had no cause to undergo phonetic change, and presumably followed by analogy.

Of the voiced stops d, b, and g, only g with 2.64 per cent which is higher than that for any g in the table, had clear cause to undergo change, though d with 4.08 per cent is surely at its upper threshold if not above it. B, however, with .144 per cent seems well below its upper threshold and again probably followed by analogy; its change was doubtless facilitated by the fact that there was no p in the language at that time with which it might have been confused (see page 89).

Pre-Germanic dh with 3.83 per cent had clear cause to change to d since we find, by referring to our table on page 75, that 3.83 per cent is practically at the upper threshold of d and hence far too frequent for dh. Pre-Germanic bh with 1.11 per cent has a frequency in accord with that for b to which it changed. Of gh, because of confused orthography, we can say nothing with any degree of certainty.

To summarize, then, pre-Germanic t and k shifted to Germanic β and χ because they had transgressed their upper threshold, and p changed, by analogy, to f. Pre-Germanic g and possibly d changed because of excessive frequency to k and t respectively, while b followed to p by analogy. Pre-Germanic dh surely, and bh possibly, transgressed their upper thresholds of toleration, while we may say nothing with certainty about gh.

Dynamic Philology must, however, be extremely cautious in ascribing any linguistic change to the influence of analogic arrangement, especially in cases where comparative figures from the subsequent development of the language, or from that of a parallel language, are not available. For the employment of the concept of analogic change can easily, though inadvertently, disguise an unequivocal disproof of what seems to be a general law. Fortunately the subsequent independent parallel development of different Germanic dialects seems to indicate conclusively that the devastating changes described under Grimm's Law involved, in all probability, analogic changes. For example, the Germanic p which arose from pre-Germanic b by the presumed action of analogy, subsequently strengthened to pf in Old High German (see page 120) as if to bring back its magnitude of complexity more into line with its low relative frequency; so, too, in many German dialects the Germanic t subsequently strengthened by augmentative change to ts, as might almost be anticipated. In some dialects k changed to $k\chi$ * analogically with the changes of t and p to ts and pf. Indeed, the heterogeneous consonantal systems of the German dialects very probably reflect the attempt, which has lasted for centuries, to restore the equilibrium which was disturbed by the analogic sound changes of the First Germanic sound-shift.[1]

On the other hand, in modern English, Dutch, and Danish, equilibrium between the magnitude of complexity and

---

* The symbol χ represents the voiceless guttural spirant, e.g. the *ch* of German *ich* or *Buch*.

relative frequency of occurrence of the phonemes involved in the First Germanic sound-shift has been restored. It would be an interesting problem in dynamics to investigate the changes in vocabulary content, and in the rules of morphological and syntactical organization, as well as the minor phonetic changes, abbreviatory and augmentative, which have taken place in the histories of these different Germanic languages, and which have probably helped in the general restoration of equilibrium resulting from the analogic changes of the First Germanic sound-shift.

4. POSSIBLE DISTURBING FACTORS OF EQUILIBRIUM

Now that we have seen that a condition of equilibrium very probably exists in the phonemic systems of languages, and that phonetic change is in all probability the means whereby this condition of equilibrium is maintained, it is only reasonable to inquire into the factors capable of disturbing this equilibrium; for these factors are the ultimate causes of phonetic change.

Since morphemes, words, and sentences are all composed of phonemes, any factor which disturbs the relative frequency of usage, or the length of morphemes and words, or which disturbs the usual syntactical arrangements of sentences, may well disturb the equilibrium in the phonemic system. We have seen how words are shortened by abbreviation and truncation, and we shall see in Chapter V how sentence patterns may also change with the lapse of time and the development of culture. But perhaps neither the changes of words nor of sentence-patterns is so important in disturbing phonemic equilibrium as changes in morphological structure. Let a language elect, for example as in English, to make its imperfect tense with a d suffix, and the relative frequency of d will rapidly rise at the expense of the relative frequency of other phonemes. Or let a language employ a verbal auxiliary in periphrastic construction, as in English *do* and *did* in the periphrastic verb forms *do go* and *did go*, and once again the relative frequencies of the phonemes constituting the auxiliary will mount. So, too, the favoring of a prefix, particle, or a conjunction will likewise disturb the phonemic equilibrium of the language; the favoring of the suffixes *-er* and *-en* in modern German has so increased the relative frequencies of *r* and *n* that in many German dialects they have become unstable even to the point of disappearing in some positions.*

Once the equilibrium is disturbed, centuries may pass before it is restored, if indeed it is ever completely restored in respect to every phoneme in the system.[1] For, not only are some disturbing factors constantly present, as we shall see in the ensuing chapters, but there is always the potential influence of analogic interference. The histories of languages reveal that one change occurs only to make room for another: endings are truncated for brevity, prefixes and particles are added for clarity, the position of accent changes to effect greater vividness, often increasing the magnitude of what is stressed and diminishing or deleting the magnitude of what is left unaccented. And as the frequencies of phonemes are altered, their forms are altered, in the attempt to restore equilibrium. In this fashion a language breaks into dialects with lines of cleavage often marked by the limits of geographical, social, economic, or political groups, in which the original disturbances took place, and in which in turn, subconsciously, the attempt is made to restore equilibrium. A phonemic system may be viewed as in a constant drift toward equilibrium, a view which as we shall see in Chapter VI seems justified for nearly all phenomena of language.

---

* The colloquial speech of Berlin, for example, does not pronounce the *r* of *Berlin* or *Bier*, nor the final *n* generally in the inflectional ending *-en*, e.g. *mit den guten Frauen.*

5. CONCLUSIONS

The tendency of a phonemic system to maintain a condition of equilibrium suggests the existence of an underlying law of economy of effort. For where there are differences in magnitude, the lesser magnitudes are reserved for the more frequent occurrences. This law of economy of energy in the form and behavior of phonemes parallels closely a similar law of economy which was observed in the form and behavior of words (page 38). Furthermore, it parallels what we are about to observe in the phonemena of accent, namely, that lesser magnitudes (or lower degrees) of accent are reserved for the more frequently occurring elements.

IV

ACCENT WITHIN THE WORD

1. PURPOSE

THE purpose of the present chapter is to investigate the phenomena of accent * as manifested in the elements of a word. We shall find that the degree of emphasis of elements of words tends to bear an inverse ratio to the relative frequency of their occurrence, and that the accentual system of a language exhibits a condition of equilibrium, the maintenance of which is responsible for accentual changes.

2. THE DEFINITION OF ACCENT

For a definition of accent, we cannot do better than adopt that of Jespersen: [1] 'stress is "energy," intensive muscular activity, not of one organ but *of all the speech organs at once.*' Jespersen's description of the phenomenon of accent as applied to the most highly stressed syllable in a given word is also well worth noting: [2]

> To pronounce a stressed syllable all organs are exerted to the utmost. The muscles of the lungs are strongly innervated; the movements of the vocal cords are stronger, leading on the one hand in voiced sounds to a greater approximation of the vocal cords, with less air escaping but with greater amplitude of vibrations, and also greater rising or falling of the tone.

In other words, the accented element is more difficult to pronounce since it consumes more energy, and is more audible because of the greater amplitude of vibrations.

---

* Normally the term *accent* applies to both stress and tone accent. In this chapter its use will be restricted primarily to phenomena of stress.[3]

3. THE ACCENT OF WORDS IN THE
SENTENCE (SENTENCE-ACCENT)

The accent of words in sentences is the least difficult type of accent to understand: by giving additional stress to a given word in a sentence the intensity of that word in the sentence increases. In the sentence 'he saw her,' one may emphasize *he* or *saw* or *her*, selecting the element to which the speaker wishes to call the auditor's especial attention. Yet, while sentence-accent is the least difficult type of accent to comprehend, it is, being the most variable of all types of accent, the one most difficult to formulate into reasonably precise laws. Nevertheless, there are two features of sentence-accent which deserve present mention because they give valuable clues to other types of accent which, though difficult to understand, will ultimately yield themselves to measurement.

The most striking feature of sentence-accent is this: words which occur most frequently are generally not preferred for accentuation. That is, the articles, prepositions, conjunctions, pronouns, and auxiliaries, which are usually the most frequent words in a language are, as a rule, not accented. If we list the twenty-five most frequently used words of modern English (according to Eldridge[1]) and of modern German (according to Kaeding[2]) — which account for 41 per cent and 34 per cent respectively of total occurrences — we find words which are normally not accented:

English					German				
the	a	it	he	from	die	ein	von	aus	dass
of	is	on	will	have	der	an	nicht	sie	er
and	that	by	his	has	und	den	mit	ist	es
to	for	be	as	which	zu	auf	dem	so	vor
in	was	at	with	not	in	das	des	sich	ich

But there is a second feature of sentence-accent. Though on the whole these words are normally not accented, as is observable from the stream of speech of these languages, they are sometimes accented in unusual usage. That is, it is quite possible to devise sentences in these languages in which any of the words listed above will bear stress. Hence, unusual arrangement of words is an important factor.

Bearing then in mind that the accent tends (1) to gravitate away from words of high frequency and (2) toward words in unusual usage, let us defer further consideration of this type of accent until we have dealt with the morphological and analogical types of accent.

4. MORPHOLOGICAL ACCENT

By *morphological accent* [1] is meant the stress which, without regard for the vacillating position of sentence-accent, is regularly placed on one (or more) of the morphological elements of the word, viz. on prefix, root, suffix, or ending. For example, in the English words *wíshes* and *bespéak* we accent a morphological element, and in each case the root *wish-* and *-speak*. In the German word *Ánfang* 'beginning,' the prefix *án-* is accented. In the Latin word *fortióribus* 'to the stronger (plural),' the suffix *-ór-* is accented. In the Greek locative *isthmoî* 'on the isthmus' the accent is on the locative ending *-i*.

For purposes of study, morphological accent has the advantage of an apparent fixity of position; it seems to adhere to a definite morpheme (*wísh-es*), or morphemes (*týpe-wrìte-er*), of the word. Morphological accent is, furthermore, as integral a part of the word as any of the constituent phonemes. Thus, an arbitrary shift in the position of accent may change the meaning of a word quite as much as an arbitrary alteration in the position of the phonemes; just as English *tab* and *bat* are different words, so German '*übersetzen*' 'to ferry across' is different from '*übersétzen*,' 'to translate.' Even in English, *próduce* and *prodúce* are by no means identical, nor is *pérfume* and *perfúme, pérmit, permít, rébel, rebél, próject, projéct*.

Let us continue our investigation by examining the accent, clearly morphological, of the words *wíshes* and *bespéak*. The question at once arises why accent selected as its resting place here the roots *wish* and *speak* rather than the prefix (*be*-) or the ending (*-es*). The explanation offered by Jespersen [1] for extensive root-accent (for example in English) is that the root is more important than the prefixes, suffixes, and endings. Whether Jespersen's explanation is valid, we must discard it as unserviceable for a measuring rod; for we know empirically little about the laws of 'importance,' nor will Jespersen's suggested recourse to 'psychological value,' [2] about which even less is known empirically, aid us at this time.

a. Fixity of the Position of Accent in English

Let us begin by asking if in a given language — our first example will be English — morphological accent is always so rigidly attached to, or so thoroughly a part of, the accented morpheme as never to deviate in position. For example, may we say that in a given English word the accent is 'fixed'? We obviously do say this, and English dictionaries ordinarily indicate a 'correct' accent for every polysyllabic word. It is true that the Englishman may accent *labóratory* on the second syllable, whereas the American accents it on the first, *láboratory*, yet the Englishman and the American are each quite consistent within their own speech-groups. Let us, however, scrutinize more closely this so-called 'fixed' accent in English. We all agree, I think, with the dictionary that *unbínd, unbólt, unbráid*, and *unlóad*, are each accented on the last syllable, which also happens to be the root, and we should follow the dictionary in uttering the sentence (*A*): 'God is all-powerful;

He can unbínd, unbólt, unbráid, and unlóad.' Having constructed a sentence which does not disobey the accepted position of accent in these four words, can we now compose one which does? Designating the above sentence as A, let us compose sentence B: 'God is all-powerful; He can bind and unbind, bolt and unbolt, braid and unbraid, load and unload.' If the reader declaim sentence B with some emphasis, he will notice, unless I am much mistaken, that in sentence B the first (prefix) syllable un (unaccented in sentence A) has taken on more accent, and at the expense of the syllable which in sentence A had the normal chief accent. The root-syllable has become less accented, the prefix more accented.*

b. *Intervals Between Occurrences*

Confining our attention to sentence B, we feel that the reason for this shift of accent from the root to un is because in sentence B the prefix un points out a sharp contrast, e.g. *bolt* and *unbolt*. Indeed, in sentence B, un points out a maximum contrast, inasmuch as, being the negative, it marks the opposite to the positive used in close conjunction with it. Nevertheless, the shift of accent from the root to un in sentence B cannot be explained solely on the grounds of contrast or of maximum contrast. That the presence of a mere contrast is not a sufficient explanation is at once clear when we remember that every word, syllable, or sound, unless it be a repetition, points out some sort of contrast from what has preceded or is about to come. So too the shift in accent cannot be exclusively a matter of maximum contrast, for we could devise a sentence B, consisting of word-pairs like *submit* and *remit*, or *accuse* and *excuse*, which

---

* I need not point out that, though we speak of primary and secondary accent and unaccentedness, accent is really a matter of degree; every syllable must have some accent in order to be audible.

would show the same tendency for accent to shift (to the prefixes *sub*, *re*, *ac*, and *ex*), even though the two words in each pair are not the negatives of one another and hence do not mark a maximum contrast. If contrast is a factor in the accent shift in sentence *B*, it is evidently not the only factor, nor necessarily the most significant factor.

Now, let us examine the differences between sentences *A* and *B* objectively, as if they were in no way potentially connected with our own behavior. Let us regard each sentence as a succession of morphological elements rather than of words. In doing this, we see at once that, aside from accent and length, sentence *B* differs from sentence *A* also in this respect: in each of the contrasting word-pairs in sentence *B* we have doubled the number of the morphological elements, except the prefix *un*. The same would also hold true of a sentence made up of couplets like *conceive* and *perceive*, or even *conception* and *perception*. In sentence *B* the morphological elements have been doubled except *un*, and to this *un* the accent has gravitated. But we must be careful in taking an entire sentence (such as *B*) as a measure of accent, for it is perfectly possible to write a sentence *C* in which, for example, *bolt* and *unbolt* are not placed so close to one another, and where the accent shift noted in *B* does not take place: 'God is omnipotent: He can *unbind*, *unbolt*, *unload*, *unbraid*, *bind*, *bolt*, *braid*, and *load*.' In sentence *C*, as in *B*, we have doubled the morphological elements of *A* with the exception of the prefix *un*, yet we find nevertheless that the accent of each word in *C* is as marked in the dictionary, the same as in sentence *A*. The reason why we cannot take the sentence as a measure of accent, and merely add up like morphemes as though we were sorting and counting apples and prunes in a basket of fruit, is that such a procedure ignores both the stream of time and the succession of words in time, a succession in which position, as we know, is of vital importance.

But may we not adopt the interval between occurrences

of a given morpheme as a measure of accent? In sentence
A, the interval between *un* and the next following occurrence was, save for the last word, roughly one morpheme;
whereas the intervals in sentence *A* between the occurrences
of the morphemes *-bind*, *-bolt*, *-braid*, *-load* may be termed
infinite, since there was no second occurrence of any of these
in sentence *A*. In sentence *B*, however, the length of the
interval between the occurrences of *un* was more than
doubled, whereas the intervals between the other morphemes
shrank enormously. We can, therefore, say with assurance
that sentence *A* differs from sentence *B* in the length of
intervals between the occurrences of similar morphemes.
As far as these two sentences are concerned, the accent has
in *B* passed from the morphemes between which the intervals have become shortened, to morphemes between which
the intervals have become longer.

c. *Average Intervals Between Like Occurrences*

If we take a language as a whole, considering it as a long
stream of speech, we may not only determine from selections
of sufficient length what morphemes occur, but we may
compute the average interval between the occurrences of
like morphemes. That is, we can view morphemes precisely
as we previously viewed words (page 45), and consider the
average interval (the reciprocal of relative frequency) of a
morpheme, as the 'wave length' of the morpheme. If a
morpheme-count reveals the fact that accent tends to settle
on morphemes of the greatest average interval ('wave
length'), that is, on the morphemes of the lowest relative
frequency, we shall have reached the very heart of the
dynamics of accent.

The practical difficulties in the way of such a morpheme-
count are manifold: a morpheme may be accented in one
word and unaccented in another, e.g. *ad* in 'ad*míssible*' and

'*ád*equate'; morphemes of different meaning may possess the same phonetic form, e.g. *in* in '*ín*stant' is not the same morphologically as the *in* in '*in*ádequate.' In addition to these practical difficulties is the fact that *in*, for example, occurs in English also as an independent word, the intensity of which may vary according to sentence-accent (see page 131 f.). To avoid difficulties which introduce significant possibilities of error that in turn might vitiate fundamentally sound conclusions, we must limit our investigation.

It would of course be ideal if we might limit our examination to the category of prefixes, or of suffixes, or of endings, in which the specific morphological elements constituting the category fall into the class of those *always* accented, and those *never* accented. For example, if we could find a language in which, say, part of the endings are *always* accented, and the balance *never* accented, we could determine whether those which are *always* accented have a lower relative frequency than the *never* accented. But to my knowledge a modern language possessing this idiosyncrasy does not exist. Indeed, a language, if our hypothesis of relative frequency is true, could not possess this idiosyncrasy for long, since the categories of endings, suffixes, and prefixes represent, as we shall see, morphological elements of such high relative frequency, that accent would tend to recede from them speedily.

Nevertheless, Dynamic Philology is fortunate in having the precise evidence of one ancient language, Sanskrit, which sheds valuable light on the nature of accent. If in some quarter of the earth a living language can be found in which accentual conditions are similar, it, too, if our conclusions are correct, should support the conclusions deduced from this ancient language.

d. The Masculine Consonantal Declensions in Sanskrit

The earliest Sanskrit literature (the *Rigveda*) still clearly reflects and frequently marks the original morphological accent of Indo-European, for our purposes especially interesting as it appears in the masculine consonantal declensions. In prehistoric Sanskrit all the endings of the singular and plural masculine possessed accent, with the exception of three: the nominative and accusative singular and the nominative plural. To make this more graphic, let us list all the cases in the singular and plural masculine, putting in capital letters the names of the three cases which have no accent on the endings. The illustrative word is the pre-Sanskrit form of the masculine present participle of the root *as* 'to be,' meaning 'being' (hyphens added for convenience):

	Singular			*Plural*	
NOMINATIVE	sánt-s *		NOMINATIVE	sánt-as	
ACCUSATIVE	sánt-am		accusative	sat-ás	
instrumental	sat-á		instrumental	sad-bhís †	
dative	sat-é		dative ⎱	sad-bhyás †	
ablative ⎱	sat-ás		ablative ⎰		
genitive ⎰			genitive	sat-ám	
locative	sat-í		locative	sat-sú	

It is clear that the presence or absence of accent was coupled with the ending of no particular number or case. If the lack of accent were a sign of the nominative, why was the accusative singular also unaccented? If lack of accent was a sign of the nominative and the accusative together, why did the endings of the accusative plural possess accent? Since all the endings of these declensions behave alike in every respect except that of accent, the conditions are ideal for the investigation of a possible correlation of relative frequency with the degree of accentual intensity. For, if

* Restored form.   † Restored only in respect to accentuation.

accent is immediately connected with relative frequency of occurrence, an examination of the relative frequency of inflectional cases as they occur in the *Rigveda* will establish this connection and reveal the nature of the correlation. An analysis [1] of the frequency of the case endings of all nouns in the *Rigveda* yields the following:

Singular		*Plural*	
NOMINATIVE	24,286	NOMINATIVE	10,981
ACCUSATIVE	17,551		
		accusative	5,353
instrumental	4,234	instrumental	3,360
dative	4,092	dative	363
ablative	923	ablative	124
genitive	5,274	genitive	1,595
locative	3,789	locative	1,546

The most striking feature of these statistics is that the three unaccented cases are enormously more frequent than the accented cases. If comparative philology has been unsuccessful in explaining the reason for the seemingly irrational accentual differences in these declensions, dynamic philology can at least point out that lack of accent was coupled with markedly high relative frequency.

Now at that same stage of linguistic development of Sanskrit when this accent variation existed in the endings of the masculine consonantal declensions, one may reasonably ask if there were not perchance other accent variations which revealed similar tendencies. For surely it would be strange if an accentual variation of this type were restricted to the masculine consonantal declensions, even granted that these declensions did include a large number of frequently used substantives and adjectives. That this was not an isolated phenomenon is evinced by the Sanskrit verbal system, in which there were similar variations in accent, still maintained to a considerable extent in earliest Sanskrit.*

* The exact position of the original Indo-European accent in the verbal system is attested in other languages by the vowel weakenings which resulted from the original position of the accent. Since these accentual differences have been discussed in considerable detail elsewhere,[2] the material does not require repetition here.

e. The Strong Verbs in Sanskrit

Originally the strong verbs in Sanskrit (that is, the athe-matic conjugations, or Sanskrit classes, II, III, V, VII, VIII, IX) regularly accented the endings throughout the entire indicative of the present stem except in the singular active.[1] Likewise the endings of the perfect tense had origi-nally no accent in the singular, whereas in the dual and plural the accent was for the most part on the endings. Hence the difference in accentuation was clearly one between the present singular active indicative on the one hand, and the present dual and plural active indicative plus the entire middle voice indicative on the other.* To make this rela-tionship clearer, let us print again in capitals the names of those forms of the indicative of which the endings were not accented:

Present Indicative

	Active			*Middle*		
	Singular	dual	plural	singular	dual	plural
Persons	First	first	first	first	first	first
	Second	second	second	second	second	second
	Third	third	third	third	third	third

If we take the Sanskrit root *dvis,* 'hate,' and inflect it in the present indicative, we have the following paradigm (hy-phens added for convenience):

Present Indicative

Active

Singular	dual	plural
1. dvéṣ-mi	dviṣ-vás	dviṣ-más
2. dvék-ṣi	dviṣ-ṭhás	dviṣ-ṭhá
3. dvéṣ-ṭi	dviṣ-ṭás	dviṣ-ánti

Middle

1. dviṣ-é	dviṣ-váhe	dviṣ-máhe
2. dvik-ṣé	dviṣ-áthe	dvid-dhvé
3. dviṣ-ṭé	dviṣ-áte	dviṣ-áte

* See footnote †, page 143.

So, too, the imperfect * and perfect indicative of these classes reveal what was an analogous relationship of accent, though differing in augment, reduplication, or endings. Now if we can show statistically from the *Rigveda* that the singular active was more frequently used throughout the language than the other five numbers (dual and plural active plus the entire middle) we have found a probable reason why the accent was not compelled to settle on the endings in the present singular active.

With recourse again to the *Rigveda*[1] and by adding together all the occurrences of the first, second, and third persons, singular, dual, and plural for the active and for the middle, including, moreover, all moods and tenses of all classes of verbs so that we may get a clear idea of the comparative use of the three *numeri* in both the active and passive, we shall approach as nearly as will ever be possible the ratios that existed when this accentual difference was still existent. The summarized results are:

	Active		
	Singular	Dual	Plural
1.	612	17	932
2.	4,378	1,143	963
3.	5,467	265	2,692
	10,457	1,425	4,587

	Middle		
1.	428	11	512
2.	914	120	166
3.	2,257	92	1,589
	3,599	223	2,267

Here again high frequency is coupled with lack of accent; only the relatively less frequent endings possess accent. The singular active, whose endings have no accent, is more frequent than the rest of the active, and more frequent than the entire middle.

It may be felt that we should not lump together the occur-

* But see page 144, and footnote, * page 144.

rences of the three different persons for each number, but should rather segregate the frequencies of each person, e.g. the first singular present active, the second singular present active, and so throughout the entire list, comparing the relative frequencies of 18 persons instead of 6 different numbers. If we did this, we should find some accented endings occurring more frequently than some unaccented endings (e.g. the accented third plural active with 2,692 occurrences, and the unaccented first singular with 612 occurrences). It might be suggested that the method of analysis employed is justifiable only if the entire singular active, for example, had only one ending, and correspondingly the duals and plurals. But let us consider the matter more closely. Let us first ask the question: would such an investigation be justified, if, without deleting the various endings which distinguish persons (as well as number and voice), we had in the Sanskrit conjugation an additional special syllable in the singular active and another different special syllable in both the dual and plural active and the entire middle? These special syllables by their presence would make the singular active easily distinguishable from the other numbers. The obvious answer is that such an additional syllable, if it were also accompanied by a difference in accent, would designate this contrast sufficiently to justify our proceeding with a frequency count. But is a whole extra syllable necessary? From what we have observed in Chapter II dealing with abbreviation, we might easily conclude that the existence of such an extra syllable would be doomed because of its enormous frequency, especially because it would be tautologous. After all, the ending *-mi* of the first singular active indicative names not only the person, but also the number, voice, and mood. If instead of a special syllable to mark the present singular active indicative, let us suppose we had a single phoneme present in each ending in the present singular active. If a special syllable could designate the entire singular indicative active, there is nothing to prevent a single phoneme from doing the same, since there is nothing in the nature of meaning which prevents it from being conveyed by one speech-element rather than another, provided that the meaning once becomes established in the symbol. By an examination of the endings of the present indicative we can observe whether these endings actually have such an element in common for the different numbers in Sanskrit:

	Present Indicative				
	Active			*Middle*	
SINGULAR	dual	plural	singular	dual	plural
1. *m-i*	*v-as*	*mas*	*e*	*vaḥ-e*	*mah-e*
2. *s-i*	*th-as*	*tha*	*s-e*	*āth-e*	*dhv-e*
3. *t-i*	*t-as*	*anti*	*t-e*	*āt-e*	*at-e*

It is quite evident in the endings *mi, si, ti* of the present singular active indicative, that *i* is shared in common; each ending is a monosyllable ending in *i*. The *i*, whether intentionally or accidentally, does in fact represent the present singular active indicative and did represent it at the time when this accent variation was in force.* Because of this distinguishing phoneme which the 1st, 2d, and 3d persons singular active present indicative had in common and which thus — by chance or purpose — formed a special category,† we are justified in considering in this instance *number* and not *person*,‡ and to regard these positive results as a confirmation of our findings in the masculine consonantal declensions, namely, that, other things being equal, inten-

---

* Indeed, the endings -*mi*, -*si*, -*ti* were the endings in proethnic Indo-European.

† Having established this category for the present singular active indicative we need not further consider the other numbers and voices of the present, inasmuch as individually as persons, or collectively as numbers, they are far less frequent than the entire singular active indicative reckoned together. In the table on page 141 it is evident that the singular active indicative occurs more often than the dual and plural active indicative together, or the entire middle together.

‡ It may profitably be remembered, incidentally, that a change from direct discourse to indirect discourse, and *vice versa*, however much it may alter the *person* of the verb, normally does not alter the *number* of the verb. E.g. *We have come*, and, *Mary says that they have come.*

sity of accent bears an inverse (not necessarily proportionate) relationship to relative frequency of usage.

Doubtlessly the endings of the present singular active
indicative were originally also accented.   But since they
were presumably the more frequent, they were also the more
expected endings in the stream of speech, the more usual
endings, endings which were less in need of accent. Subsequently, after the earliest times, the accent shifted likewise
from all the other (less frequent) endings as well, settling
upon other parts of the word for a reason of which the
underlying principle will be presently clear when we examine analogical accent.   It is only fair to interpose that the
full history of the earlier accentual differentiation between
the present singular active and the other forms is obscured
in the darkness of prehistoric times.*

There is a third instance of differences of accent in the
pre-Sanskrit verbal system which yield the same conclusions as those derived from an analysis of the endings of the
masculine consonantal declensions and of the strong verbs.

f. Verbal Stem-Formatives † in Sanskrit

In Indo-European times the accent of the present tense
of a verb as it appeared in the stream of speech was either
on the ending, or the stem-formative (suffix or infix), or on

---

* The comparative philologist may wonder at our use of the *mi, si, ti* endings of
the present active indicative, without mentioning the fact that in the imperfect
active indicative where the endings were unaccented this *i* was not present (e.g.
endings: -(*a*)*m*, -*s*, -*t*).   In reply, it may be pointed out that in Sanskrit the augment *a*- placed at the beginning of the word in the imperfect and a sign of the
imperfect (although it was creeping in elsewhere), had drawn the accent onto itself
throughout the entire imperfect.[1]   Undoubtedly we must conclude from the strong
form of the stem in the imperfect singular active that the accent was originally
(perhaps before the augment became crystallized) on the stem and not on the endings.   Since the accent was on the augment, even in Rigvedic times, we cannot extend our investigation to include the various *numeri* of the imperfect in the *Rigveda*.

† A *stem-formative* (or *stem-formant*) is a morpheme added to the root either at the
beginning (prefix) or at the end (suffix) or tucked inside (infix) to make the *stem*
(root plus formant) to which endings are added.

the root, depending primarily upon the class to which the verb belonged. For example (forms taken from Sanskrit), in Class I the accent was regularly on the first syllable of the root (e.g. *bhávati*, third singular present of root *bhū* 'to become'). In Class V the stem was made by adding the suffix (stem-formative) *nu* when the accent was on the endings (see pages 140 ff.) but by adding the suffix (stem-formative) *nō* which had the accent when the accent was not on the endings, e.g. *sunóti* 'he presses out,' but *sunumás* 'we press out' from the root *su*, 'to press out.'

Of the nine classes of verbs, Classes IV, V, VI, VII, VIII, and IX, as they appeared in Sanskrit, give unmistakable evidence that the accent in the present tense was *always* on the stem-formative when the accent was not on the endings.[1] In other words, in these six classes, when the accent, for reasons which we saw in pages 140 ff., was not on the endings,* it was always on the stem formative (suffix or infix) and not on the root-element.

In Classes I, II, and III, on the other hand, conditions differed from those of the above six classes. In Class I the accent was never either on endings or on stem-formative, but invariably on the first syllable of the root-element (e.g. *bhávati*, cf. above). Since neither Class II nor Class III made use of a true stem-formative in the present system, they are not comparable with the other classes. Class II adds the endings immediately to the root (e.g. *ás-ti* 'he is,' from the root *as* plus the ending *ti*), and Class III adds the endings immediately to the reduplicated † root (see page 82) without a formative (e.g. *juho-ti* 'he sacrifices,' from the root *hu* with reduplicating syllable *ju* plus the ending *ti*).

---

* In Class VI the accent was never on the endings.

† The reduplicating syllable might in a certain sense be viewed as a stem-formative, but not in the same sense as the stem-formatives of Classes I, and IV to IX, because the reduplicating syllable differs according to the initial phonemes of the individual roots of the reduplicating verbs, whereas the stem-formative of each of the remaining classes which employ stem-formatives is constant for all members of the class.

Now, discarding Classes II and III as being non-comparable, we find in the remaining seven classes that Class I *never* has accent on the stem-formative,* and that Classes IV, V, VI, VII, VIII and IX *always* have accent on the stem-formatives when not on the endings.

Now if the deductions made from the masculine consonantal declensions (page 139) and from the endings of strong verbs (page 141) are correct, we should expect to find that the stem-formative of the verbs of Class I, which never have accent, will have a higher relative frequency than the stem-formatives of each of the Classes IV, V, VI, VII, VIII, and IX respectively, which always have the accent when the accent is not on the endings.

A statistical analysis [1] of the occurrences of these verbs in the *Rigveda* yields the following evidence:

Sanskrit Classes	*Unaccented Stem-Formative*	*Accented Stem-Formatives*					
	I	IV	V	VI	VII	VIII	IX
Totals	5622	977	877	663	478	272	259
Percentages	38%	6.5%	5.9%	4.5%	3.2%	1.9%	1.6%

In other words, the verbs of Class I in which the stem-formative is unaccented are not only more frequent than any of the other six classes, but more frequent than all the other six classes together.

* I am well aware of the fact that the Indo-European stem-vowel *ĕ/ŏ* (Sanskrit, *ă*) of the first class of verbs may in some instances have been the second syllable of a 'disyllabic base' (i.e. disyllabic root). But, since the contrast about to be made is between verbs *always* accented on the first syllable of the root (e.g. verbs of Class I), and verbs *never* accented on the root, but always on the stem-formative or ending (e.g. Classes IV–IX), nothing is gained by introducing here the complex theory of disyllabic bases.

g. *Conclusions from the Sanskrit Examples*

The three examples of morphological accent presented thus far indicate unmistakably that accent, or rather, the degree of accent * of a morphological element is connected with the relative frequency of its occurrence, in the sense that the one bears an inverse relationship to the other,† high frequency being coupled with a low degree of accent.

We must, of course, not forget that these accentual schemes which we have just observed were only in complete force before the dawn of history and had already commenced to exhibit instability at the time of the earliest document (*Rigveda*), which was the material for our analysis. Yet though these accentual schemes were not still completely in force in Rigvedic times, they were still sufficiently in force so that only in negligibly few instances is comparative philology in the slightest doubt as to the position where in all probability the original Indo-European accent rested. And since the statistical data is clear-cut and unequivocal, dynamic philology in viewing these conclusions seems reasonably justified in pursuing in other languages the very decided clue offered by this one ancient language which has preserved adequate vestiges of this very illuminating system of accent.

The reader may wonder why accent remained on endings or stem-formatives at all in Sanskrit, since these were probably the most frequent of all morphological elements, either individually or as categories. The answer is: the

---

* The question of accent is really one of degree, from the strongly accented to the 'unaccented.' Even the 'unaccented' speech-elements possess some accent, though only a low degree thereof. There can be no utterance without some degree of loudness or stress (see definition, page 130); only the un-uttered speech-element is truly unaccented. Hence, in employing the traditional term 'unaccented,' a low degree of accent will be understood. See footnote, page 134.

† Not necessarily proportionate; possibly some non-linear mathematical function.

accent did not remain there, but subsequently shifted to other parts of the word, a shift which was already in progress in Rigvedic times. The reader may also wonder why the accent ever rested on the frequent endings and formatives; a possible answer to this query will be suggested later (page 260) after we have further investigated the phenomena of accent and investigated sentence-structure.

But if the degree of accent of a speech-element bears an inverse ratio to its relative frequency of occurrence, we should be able to find this condition in the accentual systems of other languages. And where this relationship is not clearly perceptible, we are justified in seeking secondary factors which may modify the influence of relative frequency.

h. Prefixes of Modern German

Now that we have examined the relative frequencies of endings and formative elements, it would be ideal if we might turn our investigation to prefixes, and to prefixes, which, like the Sanskrit endings, are either *always* accented or *never* accented. But to my knowledge a language happening to possess this idiosyncrasy does not exist. Modern German has, however, prefixes that are *never* accented, and others which are *practically always* accented; and if an analysis of a sufficiently long piece of German reveals that the *never* accented prefixes are notably more frequent than the *practically always* accented, we have made progress.

Kaeding [1] gives the comparative frequencies of all prefixes among 10,910,777 running words of German. From his extensive list, arranged in the order of decreasing frequency, I here present the first twelve prefixes (the prefixes which are *never* accented are in *italics*):

$$
\begin{array}{lr}
ge & — 443,639 \\
be & — 226,827 \\
ver & — 195,412 \\
er & — 122,662 \\
\end{array}
$$

an — 85,473
zu — 75,218
vor — 59,132
aus — 52,778
un — 49,831
ent — 48,456
da — 48,252
ein — 45,645

The prefixes (*ge-*, *be-*, *ver-*, *er-*) which head the list with relative frequencies considerably higher than any that follow, and hence occur at correspondingly shorter average intervals in spoken German, are chief among the *never* accented. Thus far the conclusions derived from our Sanskrit examples (pages 139, 141, 146) are substantiated. But unfortunately the prefix *ent* (48,456 occurrences) which, too, is *never* accented, is not in this group of prefixes of highest frequency, while *emp* (variant of *ent*) with 8,050 occurrences, and *zer* (with 5,385 occurrences) are not even among the first twelve listed above, though they, too, are *never* accented.

i. Variability in Position and the Degree of Crystallization of the Configuration

We may reasonably ask if there is perchance some other factor which in determining the accent of German prefixes may modify the influence of relative frequency. One thing can be said definitely: all of the *never* accented prefixes in German occur only as prefixes, whether to substantives or verbs. On the other hand, most of the *practically always* accented prefixes (to verbs) not only *may* be placed elsewhere than immediately before the verb without in any way essentially altering the meaning of the word, but they often *must* be placed elsewhere, indeed sometimes as far after the verb as possible without leaving the clause. In other words, the accented prefixes of verbs are always separable. Without in any way changing the basic meaning of the verb, one uses *an-fangen* (3d plural), *fangen — an* (3d plural), *an-zu-fangen* (gerund), and *an-ge-fangen* (past participle). These shifts may represent morphological and syntactical differences, yet there is generally less difference in basic word-meaning between *an-fangen* (3d plural) and *fangen — an* (3d plural), for example, than in English between *were I* and *if I were*. This variability in position accounts for the seeming discrepancy in the figures. Since Kaeding counted every occurrence of the prefix-morpheme as a prefix, regardless of its position,* Kaeding's figures for separable prefixes include occurrences where the prefix is really an independent word. Nevertheless, Kaeding's procedure, far from invalidating the figures for our use, unexpectedly sheds considerable light on the problem of accent. For *variability in position* of a morphological element seems in all probability to be a determining factor in the degree of accent of that element; that is, the tendency of accent to diminish in (or recede from) a morphological element of high relative frequency is offset by the *variability of position* of that morphological element.

Since *variability of position* of morphemes probably played an important role in some period in the development of the accentual system of every language, and since, as we shall see in Chapter V, *variability of position* is likewise a significant factor in sentence-accent, it merits discussion in considerable detail. Restricting our examples to present-day German, let us commence our investigation by viewing the stream of modern German speech, first, as a succession of morphemes, and, second, as a succession of words made up of these morphemes. In adopting this double point of view, we shall see: (1) that *variability in position* is a matter of degree which is computable; and (2) that *variability in posi-*

---

* E.g. in both *an-fangen* and *fangen... an*, the morpheme *an* was counted as a prefix, although in *fangen... an*, the *an* cannot be regarded, strictly speaking, as a true prefix.

tion is intimately connected not only with accent, but also with what may be termed (*a*) the *degree of crystallization of the configuration* on the one hand, and (*b*) the *distinctness of meaning* on the other, both of which are extremely important factors in the phenomena of language, and neither of which are computable.

(*i*). *Variability of Position in Modern German Prefixes*

An inseparable prefix, inasmuch as it is always attached to the rest of the word, is patently less variable in position (being in fact invariable) than a separable prefix which by definition does not always occupy the same position in reference to the stem to which it is sometimes prefixed. Of the German inseparable prefix *ver-* in the verb *vergessen* 'to forget,' one can predict that whenever the verb *vergessen* appears, the *ver-* will immediately precede the root-element; on the other hand, the separable prefix *vor-* in the verb *vorlesen* 'to read aloud' is so variable in position that it will often be separated from the root of the verb by a considerable number of words. Now if one views the stream of speech of German as a succession of morphemes, one can predict more accurately the probable morpheme or morphemes which will follow a given inseparable prefix (say *ver-*) than those which will follow a given separable prefix (say *vor-*). To predict with a reasonable degree of approximation what specific morphemes will follow the inseparable prefix *ver-* in the stream of speech of an individual German, or of a German speech-group, one need merely (1) obtain a sufficient sampling of his or its speech, (2) list the different morphemes which immediately follow *ver-*, (3) divide the total frequency of occurrence of *ver-* by the frequency of occurrence of each morpheme in the list under the combination with *ver-*. Thus, to illustrate from Kaeding's analysis,[1] in the 195,412 occurrences of *ver-*, the combination *vergess-*

occurs 1578 times; hence the chance is approximately 1 out of 124 that the prefix *ver-* will be followed by the root *-gess* in the speech-community from which Kaeding took samplings. By further consulting the evidence in Kaeding (pages 372–385) one can determine the probabilities for all the remaining morphemes which follow *ver-*. Hence the inseparable prefix *ver-* is 100 per cent predictable in respect to its following element: that is, one can establish all possible following elements and estimate for each its chances of occurrence.

But imagine adopting a similar procedure for the German separable verbal prefix *vor*! Of course for some of the morphemes which may immediately follow *vor-*, one can estimate probabilities of occurrences as accurately as for the morphemes following *ver-*. For example, in the total number of occurrences of the morpheme *vor-*, which in Kaeding is 62,477,* the chance is at least approximately 1 out of 34 that the morpheme *vor* will be followed by the morpheme *aus*; there is also an additional chance (e.g., '*Lies vor! Aus diesem Buch!*') that *vor* may be followed by *aus* in instances not covered by the probability 1 to 34. But to attempt to compute the probabilities of all the morphemes which may possibly follow *vor-* is a task which is practically impossible; indeed *vor-*, since it may occur at the end of a sentence, may be followed by any morphological element with which a following sentence may commence. The morpheme *vor-* is to a certain degree predictable, in the sense that the minimum probability for the occurrence of some certain following morphemes may be established; but it is not completely predictable in the same sense as is the inseparable prefix *ver-*.

With the method employed for *ver-* and *vor-*, one can determine for each prefix-morpheme, or for each prefix, or for every morpheme, the extent to which the following element

---

* Obtained by adding (Kaeding, page 465) the frequencies of following prefixes: *vor*, 59,132 (the frequency presented, *supra*, page 149); *voran*, 257; *vorauf*, 24; *voraus*, 1,831; *vorbei*, 205; *vorher*, 330; *vorhin*, 5; *vorüber*, 693.

(or the preceding element, or any other element in reference to it in the stream of speech) is predictable. The inseparable prefixes are completely predictable in the sense in which we have been using this term. The separable prefixes will differ in the extent to which they are predictable, and may be arranged in descending order of their predictability.

Now, it seems that as the predictability of a morpheme becomes less and less, that is, as it becomes more and more variable, it also becomes less a morpheme and more a word. Conversely, as the predictability of a morpheme becomes greater and greater it becomes less and less an independent word, and more and more a dependent morpheme; that is, its behavior (see Chapter V) is governed more by the laws of inflection and less by the laws of sentence-structure. Thus, the German prefix *vor* which has a high degree of variability in position, and hence a low degree of predictability, is both a word and a morpheme: (1) as a preposition, *vor* 'in front of' is a word, e.g. *vor dem Hause* 'in front of the house'; (2) as a morpheme it is (*a*) either completely variable in some instances, e.g. *vorlesen* 'to read aloud,' or (*b*) firmly crystallized with another morphemic member to form a larger speech-element which in turn is variable, e.g. *vor + aus* in *voraus-gehen* 'to go ahead'; or (*c*) it is a completely crystallized invariable prefix as in many substantive compounds, e.g. *Vorsicht* 'foresight.' The German prefix *wider* 'against' was once like the prefix *vor-* in all respects, but has almost entirely lost its usage as an independent word and has entirely lost its usage as a separable prefix, having become an inseparable prefix.

(*ii*). *Degree of Crystallization of the Configuration*

In viewing the stream of speech as a succession of morphemes we may speak in terms of *variability in position*, that is, of the extent to which the occurrence of specific morphemes in stated positions may be predicted. But if we view the stream of speech as a succession of words composed of these morphemes, we have a different picture. We see, for example, that the word *vergéssen* is a more completely crystallized configuration than the word *vórlesen*. The more variable in position a morpheme is, the less crystallized is the word of which it is a part. Hence, words may differ in the degree to which they are crystallized, or, in the *degree of crystallization of the configuration*.

For practical purposes, the degree of crystallization of a configuration can perhaps never be arithmetically computed with complete accuracy. But the significance of the term is easily apprehended against the background of our statistical analyses on the one hand, and with one's experience with language on the other. The degree of crystallization of the configuration of a word implies little more than this: the more firmly agglutinized, that is, the more immutable in arrangement, the constituent morphemes are in a word, the greater is the degree of crystallization.

The differing degrees of crystallization of configurations can perhaps be best apprehended by comparing the crystallization of phonemes in a morpheme-configuration, of morphemes in a word-configuration, and of words in a sentence-configuration; phonemes are normally far more crystallized in their configuration in a morpheme, than morphemes in a word, and morphemes in a word more crystallized than words in a sentence. In the decreasing order of crystallization from phoneme through sentence, there is increasing degree of choice in arrangement. We shall find that these differences in the degree of crystallization are closely associated with other phenomena of language.

If we judge from the German separable prefixes, the position of accent seems to be determined to a considerable extent by the degree of crystallization of the configuration. That is, what appears to be the normal tendency of accent to diminish in, or recede from, a prefix of excessive relative frequency is counteracted, or offset, by a low degree of crystallization of the prefix. So too, conversely, the tendency of accent to increase in, or to be attracted to, a morphological element may be counteracted or offset by a high degree of crystallization of a configuration. Thus, on the one hand, the German separable prefix *vor* is accented, in spite of its high relative frequency, because it has a comparatively low degree of crystallization of configuration; on the other hand the German separable prefix *zer-* is unaccented in spite of its low relative frequency because of its high degree of crystallization of configuration. Hence, the dynamics of accent include at least two determining factors: relative frequency and the degree of crystallization of the configuration. We shall now see that there is a third factor, a factor that may appropriately be termed 'the degree of distinctness of meaning.'

j. The Degree of Distinctness of Meaning

The distinctness of meaning of a morphological element varies also according to the relative frequency and the degree of crystallization of the morphological element. That is, an increase either in relative frequency or in the degree of crystallization of a morpheme, or both, will decrease the distinctness of the meaning of the element. Since the phenomena of meaning do not lend themselves to quantitative analysis, this tendency of the meaning of a morpheme to be less distinct when it is of high relative frequency or of a high degree of crystallization of configuration can only be apprehended and not quantitatively established.

The apprehension of this tendency in meaning is perhaps easiest in the case of two prefixes of like high degree of crystallization yet of significant differences in relative frequency; for, in two prefixes of this type where all else is constant except relative frequency, we can observe differences in the degree of distinctness of meaning. For example, the German prefixes *ge-* and *zer-* are each unaccented and, being always inseparable, have a very high degree of crystallization of the configuration. But *ge-* with a frequency (according to Kaeding [1]) of 443,639 in 20 million syllables is over eighty times more frequent than *zer-* with a frequency of 5,385. On the other hand, the prefix *zer-* of low frequency is far more distinct in its meaning than the prefix *ge-* of high frequency. Indeed the meaning of *ge-* is so indistinct that it is impossible to determine its meaning; * the meaning of *zer-*, however, is 'to pieces,' precisely and invariably, e.g. *reissen* 'to tear,' *zerreisen* 'to tear to pieces.' Hence we see from this example that with all else constant, the degree of distinctness of meaning of a morpheme seems to bear an inverse relationship to its relative frequency. Naturally, since meaning is subjective and does not lend itself to quantitative measurement, a precise measurement of this relationship can probably never be made.

The relationship between (1) the *degree of distinctness of meaning*, and (2) the *degree of crystallization of the configuration*, and (3) the *degree of accent* of a morpheme can be illustrated by the so-called 'doubtful prefixes' of German. For example, the prefixes *durch, über, um, unter, wieder* occur in verbal compounds both with and without accent, and hence are both separable and inseparable. When the verbal prefixes are inseparable, they are unaccented, and *vice versa*. Thus *dúrchblicken* means 'to look through,' *durchblícken* 'to peruse'; *übersetzen* means 'to ferry or set across,' *übersétzen* 'to translate'; *úmziehen* 'to move one's residence,' *umzíehen* 'to surround'; *úntergehen* 'to sink,' *untergéhen* 'to undergo'; *wíederholen* 'to fetch back,' *wiederhólen* 'repeat.' In these examples it is observable that the higher degree of crystal-

---

* Even if in *Gefilde, Gebrüder, Gebirge*, etc., the *ge-* designates a generic category, still one cannot say that *ge-* invariably designates a generic category since the chief use of *ge-* is as a sign of the past participle. Moreover, where *ge-* does indicate a generic category, one can by no means say that its meaning is particularly precise.

lization is coupled with a lower degree of accent. But more than that. Separable composition, or separability, which accents the idea of the prefix, is, according to an established rule of German grammar, more 'literal' in its meaning than the inseparable unaccented composition in which the meanings are more 'figurative.' In other words, like the English verbs *undergo, go under, undertake, take under*, etc. the meaning of the German separable compound is more distinct than the meaning of the inseparable compound, that is, distinct in the sense that the meaning of the compound is transparent from the meanings of the constituent morphological elements.

k. Equilibrium in an Accentual System

From the accentual phenomena discussed to this point, we may deduce with considerable plausibility the existence of a condition of equilibrium in the accentual system of a language. In this condition of equilibrium there appear to be at least four determining factors: (1) relative frequency (F); (2) the degree of intensity of the accent (A); (3) the degree of crystallization of the configuration (C); and (4) the degree of distinctness of meaning (M). These four factors seem to stand in this relationship: A (accent) and M (meaning) seem to bear an inverse relationship to F (frequency) and C (crystallization). Indeed, it is possible that the phenomenon is representable by the formula $FACM = K$ (constant), although (because the distinctness of meaning cannot be reduced to quantitative measurement) quantitative values can probably never be substituted for the symbols of this formula. Hence the chief value of the formula, if true, will be as a help in gaining insight into the phenomena.

Of these four factors, the relationship between F (relative frequency) and A (degree of accent) seems to be fundamentally most vital, for in the Sanskrit examples of accent adduced above (pages 138–148), we find accent and relative frequency in an inverse relationship,* in the many instances in Sanskrit where C (degree of crystallization) and M (degree of distinctness of meaning) seem constant. That is, the Sanskrit suffixes and endings which we considered were invariable in position, and the meaning of one was presumably neither more nor less distinct than the meaning of another.

The existence of a condition of equilibrium among the four factors enumerated above is not difficult to comprehend. A little reflection upon our own English assures us that certain speech-elements (such as the endings -s, -ing, -ed or the words the, of, a) are so expected in the stream of speech that they merit little emphasis: the usual is not emphatic especially when it occurs in a familiar arrangement crystallized by generations of usage. But if a speech-element is frequent and yet occurs now in one arrangement (in reference to some one member of the configuration) and now in another, manifesting thereby a low degree of crystallization, it is likely to be more emphatic than a speech-element with the same frequency whose occurrences are always in easily predictable surroundings. So, too, the meaning of a speech-element is likely to be less precise, less individual, more blurred, if it occurs in firmly crystallized sequences than one which is now in one position, now in another. For example, the th-morpheme in English truth, heighth, breadth, which has been crystallized since time immemorial, is less precise, less individual, and more blurred in its independent meaning than the ie-morpheme of English Johnnie, mommie, Lindie (written Lindy) which can be, and in familiar family language frequently is appended at will to almost any substantive; both the -th and the -ie modify the meaning of the word-configuration, but the latter, being less crystallized, has 'more meaning' in its own right. In these illustrations

* Not necessarily proportionate.

we have spoken of speech-elements instead of morphemes, although the general discussion has been of morphemes, for as we shall see in the following chapters, this condition of equilibrium between these four factors, though most easily illustrated from the behavior of morphemes, is not limited to morphemes.

Now that we have observed the probable existence of this condition of equilibrium in the accentual system of speech, the question naturally arises as to a causal relationship between relative frequency, degree of accent or intensity, degree of crystallization of the configuration, and the degree of distinctness of meaning. The probable causal relationship can here, as with phonemes (pages 81 ff.), be best demonstrated by investigating an instance of accentual change. Our example will be the accent of Latin from the earliest times to classical times. The advantage offered by Latin is not only that it sheds light on the causal factors in maintaining equilibrium but also that it illustrates a second type of accent, *analogical accent*, and thus gives us in the most expeditious manner a fairly complete picture of most, if not all, the chief dynamic forces of accent. In our discussion of Latin accent we shall observe first, that relative frequency is the motivating factor upon which accent, meaning, and crystallization seem to depend; and secondly, that the influence of pattern, as will be explained later, may modify the direction which a change in accent takes. The present investigation of analogical accent will be of special interest because it is the system of accentuation usual in many western European languages.

5. ANALOGICAL ACCENT AND ACCENTUAL CHANGE

In turning to *analogical accent* we are confronted by a system of accent which differs significantly from that of morphological accent. In systems of morphological accentuation, the position of the accent is determined for each word by the nature of the actual morphemes in the word without respect for the numerical position of the morphemes in the word; for example, in pre-Vedic Sanskrit, the accent might be on the last syllable, the next to the last, or on any other syllable or morphological unit; no morpheme was disqualified for accentuation because of its nearness or distance from the beginning or end of the word. But not so in systems of analogical accent where nearness or distance from the beginning or end of the word is of paramount, indeed of sole importance. In languages possessing the analogical type of accentuation, the position of accent can be predicted for any word by simple rules of thumb valid for the entire language and without any previous knowledge of the morphology of the language: thus a language of this type may invariably accent the first syllable, or the last syllable, or the third syllable from the end, irrespective of whether the accented element is a prefix, root, suffix, or ending. In systems of morphological accentuation, the position of accent is a matter of the *morphemes*; in systems of analogical accentuation, the position of accent is non-morphological, in the sense that *words* have accent, the position of which is arbitrarily determined without reference to the morphemes. In morphological accentuation, the position of accent may be of valuable secondary service in differentiating cases, tenses, voices, or moods; in analogical accentuation, the position of accent generally helps in no way to distinguish cases, tenses, voices, or moods. But though these two types of accentuation are significantly different, we shall see that the morphological may easily develop into the analogical type. Indeed, without a knowledge of the antecedent morphological accent of a language, one is often at pains to comprehend the arbitrariness of the subsequent analogical type.

The accentual system of Classical Latin was typically and entirely analogical. In the inflected form of each word the accent was definitely 'fixed' according to the mechanical rule

that the third syllable from the end of the word always bore
the chief accent unless the second syllable from the end were
long, in which case the chief accent fell on the long second
syllable. Hence the accent might fall in different places in
the various inflected forms of the same stem if the forms happened to vary in the number of their syllables: e.g. *pórto* 'I
carry,' but *portămus* 'we carry'; *hómo* 'man' (nominative
singular), but *homínibus* 'men' (dative-ablative plural); *mú-
lier* 'woman' (nominative singular) but *muliéribus* 'women'
(dative-ablative plural); *fórtis* 'strong,' *fórtior* 'stronger,'
but *fortióribus* (dative-ablative plural).

Such a placing of accent seems too arbitrary to be comprehensible from the point of view of the relative frequencies of
the various structural elements involved. Furthermore, considerations of the comparative importance or 'psychological
value' of the respective accented and unaccented elements,
so often advanced as probable causes in all accentual phenomena, appear offhand quite gratuitous here. Nevertheless, both relative frequency and the comparative importance
(or 'psychological value') of speech-elements are, as we shall
see, deciding factors in analogical accent. Though we may
approach the problem of analogical accent in Latin either
from the angle of relative frequency or from the angle of comparative importance, it will reward us at this time to investigate it from the angle of comparative importance, a course
which is especially recommended because we all feel — and
quite rightly — that accent and importance are linked together.

Now even from our very cursory view of the few isolated
accentual differences whose vestiges are preserved in very
early Sanskrit, we have observed that the original accent of
Indo-European, the prehistoric mother tongue, though fixed
for individual words, did not show a thoroughgoing preference
for endings, suffixes, roots, prefixes, long syllables or short
syllables, for the last syllable or the next to the last, or the
third from the last. Indeed, without appeal to relative fre-

quencies it would be difficult to determine why the accent was fixed where it was in any single paradigm.

Let us, for the sake of argument, assume that the position of accent was fixed by the 'importance' of the syllable in the word. Although our ideas about 'importance' must in general be somewhat vague, let us venture the assumption that accent in each word actually gravitated to the most important syllable. The question then arises, how are we to account for the shift in accent which took place in almost every Indo-European dialect after the pro-ethnic parent language broke up in toits dialects? Why did pro-ethnic Germanic* shift its accent toward the front of the word, so that in the nouns, for example, it became fixed to the first syllable? Why did a sweeping shift to the first syllable take place in primitive Latin? It is indeed difficult to understand how a shift in meaning or 'importance' of syllables sufficiently general could have taken place to precipitate such an all-embracing accentual change.

But even if it were possible to explain this early shift in Latin on the basis of 'importance' or value, how could we explain the second shift which subsequently took place in Latin whereby the accent became fixed to the second or third syllable from the end, yielding the system of accentuation familiar in Classical Latin? What 'importance' or value could have been regularly attached to a long second syllable or the third syllable preceding a short second? The distorting effect of this second shift in Latin from the earlier system of first-syllable accent can indeed only be fully appreciated if we think of our own language, which has primarily a first-syllable accent, and try to imagine a wholesale shifting of accent in all words to the penult or antepenult, e.g. *áwfully* becoming *awfúlly*, *prepáratory* becoming *preparátory*, *díscipline* becoming *discípline*.

---

* The period before Germanic broke into East, West, and North Germanic.

a. Prehistoric Latin and its First-Syllable Accent

Before we can explain the accent of Classical Latin,* we shall first have to explain why the Indo-European accent had in prehistoric Latin shifted everywhere to the initial syllable. The causes of this prehistoric shift are not difficult to identify since in all probability they are associated with the early development of Latin prefixes. One commonly infers from the nature of early Sanskrit and Greek, that in late Indo-European times the prefixes — like some in Modern German (page 148) — were separable; but at some later period, albeit before historical times, these same prefixes gradually became non-separable, a condition in which we find them even in the earliest stage of recorded Latin, where, for example, we have the familiar Latin compound-verbs such as *confacere, dismittere, invenire,* etc.

Now the purpose of a compound is to express a shade of meaning not expressible by the simplex; indeed, we can constantly observe in daily speech that such differentiation in meaning is the very purpose of compounding. Hence, from the very earliest time, the Latin compounds *confacio, dismitto, invenio,* and *prodouco* must have differed in meaning from the simplexes *facio, mitto, venio,* and *douco.* And since *facio, mitto,* etc. were common in both the simplex and the compound, the difference in meaning rested primarily in the prefix. The prefix *con* distinguished not only the compound *confacio* from the simplex *facio,* but from such other compounds as *adfacio, infacio, obfacio,* etc. In the light of these considerations we can say that the prefix was the most important element in the contrast between simplex and compound and hence, if 'importance' is decisive, the prefixes

---

* Chronologically the presumed stages in the development of Classical Latin accent are as follows: (1) the Indo-European accent (prehistoric), (2) the Latin first-syllable accent (prehistoric), (3) the pre-Plautine accent (historic),[1] and (4) Classical Latin accent.

naturally enough bore the chief accent. This 'importance' satisfactorily accounts for the first syllable accent on all prehistoric Latin compounds though not for the first syllable accent of simplexes.

The simplexes, having no prefix, had as their first element the root. If we proceed with the simplexes as with the compounds, saying now, however, that the root is more important than the endings, that in *mitto* the *mitt-*, for example, is relatively more important than the *-o*, inasmuch as *mitt-* distinguishes the verb *mitt-o* from *faci-o*, from *veni-o*, and from *douc-o*, it is natural that the accent should in simplexes as in compounds gravitate to the initial element. We have thus accounted for the first-syllable accent in *all* words in prehistoric Latin. But why, once the accent had under such normal conditions settled on the first syllable, did it later shift again?

At the beginning of compounding, the use of prefixes must, of course, have been only occasional and compounds were made only to meet exigencies of the speaker's thought of the moment. A root must have been considered the common denominator to the various prefixes with which it was compounded. But as the process of compounding continued, and the prefixed verbs and nouns became almost as abundant as the corresponding simplexes, the compound began to be felt less and less as a compound and more as an individual word. In the assimilated form *colligo*, the prefix was not as easily discernible as in the older unassimilated *conligo*. As compounding extended further, providing an ever-increasing host of different compounds for a still greater host of different roots, it was no longer so much a question of distinguishing between *duco* and *conduco*, as of distinguishing *conduco* from *conficio*, *conicio*, *confero*, and the like. Since the number of available prefixes in Latin was much smaller than the number of available roots, it was only reasonable that the root-syllable should again be deemed the important feature, and the one worthy of chief stress. Hence, after compounding had become extensive, the individual members of the small score of Latin prefixes must have been looked upon by the speakers as common denominators (like the endings), in contrast to which the scores upon scores of different roots were deemed the 'important' part of the word, the part worthy of special accentual distinction. So long as prefixing was rare, the prefix was the more important element in the compound; as prefixing became more generalized, the root regained its position as the significant element in the compound.

That compounding with prefixes attained such proportions in Latin that the root in its various compound forms was quite as common in occurrences as the root in uncompounded (simple) form, is fortunately something more than mere hypothesis. If we consult, for example, Lane Cooper's *A Concordance to the Works of Horace*,[1] and select at random a few simple verbs, noting how often they occur in all their tense forms, participles, infinitives, gerunds, gerundives, we shall obtain statistical proof of the validity of this hypothesis, since for each verb-simplex we are also able to note the corresponding occurrences of all its verb-compounds.[2] In the following list only the most frequent simplexes have been considered: *

	Simplex	Compounds
dare	122	238
agere	83	57
videre	107	58
ire	63	171
ferre	118	140
facere	123	43
legere	31	46
ducere	66	67
capere	23	111
dicere	193	22
	929	953

In Horace, then, the compounds are approximately as abundant as the simplexes if we may accept as criteria the

* I have omitted *esse* because of its extensive use in periphrastic constructions.

evidence of these ten words. Yet equally important for our purposes is the safe inference from the body of Latin literature: the number of different *verb-stems* and *noun-stems* which enter into compounds far surpasses the number of available prefixes which may be used in compounds; that is, the variety of different roots is far greater than the variety of different prefixes. Since the Latin verb-compounds are approximately as frequent as their corresponding simplexes, and since the number of different roots far surpasses the number of different prefixes, we may reasonably assume, even in the absence of statistical data, that the average relative frequency of prefixes in Classical Latin was much higher than that for roots. Hence, it seems to make little practical difference in this instance whether we say that accent tends to gravitate toward the relatively more important element (i.e. the element of a word more worthy of distinction), or away from the relatively more frequent. Both lead to the same conclusion, that high frequency and low intensity are linked. And since the procedure which we have just followed for the accent of early Latin might likewise have been followed with the previously given examples of morphological accent in Sanskrit, may we not perhaps say that much of what we call 'important' in language is somehow connected with infrequency of usage?

After this preliminary survey of the working of morphological accent in the earliest Latin accentual system, let us now turn to the accentual system with analogical basis which prevailed in Classical Latin.

b. Classical Latin and its Analogical Accent

While the foregoing analysis of earlier Latin * accent has shown us why the accent abandoned in favor of the root (1) the ever-recurring prefixes of compounds and (2) the ever-

* The period of development after the Indo-European accent and before the pre-Plautine accent; cf. footnote and reference to page 163.

recurring suffixes and endings of both compounds and simplexes, it has not explained the subsequent history of accent
in Latin. One may be inclined to feel that the earliest first-
syllable system of accent in Latin was followed by a system
of *root-accent* (i.e. in which the root was invariably accented);
but this feeling is unjustified for two reasons: (1) after the
accent settled rigidly on the third from the last syllable of all
words of three or more syllables except those in which the
second syllable was long, the accent found itself by no means
necessarily on the root, but now on a prefix (*cón*-ficit), now
on a root (con-*féc*-i), and now on a suffix (confēc-*ís*-tis); (2)
it must, in subsequent years, have been difficult if not impossible for native Latin speakers to distinguish in many
compounds the root-element as such. For, at the time when
the accent fell uniformly on the first syllable (say a prefix),
the roots of such compounds, deprived of their earlier accent,
did not always remain unchanged; on the contrary, the unaccented root-vowels of compounds frequently weakened
(see pages 176 ff.) so that roots which were once identical now
become quite different. For example, all unaccented short
a's in an open syllable became short *i* (**cónfacio > confício*);
in an unaccented closed syllable, short *ă* became short *ě*
(**cónfactus > confectus*). The result of these vowel weakenings [1] was that many hitherto identical roots had several
phonetically different forms (e.g., *fac-, fic-, fec-*). Furthermore, the roots in Latin were not the only morphological elements which exhibited phonetic instability; the prefixes —
after the accent began to recede from them — tended to be
assimilated to the root, e.g. *exficere > efficere, adficere > af-
ficere, conligo > colligo*. Hence there were not only variations
in the form of the root, but also variations in the form of the
prefix, variations which were unimportant morphologically.
To summarize, the compound with passing time came in
many cases to be felt less as an arrangement of its component
morphemes and more as an individual word (i.e. an arrangement of phonemes): *colligo* being one word, *lego* another, *in-*

tellego a third. The same development is frequent in other languages and easily understandable from such an example as English *undertaker*, where the component elements are even more obvious than Latin *sufficere*, but where the original sense of the compound is lost.

Hence, though we today may say that the accent tended to recede from the prefix to the root for reasons of the comparative importance of the various morphological elements, such a statement in Caesar's day would have meant little to the average Roman, who was losing in many cases any precise feeling for what was root and what prefix. To a Roman the position of the accent, if he gave the matter thought, must have seemed arbitrary and confused, now on the first syllable, now not; for him it would probably have been impossible to perceive the etymological relationship of *difficilis* 'difficult,' with *proficisci* 'to set out,' and *facinus* 'act, crime.'

Nevertheless, if the accentuation of Classical Latin is not always explicable from the point of view of the morphemes of a word, it is explicable from the point of view of the syllables of a word. The accent adhered to the first syllable of simplexes and tended to abandon the first syllable of compounds in order to rest upon some other syllable in the compound. For example, when the accent left the *con-* of *confectus*, it had a choice of settling only on the root *-fec-* or on the frequent affix *-tus*. Yet the same force of high relative frequency which shunted the accent away from the prefix *con-* must also have restrained the accent from becoming attached to the highly frequent affix *-tus*, even though the tendency of accent in compounds was to gravitate away from the beginning of the word and toward the end. In many compounds, such as *con-fec-tus* or *con-fic-ere*, the accent would perforce have fallen on the second or third syllable from the end. Indeed, many Latin words, simplexes or compounds, would tend to carry accent on the second or third syllable from the end, because (1) the final syllable was more than likely an affix and (2) the fourth syllable from the end was quite likely to be a prefix. Hence the second and third syllables from the end were doubtless favored syllables for the accent in many words.

Now if it happened in a sufficient number of cases (1) that the accent in remaining on the first syllable of simplexes also happened to be resting on a long second syllable (e.g. *féci, hómo, cáptus*) or on the syllable preceding a short second syllable (e.g. *fácere, hóminis, cápere*), and (2) that the accent in receding from the prefix to the syllable immediately following the prefix accidentally rested on a long second syllable (e.g. *conféci, conféctus, exáctus*) or on the syllable preceding a short second syllable (e.g. *confícere, exígere, difícilis*) — then there would have accidentally arisen a slight consistency in the otherwise motley accentual system in Latin. To be sure, this consistency would be accidental and at most a marked tendency. Yet it is quite possible to understand how such a marked tendency, supported by a favoring probability, might develop and extend itself by analogy to assimilate other words the position of whose accent would normally be elsewhere. For analogy is clearly a powerful force in all linguistic development; it manifests itself with regard to accent, for example, in such English substantives as *prómise* and *párliament* where the accent has moved from the older *promíse* and *parlemént* to the first syllable, only because of analogy with the prevailing tendency in English to accent (most of the usual substantives) on the first syllable.

Though analogy is assumed to be a powerful force in linguistic change, nevertheless, before one ever ventures to employ the concept of analogy in a given problem, one must first clearly demonstrate the preponderant frequency of the attracting 'natural' form over the forms which are attracted analogically, namely, the 'analogical' forms.

If on the basis of a piece of Classical Latin prose we find sufficiently numerous instances of words in which the accent (1) in receding from the prefix of compounds to the next following syllable and (2) in remaining on the first syllable of simplexes (as in *confēci*, *confīcere*, and *fácere*, *fēci* respectively), *ipso facto* fulfilled the conditions of the three-syllable law, it is then quite conceivable that the accent of other words may, for the sake of regularity, have drifted to the second or third syllable from the last out of respect for the predominant pattern.

In an examination of the first and third books of Caesar's *Gallic War* I arranged the individual words of the text into six categories according to the actual position of the accent as it appeared in the various inflected forms.

Category 1: Prefixed compounds having accent on the prefix.
Category 2: Prefixed compounds having accent on the syllable immediately following the prefix.
Category 3: Prefixed compounds having accent elsewhere than in Categories 1 and 2.
Category 4: Simplexes having accent on the first syllable (i.e. the root-syllable).
Category 5: Simplexes having accent elsewhere than on the first syllable (i.e. on suffixes or endings).
Category 6: Monosyllables.

All the words in Caesar follow, of course, the three-syllable law of accent of Classical Latin. Categories 2 and 4, however, represent forms which simultaneously obey the previous law of morphological accent as explained above (pages 132–159); that is, Categories 2 and 4 embrace words in which the accent in receding from the prefix of compounds to the next following syllable, and in remaining on the first syllable of simplexes automatically conformed to the Classical three-syllable law of accent, e.g. *confício*, *confícere*, *confēci*, *conféctus*, *fácio*, *fácere*, *fēci*, *fáctus*.   If our hypothesis of analogical influence be correct, these 'natural forms' (words of Categories 2 and 4) should be appreciably more frequent than the words of Categories 1, 3, and 5, 'analogous forms,' with the result that the pattern accidentally established by the 'natural forms' would be sufficiently conspicuous to attract the other words — the 'analogous forms.' Let us turn to the analysis:

Natural Forms

(2)	(4)		Total of 2 and 4
691	3009		3,700

Analogous Forms

(1)	(3)	(5)	Total of 1, 3, 5
214	514	1413	2,141
			5,841
		Plus 1692 monosyllables	1,692
		Total words examined	7,533

Disregarding monosyllables which had no choice in the matter of accent, we find that the total number of 'natural forms' (3700) is 72 per cent *more frequent* than the 'analogous forms.' The excess of 72 per cent of 'natural forms' over the 'analogous forms' is itself a sufficient justification for the operation of analogy. If we consider the frequency of individual categories which might establish the type for accent, we find that the two most frequent categories are 4 and 5; of these, 4 is more than twice as frequent as 5. Moreover, 4 is a homogeneous category containing only words accented on the root while 5 is heterogeneous containing words accented either on the suffix or endings.[1]

In concluding with Latin accent, we must say that two powerful forces were at work: first, relative frequency, and second, analogy. The fact that secondary accent and syncope undoubtedly assisted in this shifting of the accent does not in any way weaken the force of our conclusions. After all, syncope, which occurs only when a syllable is unaccented, is but a form of abbreviation which in turn is presumably dependent upon relative frequency; secondary accent of a given word is but a lower degree of accent than the primary accent of the word, and hence is probably somehow connected with relative frequency, though this important aspect of accent has never been statistically investigated.

It is perhaps worth indicating that in our investigation of the development of Latin accent from Indo-European to Classical times, the degree of accent has seemed to be a function of relative frequency and not *vice versa*. That is, it seems that a speech-element became less accented or more accented because it became relatively more frequent or less frequent, and not the reverse. So, too, it seems that the higher degree of crystallization and lower degree of distinctness of meaning have attended upon loss of accent and hence are dependent upon relative frequency. Though the author feels that this is a true statement of the causal relationship, yet in view of the difficult nature of the evidence (coming from remote times) he offers it as but his surmise.

6. RELATIVE FREQUENCY AND THE LENGTH OF MORPHEMES

Having seen that the accentual intensity of morphemes depends to a considerable extent upon their relative frequency of occurrence, let us now turn to a brief investigation of the comparative length of morphemes. In light of Chapters II and III it is not presumptuous to expect that the length or total magnitude of complexity of a morpheme will depend to a considerable extent upon its relative frequency, and for the same reasons which were valid for the magnitude of words and phonemes.

The ideal data for our present purposes would be a statistical investigation of the relative frequencies of morphemes as they occur in the stream of speech of some language over a considerable period of time; that is, an investigation of morphemes similar to, say, Eldridge's investigation of words in English. Yet an investigation of this sort has, to my knowledge, never been made. Hence, until such valuable data are available we are forced to use the material provided for modern German by Kaeding. Though the Kaeding material has, as we shall see, decided shortcomings, it possesses, nevertheless, sufficient merit to justify presentation, and unmistakably indicates that the length of a morpheme tends to bear an inverse ratio to its relative frequency of occurrence.

In the 20 million syllables of connected German, Kaeding investigated the frequencies of (1) prefixes (*Vorsilben*), (2) stems (*Haupt-* or *Stammsilben*), and (3) suffixes (*Nachsilben*), for which he gives figures on pages 464, 424, and 468 respectively. Let us briefly consider Kaeding's treatment of each category.

In his investigation of German prefixes,[1] Kaeding included not only the autochthonous German prefixes such as *ge, be, ver, zu,* etc. but also prefixes borrowed into German from Latin (e.g. *extra, super, praeter*) and from the Greek (e.g. *kata, ortho, mono, eu,* etc.). These borrowed prefixes, though in use in German today, can scarcely be considered living morphemes, as they were in Latin and Greek; in German they are generally an integral part of the words in which they occur, without any individuality of their own. Thus, in the words *Paragraph, Katarrh, Monopol,* and the like, the average German speaker very probably is unaware of even the existence of an underlying morphological structure, and certainly of its nature. Hence we may exclude these foreign prefixes from consideration. Since they are of comparatively rare occurrence, their exclusion, moreover, matters but little.

The second disadvantage of Kaeding's investigation is for our purposes more serious though again not irreparable. Taking the morpheme *vor* for illustration, we find an entry for *vor* under the list of stems (page 423) giving 25,953 as the number of occurrences of *vor* as an independent word; on page 464 in the list of prefixes we find separate entries for the morpheme *vor,* i.e. *vor* (59,132), *voraus* (1831), *vorüber* (693), *bevor* (657), *vorher* (330), etc. An investigation undertaken for the specific purposes of establishing the relative frequencies of morphemes in German would have one entry for the morpheme *vor* which would include its occurrences as an independent word and as a prefix and as a part of a prefix. Kaeding's list of suffixes and endings (page 468 ff.) meets with a similar objection: for example, Kaeding gives the frequency of the suffix-ending *-e* (1,287,899) and *-ig* (197,679) and also for the combination of the two, *-ige* (32,222). Though the additional information about the frequencies of occurrence of certain morpheme combinations is extremely valuable, information about the frequencies of occurrence of the uncombined morphemes is essential.

Nevertheless, the data furnished by Kaeding are of considerable value if used with discretion. If we limit our investigation, for example, to the thirty most frequent autochthonous German prefixes we have a list which includes 25 per cent of the different available autochthonous prefixes, and over 95 per cent of the occurrences of all prefixes. In these 30 prefixes, only *zurück* (7560) and *zusammen* (6621) consist of more than one morpheme.* If there is, then, any correlation between the lengths and frequencies of morphemes we should expect to find in this arbitrarily selected category of prefixes that the average length of the thirty most frequent prefixes would increase as we proceed down the list which in Kaeding is arranged in the order of diminishing frequency. And this correlation is indeed substantiated by Kaeding's figures. Arranging the thirty prefixes into six groups of five each, and counting the total number of phonemes (standard pronunciation) in each group, we find

Group	Total Number of Phonemes	Average Number of Phonemes
I (1 through 5)	11	2.2
II (6 " 10)	12	2.4
III (11 " 15)	12	2.4
IV (16 " 20)	16	3.2
V (21 " 25)	16	3.2
VI (26 " 30)	20	4.0

* *Zurück* is frequently condensed into what seems to be one morpheme in rapid colloquial discourse, e.g. *zrück*.

There seems here a clear tendency for average length to increase as average relative frequency decreases.

Similarly with the stems. If we select the 400 most frequent stems, which include all stems occurring more often than 5010 times which are arranged (pages 424–425) according to diminishing frequency, we have eight groups of stems, each group containing 50 stems. Again the average number of phonemes per stem in each group seems to increase as the frequency decreases:

Group	Total Number of Phonemes	Average Number of Phonemes
I (1 through 50)	136	2.72
II (51 " 100)	156	3.12
III (101 " 150)	154	3.08
IV (151 " 200)	158	3.16
V (201 " 250)	167	3.34
VI (251 " 300)	171	3.42
VII (301 " 350)	171	3.42
VIII (351 " 400)	176	3.52

Similarly with the suffixes. Disregarding Kaeding's additional notations of combinations of morphemes in the list (pages 468–469) which is arranged according to decreasing frequencies, and dividing the thirty most frequent suffixes into six groups of five each, we find:

Group	Total Number of Phonemes	Average Number of Phonemes
I (1 through 5)	9	1.8
II (6 " 10)	12	2.4
III (11 " 15)	10	2.0
IV (16 " 20)	12	2.4
V (21 " 25)	12	2.4
VI (26 " 30)	14	2.8

Here again, though not so marked, there seems a tendency for an increase in magnitude to be coupled with a decrease in relative frequency.

In spite of the obvious limitations of these Kaeding figures, they reveal a reasonably clear correlation between the relative frequency of morphemes and their magnitudes of complexity, in this sense: the magnitude of complexity of a morpheme bears an inverse * relationship to its relative frequency. Naturally the evidence from which this conclusion is drawn is not as perfect from the point of view of our science as we might wish, but it is adequate, and the method of procedure to be adopted in making an ideal frequency count of morphemes is, I think, sufficiently clear so that in the future Dynamic Philology may check the accuracy of the above conclusion by independent investigations.

The next obvious step would be to establish a causal relationship between the magnitude of complexity of morphemes and their relative frequency in the manner adopted for words (page 29) and phonemes (page 81). But limited space forbids tarrying on this point; let us therefore assume that the magnitude of complexity depends upon relative frequency of occurrence, an assumption which in all probability is correct, and one which could be tested in the same general manner adopted in the analogous cases for words and phonemes.

The value of the assumption of the above causal relationship is twofold: first, it sheds light on the phenomenon of accentual phonetic changes (page 90), and second, it offers a possibility of determining the comparative magnitudes of many vowel phonemes. Since both of these problems may be not without some interest, let us turn to a brief discussion of them.

a. *Accentual Phonetic Changes*

On page 90 it was remarked that vowels sometimes undergo change in an unaccented syllable. An example of this is the familiar changes in prehistoric Latin in which an unaccented short *a* shifted in an open syllable to short *i*, while

---

* Not necessarily proportionate; possibly some non-linear mathematical function.

an unaccented short *a* shifted in a closed syllable to short *e*. Thus, in prehistoric times

cón-fă-cere became *cón-fĭ-cere*

cón-făc-tus " *cón-fĕc-tus*

This phonetic change in Latin was phonemically significant, since both before and after the change the short vowels *a*, *c*, and *i* were three different phonemes.

The reason for these phonetic changes in Latin was probably the general shift of accent in Latin, of which the causes were discussed on pages 163 ff. Now, if we remember (1) that the degree of accent of a morpheme tends to vary in an inverse relationship with its relative frequency, and (2) that the magnitude of complexity of a morpheme tends to stand in an inverse relationship to its relative frequency, it does not seem an overbold step to correlate these two factors in these vowel changes of prehistoric Latin. That is, the total magnitude of complexity of the root-morpheme *fac*, a typical example, was diminished, not by truncation of an entire phoneme, but by a decrease in the total magnitude of complexity of the root-vowel. In a roundabout way, then, this change in Latin can be correlated with relative frequency.

But we must be cautious in universalizing this probable correlation in Latin; for, first of all, not all vowels were changed in unstressed syllables in Latin, for example, the long vowels *ā* and *ē* (e.g. **dēlātus* > *delātus*, and **cónfēci* > *confēci*). Furthermore, modern languages that use stress as a distinctive feature are not consistent in their treatment of unstressed vowels. English, for example, generally modifies unstressed vowels; compare the pronunciation of the vowels of the similar syllables of the pairs: *cóncert, concérted; áddress* (noun), *addréss* (verb); *átom, atómic; rélay, retúrn*. On the other hand, languages like Italian, Spanish, Czechish, Polish, do not use special variants for any of the unstressed vowels: the vowel is the same, with or without stress. In the Germanic languages, except English, only the one vowel, short *e*, appears in a variant form when unstressed: e.g. German *éssen* but *hátte* (the *e* of *hatte* pronounced as *a* in English *China*).

It is indeed difficult to account for this inconsistency in the behavior of comparable vowels in unaccented syllables of different languages. There is, however, a relevant consideration which seems to merit mention, viz.: a vowel, stressed or unstressed, is a member not only of the syllable or morpheme in which it occurs but also of its phoneme-type; that is, the vowel, short *a*, of Latin was a member not only of the specific morphemes *fac*, *ag*, etc. in which it occurred but also of the phoneme category, short *a*. Now, in view of our deductions made about the phoneme (Chapter III), short *a* might either change 'spontaneously' because of its excessive frequency as a phoneme, or, as we have surmised (pages 177 ff.), it might merely change in unstressed morphemes to represent a diminution in the total magnitude of complexity of the morphemes (or syllables). The change of West Germanic *ă* to *æ̃* in Old English (*ĕ* in Old Kentish and Old Frisian) was a 'spontaneous' phonetic change affecting every occurrence of short *a* wherever specific conditions were fulfilled; the instability of short *a* in Old English, accented or unaccented, was the instability of a phoneme type. Now, it is possible that short *a* in Latin at the time of the first syllable accent had tendencies toward instability because of a high relative frequency; and hence that it weakened where conditions were propitious for a weakening — in unstressed syllables. Presumably long *a* and long *e* were not excessively frequent in the Latin of that time and hence remained generally stable even in unstressed syllables.[1] Had vowels other than short *a* and short *e* been in general excessively frequent in the Latin of that time, they would presumably have shown tendencies toward weakening in a manner analogous to that of short *a* and short *e*.[2]

Hence, what we have termed (above) an inconsistency

in the behavior of comparable phonemes in unaccented syllables of different languages is only an apparent inconsistency.
If our analysis is correct, the phenomenon of accentual vowel
change in unstressed syllables might be formulated thus:
when a vowel because of excessive relative frequency tra-
verses the upper threshold of toleration, it may weaken in
unstressed syllables, thereby helping to restore a condition
of equilibrium. If the vowel has only a normal relative frequency compatible with its magnitude of complexity, the
vowel may well resist change even in unstressed syllables.

Unfortunately there are no statistical data yet available to
substantiate this explanation of accentual phonetic change,
which must be accepted or rejected according to its appeal to
one's reason. An investigation of comparable phenomena in
some modern language would be most rewarding; for an
understanding of accentual change will probably lead to a
valuable understanding of the dynamics of vowels, and of the
comparative degrees of complexity of vowels in a given
language.

b. Comparative Degrees of Complexity of Vowels

In discussing the comparative degree of complexities of
vowels (pages 76–78) we found no ready method for comparing the magnitude of complexity of one short vowel with that
of another short vowel, or that of one long vowel with that
of another long vowel. As far as we could judge at the time,
short *i, e, a, o, u*, for example, represented equal magnitudes
of complexity. However, the behavior of these vowels in unstressed syllables in a language may well give a clue to their
comparative degrees of magnitude of complexity in that
language. For example, in Latin we have the phenomena of
short *e* in an open unaccented syllable becoming short *i*,*
while short *a* became short *e* or short *i*. We should expect,

---

* E.g. *cóntĕneo* became *contĭneo*, or *óbsĕdeo* became *obsĭdeo*.

therefore, that these three vowels in the Latin of the time of this change would be arranged thus in the order of decreasing magnitude of complexity: *a, e, i.** If this arrangement is correct, we should also anticipate (cp. conclusions, pages 79 ff.) that in the Latin of that time the arrangement *a, e, i* would represent one of increasing relative frequency (see note 4b to page 78). A statistical investigation along parallel lines of analogous phenomena of a living language would then serve as an interesting test of the validity of the conclusions reached on pages 79 ff.: the total magnitude of complexity of a phoneme bears an inverse ratio to its relative frequency.

7. LENGTH, ACCENTUAL INTENSITY, AND METRICS

It is difficult to observe the phenomena of accent without being mindful of an enormous field of human expression in which the arrangement of accent often plays a significant role: metrics. To be sure, not all metrical systems avail themselves of the resources of stress accent of the language; for example, the meter of the *Iliad* and the *Odyssey* is a matter of the length and shortness of syllables without regard for the position of accent. In these two epics, a syllable containing a short vowel which is not followed immediately by two consonants is considered short, and all other syllables are considered long. And the long and short syllables thus defined are used in the Homeric dactyls with such consistency that when a short syllable actually occurs in the later text contrary to the exigencies of meter, philologists have generally demonstrated that in the original dialect, before the loss of certain consonants from 'spontaneous' change, the syllable had probably been long.

For our purposes the interesting feature of metrical systems employing differences in length (quantity) and those employing differences in accent (stress) is that the metrical patterns

---

* See page 78, note 4b.

of the one type can often be borrowed into the metrical usage of the other type by substituting corresponding differences in length for corresponding differences in accent, or *vice versa*. Thus, for example, the dactyllic hexameters of antiquity are not unknown to our own English and German poetry, with the substitution of stress for length.

Cannot this interchangeability between differences in length and differences in accent be anticipated theoretically and does not its existence shed some light on the dynamics of language? We have seen that the amount of accent of a speech-element is very probably intimately connected with its relative frequency, and we have also seen that the length of a speech-element is likewise intimately associated with its relative frequency. Length and accentual intensity, then, both seem to be functions of one common factor. Of course other factors may and probably often do play an accessory role, for example, meaning (pages 155 ff.), variability of position (pages 149 ff.), and the like.

Nevertheless, this relationship between length and intensity which we detect in language, even if ultimately perhaps only of secondary importance for linguistic research, may well supply the opening wedge to empirical investigation of an extensive field replete with interest and potential information about the inner structure and dynamics of our moods and feelings: music. That poetry and music are closely related is no new discovery; nor is it a novel reflection that differences in length and intensity may be of signal importance in both. It is perhaps worth suggesting that a statistical investigation of occurrences of differing degrees of length and intensity, which has not been without reward when made on the stream of speech, may be enlightening when applied to the stream of music. Not only may the researches conducted in the dynamics of speech be of considerable importance in helping toward an understanding of the dynamics of music, but statistical investigations of music may be of enormous importance in understanding the dynamics of speech. Naturally, the problems offered by this practically uninvestigated field are of necessity vague. Yet a discussion of accent would be incomplete which neglected mention of the possibility of an empirical investigation of the intimate connection between the accentual system of a language, its metrical system, and music.

8. SUMMARY

We have viewed the chief phenomena of accent and have gained some insight into the dynamics of accent as applied to morphemes and syllables, and have found that among other factors relative frequency of occurrence is of considerable importance. Let us, in conclusion, briefly view our findings from a distance with the intention of evaluating their significance and of bringing them more into perspective with common daily experience.

An average person, if asked about the elements of speech which he is accustomed to accent would doubtless reply that he accented the important elements; pressed further, he would probably add that these were also the significant elements, though it is doubtful that he could name all the criteria whereby comparative significance was determined. One criterion which would probably not come to his mind is that of relative frequency; on the other hand, he probably would feel that he tended to accent the unusual in occurrence, unusual in the sense either of being rare in occurrence or of being in an unaccustomed setting. For the unusual, be it rare or in unfamiliar setting, is that to which one is inclined to call attention in speech. If there is a difference in accent between the commonplace and the unusual, it is not remarkable if we find that the unusual generally possesses the greater accent. But if we view the stream of speech as gestures in arrangement, may we not say that the unusual is also the less frequent, certainly in the case of rarity, and possibly, too, at times in the case of unfamiliar surroundings; a tendency to accentuate the unusual will then reveal itself, as we have found, in a statistical analysis of relative frequencies.

Of course the above-mentioned average person in interpreting our questions would very probably refer them to his method of accenting words in sentences and not of accenting morphemes or syllables in words. As to morphological or syllabic accent he would scarcely be aware of any choice, and simply feel that he accented the elements of a word the way they 'should be accented.' Although he would instinctively detect a mistaken accent on the part of his interlocutor, he would be about as conscious of correct accent while speaking, as he would be of the operation of the physical laws.

The phenomena of word-accent are, then, roughly divisible into two types: (1) the accent of the elements within a word (morphological, or syllabic accent), and (2) the accent of the word in the sentence (sentence-accent). The latter type of accent is more difficult to study empirically than the former, if for no other reason than that in sentence-accent unusual arrangement of words, dictated by the exigencies of the particular situations in which the individual speakers find themselves, plays a far more important role than it does in morphological or syllabic accent. In the morphological or syllabic structure of words, the degree of crystallization (pages 153 ff.) is so great that unusualness in arrangement plays but a minor role. But though the two types of accent are roughly distinct, they are not absolutely distinct; for in almost any language * the most frequent words (e.g. English *the, an, of,* etc.) are also often simultaneously but morphemes and syllables. That is, the most frequent members of a language's vocabulary of morphemes, syllables, or words will be, to some extent, identical; they will not be numerous, but they will be frequent, and their behavior in respect to accent will be a matter both of morphological or syllabic accent on the one hand and

---

* Especially when, as in Chinese, the language is inflected only to a negligible degree (cp. Chap. V).

of sentence-accent on the other. Hence, in turning now to a general investigation of sentence-structure and the behavior of sentence-elements, which tacitly includes sentence-accent, we shall have at hand much serviceable information derived from our study of morphological and syllabic accent. So, too, our investigation of the word in the sentence will retroactively shed additional light on the dynamics of the structural elements of words.

V

THE SENTENCE: POSITIONAL AND INFLECTIONAL LANGUAGES

IN TURNING to the subject of the dynamics of sentence-struc-.
ture we approach a speech-element which, as it occurs in the
various languages of the earth, reveals a diversity in form
and general variegation in structure far beyond that of any
other speech-element which we have hitherto investigated.[1]
For example, some languages, such as Chinese, show the
interrelationship of the component words of a sentence
solely by the positional arrangement of these words in the
sentence; other languages, such as Latin, obviate the necessity for stringent positional arrangement by appending inflectional affixes to many of the component words of the
sentence; still other languages like modern German, employ
the devices both of positional arrangement and of inflection.
As a further example of diversity, most languages, such as
English, have the categories of noun and verb in their material for sentence-structure, but so large a number of languages makes no use of these two categories as to assure us
that they are not a *sine qua non* of sentence-formation.[2] If we
view other salient differences among languages we find: some
commence their sentences with the subject, others with the
verb, and still others commence with the subject under certain
conditions and with the verb under others; in some languages
the modifying adjective precedes its noun, in others it follows. So great, then, is the multifariousness of specific
sentence-forms that it would be unsafe to propound general
laws of sentence-dynamics on the basis of data derived solely
from a few languages. Hence, instead of proceeding from the
particular to the general, we shall proceed from the general
(in Part I, pages 187 ff.) to the particular (in Part II, pages
224 ff.).

Though Part I will be a discussion of general principles,

our investigation will not for that reason cease to be empirical, since we shall discuss primarily the data derived empirically in our preceding investigation of words, phonemes, and morphemes. For, these speech-elements which we have just studied are not only configurations in their own right, they are likewise simultaneously the structural elements of sentences. Hence for our impending investigation of the incredibly complicated field of sentence-dynamics we have already laid a substantial foundation through the study of the behavior of the component elements.

Part I will commence with a comparison of the sentence with other speech-elements, in which we shall strive to reduce the observed behavior of all these different speech-elements to one common denominator. Our second step will be an exploration of the nature of meaning and emotional intensity, and the general relation of the two both to the degree of crystallization of the configuration and to relative frequency. The third step will be the investigation of a condition of equilibrium in sentence-structure which will provide us with the key to an understanding of the grammatical rules of syntax and inflection in force in specific languages. Finally we shall examine the devices by means of which sentence-equilibrium is maintained. This examination will be conducted by briefly scrutinizing, first, types of pathological language where these devices are inadequately employed, and second, literary style, where the operation of the devices are apparent because of the perfection of their employment. This preliminary investigation of the employment of these devices in pathological language and literary style will furnish us with the necessary equipment for studying in Part II the less conscious and more crystallized use of these devices reflected in the grammatical rules of syntax and inflection of specific languages.

One may profitably remember while reading Part I that the discussions of meaning, emotional intensity, rootedness of habit, and the like have as a constant background definite problems of sentence-dynamics which will be elucidated in Part II. In occasionally illustrating linguistic principles with examples from analogous non linguistic behavior, the motive is partly the desire to present the most clearly defined examples and partly the wish to test the general validity of our principles before applying them to specific languages; it is not the intention to urge the acceptance of our principles as sufficient explanations of all nonlinguistic behavior.

Part I

General Principles

I. THE STREAM OF SPEECH

If a Martian scientist sitting before his radio in Mars accidentally received from Earth the broadcast of an extensive speech which he recorded perfectly through the perfection of Martian apparatus and studied at his leisure, what criteria would he have to determine whether the reception represented the effect of animate process on Earth, or merely the latest thunderstorm on Earth? It seems that the only criteria would be the arrangement of occurrences of the elements, and the only clue to the animate origin would be this: the arrangement of occurrences would be neither of rigidly fixed regularity such as frequently found in wave emissions of purely physical origin nor yet a completely random scattering of the same. That is, his data would reveal both regularity and suppleness of arrangement. From this peculiarity let us suppose what is by no means certain, namely, that he guesses the animate origin.

Having guessed the animate origin, what criteria would he have for determining whether the reception represented meaningful, purposeful, feeling expression? The only objective evidence in the stream of speech from which anything whatsoever could be deduced is this: (1) the speech-elements occur in arrangements which seemingly differ primarily as different permutations of the same elements; and (2) these permutations occur far more frequently in the stream of speech than can be anticipated merely from the action of probabilities. His discovering the intelligent origin of his reception would depend upon his guessing that these permutations were purposive configurations. Let us be more explicit.

2. CONFIGURATIONS

On the basis of subjective evidence we are assured (1) that configurations have meaning and purpose. We know (2) that configurations are essentially permutations or arrangements of subsidiary components. It is clear (3) that the only objective information about the existence of, or limits to, a configuration is the fact that the relative frequency of its occurrence is far above what may normally be anticipated to eventuate from the action of the sheer laws of probability.

May we now correlate the three factors mentioned in the previous paragraph? Since there are configurations other than linguistic configurations, let us in the interest of clearness illustrate with a non-linguistic example. There are two long high stone walls. On one (A) are bullet marks scattered at random such as one might find after a military engagement in the neighborhood; on the other (B) is a cluster of bullet marks such as one might find behind a target. The presumption would be that the scattering of bullet marks on A would represent accident from whatever source and not reveal in their distribution any meaningful intent; while the scattering on B would represent meaningful intent and not pure accident. The fact that bullet marks are made by bullets fabricated and generally shot by man would of course reveal to the observer that human beings were ultimately involved in both phenomena. Nevertheless, it is only in B that the type of distribution of bullet marks permits the observer to infer a purposive aiming.

If the scattering of bullet marks about B were analyzed, they would probably be found distributed about a norm (bull's eye) according to the familiar Gaussian formula indicative of random variation. But the randomness holds only for the *deviations* from a central aim, which represent chance degrees of success or failure. The occurrence of failures implies the existence of an intent from which the erroneous has deviated, while pure accident does not necessarily imply by definition the existence of intention. The target, either in its arrangement or its purpose, represents a human configuration. Yet objectively there is discernible only the peculiar arrangement.

We may then say objectively of a configuration implying purpose (without presuming for a moment that the statement is a sufficient definition) that it is an arrangement which on the whole (1) is neither completely fixed in invariable regularity nor completely random, and (2) occurs as a permutation far more often in total behavior than may be anticipated from the action of the sheer laws of probability. Only from this aspect of a configuration may we *empirically* infer anything concerning the existence or nature of meaning and purpose. What are the implications of this criterion of meaning or intent when applied to the stream of speech as by our hypothetical Martian?

3. RELATIVE FREQUENCY AS A DEFINING FACTOR IN THE DIFFERENTIATION OF SPEECH-ELEMENTS

It is common knowledge that different speech-elements have different average and actual relative frequencies of occurrence. Since relative frequency of occurrence is seemingly so important in characterizing a configuration, differences in relative frequency can presumably not exist without effecting in some way the content of the configuration in respect to meaning.

For the purpose of material for observation let us in imagination analyze an extensive sample of connected speech into its respective phonemes, morphemes, words, and sentences, and determine the individual relative frequency of occurrences of each. That is, we shall determine the relative frequency not only of a given sentence in the sample, but also of its component clauses and phrases, and of their component words, morphemes, and phonemes. Now let us arrange these classes of speech-elements from left to right on a straight line in the order of decreasing relative frequency. In the absence of actual data which would probably yield a curve of considerable interest we can only say that at the extreme left would fall the category of phonemes, next the category of morphemes, next that of words, then phrases, clauses, and finally sentences.

But these categories would not be rigidly demarcated from one another. Some phonemes may also occur as a complete morpheme (e.g. *t* in English *slept*); some morphemes would also occur as complete words (e.g. *bei* in German *Beispiel* and *bei mir*); there might be considerable doubt whether some elements were viewed best as words or phrases (e.g. German *zumute* or *zu Mute*), or clauses (e.g. French *comme il faut*), or as complete sentences (e.g. French *n'est-ce pas?*). The categories phoneme, morpheme, word, etc., though helpful in analysis, are not clearly definable nor mutually exclusive. Between the categories of phonemes, morphemes, words, etc. into which many speech-elements unqualifiedly fall, there are in each case sections containing speech-elements which belong to more than one category.

Now is it perhaps true that differences in the relative frequency of occurrence of speech-elements is definitive of their differences? That will depend entirely upon whether the attributes of a speech-element, that is, its degree of articulatedness of meaning, its emotional intensity, the degree of its

crystallization in usage, are found connected solely with differences in relative frequency. Let us then examine to what
extent these other differences between speech-elements may
be correlated with corresponding differences in relative frequency.

4. THE RELATIONSHIP BETWEEN MEANING, EMOTIONAL INTENSITY, INDEPENDENCE IN USAGE, AND RELATIVE FREQUENCY

As we progress by classes from left to right in the afore-
mentioned series, from phoneme to morpheme, to word, to
phrase and clause, to sentence, we pass (1) from the less
articulated in meaning (i.e. less precise or specific) to the more
articulated in meaning, (2) from the emotionally less intense
to the emotionally more intense, (3) from the less independent * in usage to the more independent in usage. However,
the statement of this relationship is valid only for averages.
Words are plentiful which are more precise and specific in
meaning than many a sentence that is uttered. Even a
phoneme (e.g. the English exclamation *Oh!*) may be emotionally more intense than many a word. Yet that the average sentence is both more meaningful and more intense than
the average word, and so on, is a proposition too self-evident
to justify examples.

That differences in the independence of usage of various
speech-elements attend differences in relative frequency is
equally certain, though the concept may not be as familiar
as those of meaning and intensity. Elements that are more
frequent are also found more firmly crystallized in usage
than the less frequent; an individual speaker has less choice

* The degree of independence of usage of a speech-element is the reciprocal of
its degree of dependence; the degree of dependence of usage of a speech-element
is tantamount to the totality of the degree of its crystallization in all configurations in which it occurs, or, if one prefers its average degree of crystallization.

in his formation of phonemes, say, than in that of sentences, and in this sense the phoneme is a less independent element in the usages of speech than a sentence. Though a phoneme enters into thousands of different permutations it has comparatively no freedom of change in position within these arrangements. If, next, morphemes and words are to a considerable degree likewise stereotyped in arrangement or usage, the latter are nevertheless more variable than the former, and both more variable than phonemes, that is, variable in respect either to the arrangement of their components or to their arrangement as components in a larger configuration.

For example, aside from minor personal differences in timbre, average pitch, and amplitude, most speakers of a dialect agree remarkably closely in the formation of phonemes. With morphemes there is some slight latitude; some say *doing*, others *doin'*, some pronounce the initial vowel of *either* as the vowel of *eat*, others as the diphthong of *my*, some pronounce the final *t* of *drought* as *th* (in *think*). These differences in the phonemic structure of morphemes, whatever their cause, illustrate the tolerance of at least some variability. In arranging morphemes into words there is somewhat more variability; witness: *dived, dove; showed, shown; he doesn't, he don't; you weren't, you wasn't*. The extensive choice in arranging words into phrases, clauses, and sentences, which is restrained at the most by parts of speech or grammatical rules, needs no illustration. And the arrangement of sentences into larger configurations is, comparatively speaking, free.

Hence differences in relative frequency reflect at least to some extent differences in the degree of articulatedness of meaning, emotional intensity, and independence in arrangement, respectively.

5. PATTERNS OF CONFIGURATION AS POTENTIAL ARRANGEMENTS WITH VARYING PROBABILITIES OF RECURRENCE

The question now arises whether we may not use the statistics already presented for phonemes, morphemes, and words as a background for our analysis of sentence-structure. For, because of the great variety of different sentences and their low average rate of repetitiveness, a statistical analysis of the relative frequencies of occurrences of sentences would be an enormous numerical task. But first let us ask whether sentences and, say, phonemes are commensurable.

Though a phoneme is socially more integrated than a sentence, and a sentence more individualistic than a phoneme, this condition does not necessarily render the two incommensurable, since a sentence must be somewhat socially integrated to be understood, even though a phoneme does appear to be individualistic only to a negligible extent. It is, further, not-true that they are incommensurable because a language's resources of sentences is in the domain of potentials while its phonemic system appears to be actual. Indeed, it is because they are both potentials differing only in probability of occurrences that they are commensurable; all speech configurations, as can be easily shown, are potentials, and for that reason can be shown to be commensurable.

The number of organs which may conceivably be used as vocal organs is fairly large. The possible different gestures of each of these potential vocal organs is also large. Hence the number of possible combinations of these gestures into speech-configurations is enormous. The phonemic system of a given language represents but a tiny fraction of all possible phonemes, and also but a small fraction of all known phonemes. If the phonemic systems of every living dialect today were placed side by side there would be innumerable instances of phonemes present in some and absent in others. Dialects would be found, such as the African dialects, in which would occur vital, deeply ingrained, highly frequent phonemes, such as the African clicks, which many speakers of other dialects could not articulate if they tried. Any given phoneme represents a selection from a host of potential phonemes, any one of which not only exists potentially, but may even actually arise in the future development of the language. The phonemes in English today will be the phonemes of English next year, not because they have ceased to be potentials, but because they represent potentials of a high probability of recurrence, with probabilities estimated on the basis of past performance. The resources in sentences are likewise potentials. Since sentences normally represent permutations larger than those of phonemes, there are theoretically far more different potential sentences than potential phonemes. But this difference in number does not make the one the more, nor the other the less, a potential, though the probabilities for average occurrences of individual sentences will be appreciably lower than that for phonemes. The reason we do not feel that phonemes are only potential arrangements of high degree of probability of recurrence is because their rate of repetitiveness is so great that we tacitly assume recurrence, forgetting that within the next thousand years many a present English phoneme will have disappeared. We feel that sentence patterns are only potentials in a sense in which we feel a phoneme is not, because the average rate of repetitiveness is so comparatively low that the utterance of a given sentence often impresses one as unique and unlikely to recur. That sentences do often recur is evident from the absurdity of the proposition that the scores of millions of speakers of English rarely use the same sentence again in the course of their lives. Sentences are not incommensurable with other speech-elements though they may differ in variety or probabilities of recurrence. Considerable evidence can and will be presented to demonstrate that differences in variety and probabilities of recurrence are the essential differences of speech-elements.

The relationship between the various speech-elements should not be obfuscated by the alternate uses of the terms *pattern* and *configuration* in treatments of linguistic phenomena. Every speech-element is both a pattern and a configuration. For example, a phoneme is nothing actual in the sense of having material reality, but exists only as an ideal model or copy which speakers must approximate in order to have their speech comprehended. It is real in the same sense that the center of gravity of an object is real. Every speech-configuration made in conformity with the pattern, represents the pattern and is in turn a part of the model or copy for those who are learning to speak the language. Though no two actual utterances of a given speech-element may perhaps ever be found which in the precise language of physics are completely congruent, they are configurations of speech only in so far as they do correspond. Not only is every configuration a pattern, every pattern is a configuration or arrangement. The only difference between a *pattern* and a *configuration* is that the former is the more generic and collective term. One infers the nature of speech-patterns from the exemplifications of the patterns, i.e. the configurations of speech-elements.

6. STATIC CONDITIONS: THE INTERRELATIONSHIP OF MEANING, EMOTIONAL INTENSITY, INDEPENDENCE, AND RELATIVE FREQUENCY

It has been previously observed (pages 157 ff.) that the degree of articulatedness of meaning, emotional intensity, and independence in usage in arrangement, each stand in some inverse, though not necessarily proportionate, relationship with the relative frequency of occurrence of the embodying configuration. The question now arises whether the first three factors are mutually interdependent so that a difference in the size of the one is off-set by a difference in the size of the other. For example, may we say that, with all else equal, the more articulated the meaning of a configuration the less its emotional intensity, and so on?

To demonstrate an interrelationship between the articulatedness of meaning, emotional intensity, and independence in usage in arrangement will clearly be difficult. None of these qualities of language can be measured quantitatively, and we can sense differences in degree with certainty only when they are quite large. Then too, this interrelationship may be only a statistical law representing a prevailing tendency. Though the tendency may be strong, individual examples are an unsafe criterion in demonstrating and establishing a statistical law. It is, of course, common knowledge that, say, curses and terms of abuse whose utterances normally reflect a high degree of emotional intensity on the part of the speaker are in themselves neither precise nor specific in meaning when compared with other words of a high degree of articulation of meaning, such as the words *apple-tree* or *circumference*. Nevertheless a word which is emotionally intense in one utterance (e.g. *FIRE!*) may be emotionally unintense in another (e.g. *fire*). An observation of the static condition of a cross-section of language would probably suggest that the factors of meaning, intensity, and independence in usage are in the long run somehow interrelated, yet only a study of the dynamics involved seems to offer the possibility of really proving the existence of the interrelationship while accurately describing its nature.

7. DYNAMIC CONDITIONS: THE INTERRELATEDNESS OF MEANING, EMOTIONAL INTENSITY, INDEPENDENCE, AND RELATIVE FREQUENCY

If the above three qualities and relative frequency are interrelated, a change in the development of one will be attended by a change in the development of another or others. Can we find that one of these factors by its very nature changes, and changes consistently in one direction or another?

a. The Effect of Habit on the Chances of Recurrence

There is one force about which all agree, whether we prefer to describe it in the terms of the biologist or in those of many a homely proverb: our behavior becomes on the whole ever more one of habit, and our habits on the whole ever more deeply rooted; 'as the twig is bent, etc.,' 'habit is a cable, we weave a thread, etc.'

Further, all our acts of whatever sort are performed in a stream; even when isolated every act since birth is preceded by an act, and every act up to death is followed by another. Though possibly some acts are best viewed in isolation, all acts really occur in sequential arrangement. They become ingrained in habit, either as a potential part of, or as an escort to other acts; they do not become ingrained in habit as isolated acts. Neither in language nor in any other type of behavior does an act occur or exist except in reference to a contextual setting.

Many factors probably help determine what acts will become habitual and the degree to which they will become habitual, yet the total effect of habit is on the whole the preference of the habitual to the unhabitual, if all else is equal. Hence, if all else is equal, habit increases the chances of repetition of habitual acts over unhabitual acts in the future. We can predict with greater certainty what the person will drink at breakfast who is in the habit of drinking coffee than the person who is not in the habit of drinking any one particular liquid. In other words, a chief effect of habit is its modification of the average course of events in the future. Because of the existence of this force of habit the prediction of future human events is not the same as the prediction of future inanimate events like the eventualities of tossing a coin.

The difference between the future acts of our behavior and those of a tossed coin is that the tosses of a coin represent isolated events whereas our acts are connected and their effects are cumulative. Though a true coin tossed a thousand times may fall tails a thousand times consecutively, the odds remain equal that in toss number 1001 the coin will fall either heads or tails. Not so the acts of human behavior. The more often we perform a given act in a given arrangement the more likely are we to repeat the act in the same arrangement. For instance, if in a given situation there are two equally valid and likely choices, A and B, in behavior, the chance selection of one, say A, increases the probabilities of its selection instead of B at the next occasion. If A is selected at the next occasion, its probabilities of recurrence instead of B are further advanced.* Translated into terms of linguistic phenomena, the force of habit is exemplified in many ways. For example if the only non-parental and non-alimentary words of a given small child are *bow-wow* and *moo-cow*, and a toad is protruded into his sand-box, the child has in naming the toad two equally valid choices, A (*bow-wow*) and B (*moo-cow*).

---

* If the two acts, A and B, are not of equal validity or suitability in a given occasion, the selection of the more suitable will increase its chances of recurrence above normal, and that of the less suitable below normal, presumably. Nevertheless, once the less suitable has become ingrained in habit, it is not always instantly altered when an alternative course is found more suitable. An elderly gentleman, though willing to concede and even regret the irrationality of some of his set habits, will probably persist in those habits.

Though it is probably incorrect to assume that his selection of a name is dictated solely by chance, nevertheless it was observed with one child that the name first selected, B, was subsequently generally preferred to A, and finally replaced A until the time when the toad was renamed with the child's new word for caterpillars. Similarly a people migrating to a new terrain containing unfamiliar flora and fauna which are unnamed will generally select names for the new from its stock of words and not coin new words.[1] For each new object many names are doubtless tried until one name gradually becomes completely favored by habitual usage, though the actual names selected may differ geographically in the new terrain. The probabilities of recurrence of individual speech-elements are modified, then, by the extent to which they are ingrained in habit.

That force of habit may reach such a point as to decimate or even annihilate competitive patterns is witnessed in language by *levelling* and *analogic change* (page 289). For example, if for a given inflectional usage there are two equally valid morphemes, the chance preference for the one may ultimately delete the other from the language. By first replacing the alternate form in configurations where it is least crystallized, the ascendent pattern adds to its force of habit until even the most frequent competitors have succumbed. At one time in the development of our language there were two morphemic endings for past participles, $(e)d$ (e.g. deem*ed*) and $(e)n$ (e.g. ridd*en*). Through the centuries the former has gradually been levelling out occurrences of the latter, first in the less frequent and less crystallized words and then in the more frequent. The older *holpen* has become *helped* by analogic change, while *sown* for which one frequently hears *sowed* is now in the process of being levelled.

To summarize, we may say that the operation of chance in the selection of linguistic components is cumulative in its effect, because (1) all acts of behavior are related, and (2) all acts of behavior are subject to the action of the force of habit. We shall henceforth designate this entire phenomenon with the term the *cumulative force of chance.*

b. The Effect of the Cumulative Force of Chance upon Relative Frequencies of Occurrence

The general effect in the long run of the cumulative force of chance is clearly (1) an increase in the relative frequency of occurrence of preferred configurations and (2) a corresponding decrease in the relative frequency of unsuccessful competitors. For the more *A* replaces *B*, the more the relative frequency of *A* is augmented by occurrences in which it has replaced *B*. In the long run, if all else is equal, *B* will cease to exist and have the relative frequency of zero. While there may be intermediate increases and decreases in the relative frequency of occurrences of different configurations, yet in the long run, if all else remains equal, relative frequency proceeds in only one direction, i.e. towards augmentation. And configurations whose relative frequencies do not increase will ultimately (if all else is equal) become obsolescent and obsolete. In levelling there are many other factors involved, the study of which will presently occupy our attention; hence in any given operation of the cumulative force of chance, it may not be assumed that all else necessarily remains equal.

A significant corollary to the observation that the prevailing direction of relative frequency is towards augmentation is the effect of increased frequency upon: (1) the degree of articulatedness of meaning, (2) emotional intensity, and (3) independence in usage in arrangement. Since each of these qualities was found to stand in some inverse ratio (not necessarily proportionate) to relative frequency, it follows from the effect of the cumulative force of chance on relative frequency that the prevailing direction in articulatedness of meaning, emotional intensity, and independence in usage in arrangement is from the higher degree to the lower in each configuration — a proposition which if true will surely be found of fundamental importance in the behavior of speech-patterns, especially sentence-patterns.

It has, however, not yet been shown what the precise relationship is that meaning, intensity, and independence in usage bear to one another. In the interest of clarity it may be said in anticipation of future findings that these three attributes are interrelated, but interrelated more in the sense of the interrelationship of, say, motion, heat, and electricity, than in that of the three sides of a geometric triangle. Like three forms of energy, articulatedness of meaning, emotional intensity, and independence in arrangement are each convertible, one into another. Let us now partially inspect each of these qualities in its relationship to another so that we may more expeditiously arrive at the question of equilibrium which lies at the root of the development of all sentence-patterns. In the presentation of the particular studies of these individual attributes, the repetition of some of the material already presented is inevitable.

8. ARTICULATEDNESS OF MEANING
AND EMOTIONAL INTENSITY

If we remove from consideration all other factors except articulatedness of meaning and emotional intensity, we find a curious phenomenon in many of the larger configurations: configurations of high emotional intensity or of great vividness are likely to be unprecise, indefinite, poorly articulated in meaning, and *vice versa*. Though this relationship may not be discoverable in all instances, it is apparent in enough cases to be significant, and to these latter we shall turn our attention.

All slang words, curses, terms of abuse, are of high intensity but of very indefinite meaning. Unless a person be familiar with the slang meaning of a word he often has no means of guessing it. It is common knowledge that the vividness of the slang recommends its usage; it is further-more well known that a person who habitually indulges in slang expressions often finds it impossible to articulate meaning in terms acceptable to general usage. Sometimes, to be sure, slang is in every respect very apt and occasionally it is accepted into general permanent good usage; yet on the whole it is more vivid than precise, and after repeated us-age with resultant high relative frequency has sapped its intensity, the slang is discarded. So, too, with terms of abuse: the terms *son-of-a-bitch*, *bloody* (in England), and the like are used in such various and dissimilar occasions to designate such incomparable events that the words can have little stable basic articulated meaning nor represent anything other than a high negative intensity. Similarly words of high positive intensity such as those of endear-ment (e.g. *honey*, *sweetheart*) have generally in most occur-rences little basic meaning, and tend to diminish in intensity upon increased usage; it is said that an infatuated wooer does well to introduce variety in his appellatives in order to avoid the cliché. Furthermore one finds that the impas-sioned speech which has moved the crowd or touched the jury is, when soberly scrutinized the next morning in print, generally more striking for its vividness than for its clarity and logic.

On the other hand speech-configurations which are clear, logical, coherent, and whose meaning is highly articulated, are on the whole not vivid. The words *automobile*, *oxygen*, *apple-tree*, are generally uttered with little concomitant emotional intensity. Of course, one may not forget that even as the vivid word in certain situations may also be admirably clear-cut and meaningful, so too the beautifully articulated expression may at times be rich in feeling, both on the part of its speaker and on the part of its hearer.

A general view of articulatedness of meaning and of emotional intensity sheds further light on their interrelationship. The experience of the confessional as well as that of the clinical laboratory attests for instance that a high emotional intensity diminishes upon greater articulation. Highly intense grief, remorse, or anxiety often become permanently less intense when discussed with friends, that is, when articulated in everyday terms. Hence, we find, on the whole, not only that articulatedness of meaning and emotional intensity in linguistic expression stand in some inverse relationship (not necessarily proportionate) but also that emotional intensity is, as it were, convertible into a condition which one may term articulatedness of meaning.

Nevertheless we do not seem to have reached the fundamental factor involved, inasmuch as there appears in dynamic process no readily observable reversal from high articulatedness of meaning into high emotional intensity, though we know that high emotional intensities do arise. Hence, let us limit our investigation to the particular question of the origin of high emotional intensities.

9. EMOTIONAL INTENSITY AND THE DEGREE OF CRYSTALLIZATION OF THE CONFIGURATION

If one reviews his past to inspect more closely his experiences of high emotional intensity, whether pleasant (of *positive quality*) or unpleasant (of *negative quality*), one finds that a great majority, if not all, occurred on the one hand either at the intervention of a new experience, or, on the other, at the removal or the destruction of habitual behavior or of familiar and habitual parts of environment. For example, the acquisition of considerable wealth or of the affection, love, or possession of a desired person, the attainment of a successful solution to a problem, the achievement of fame, are all attended by emotional intensity of positive quality and represent the intervention of new experience. Similarly the loss of accustomed wealth or of the love, affection, or possession of a desired person, the failure to solve a problem, the loss of reputation, failure, all of which seriously disturb if not completely destroy parts of our habitual behavior or environment, are attended by emotional intensity of negative quality.

Now, these highly intense emotional experiences, whether positive or negative, whether viewed primarily as interventions of the new, or displacements and destructions of the old, have one feature in common: each one accompanies a breach in the established patterns of behavior. Moreover, the greater the emotional intensity, the more serious do we find the disturbance in the pattern, or the more fundamental the pattern which is disturbed. All experiences of high emotional intensity are, to use a familiar term, emotional disturbances, although, from the fond belief that the positive represent the advent of a status without end, we are inclined to view only the negative experiences as disturbances.

A further characteristic of emotional conditions is that they normally run their course and come to an end, provided that the person's life does not end first. This attenuation and ultimate disappearance of highly intense emotional conditions is accomplished in many instances without the intervention of any other factor, as far as one can see, than that of the unmitigated passage of time. With positive (i.e. pleasant) emotional intensity, the effect of sheer time is understandable, for we naturally repeat as often as possible the pleasant; and the resultant increase in relative frequency will, if our various hypotheses are correct, lead of its own accord to diminished intensity.[1] Yet, on the other hand, we equally zealously shun the unpleasant, heartily disliking a condition of remorse, grief, or anxiety. With emotional intensity of negative quality it is difficult to observe that any role is played by increased relative frequency. Relative frequency cannot then be the only factor in diminishing emotional intensity.

There happens to be a practical method frequently employed therapeutically to diminish the intensity and duration of unpleasant emotional conditions, which sheds light on the nature of emotion itself. The application of this therapeutic method admittedly attempts to re-establish order in a condition of disturbance or derangement, and, as far as can be judged empirically, the effect of its successful application is reorganization. By detecting the patterns of the past which have been disturbed through exigencies of the present, by understanding their ramifications into the acts of everyday behavior, and finally, through changes in environment or in the behavior of the afflicted individual, by restoring a more harmonious adjustment between the individual, his group, and his environment, one can often effect an abatement in the condition of unpleasant emotional intensity. During this entire process the reduction of daily occupation to one of routine is a help. The success of the therapy depends almost entirely upon the degree to which reorganization is accomplished. The more rapidly and the more thoroughly reorganization is effected, the more speedily and the more durably the unpleasant emotional condition is removed.

This therapeutic method, which has developed into one of major social value, seems to indicate, as do our commonplace terms for the phenomenon, that unpleasant emotional intensity arising from derangement or disorder of the habitual course of our life is removed by the establishment of arrangement and order. Even as emotional intensity seems to attend disturbances of established patterns of behavior, so too it seems to abate upon re-establishment of patterns. Since this abatement attends either the establishment of new patterns in place of the old, or the re-establishment of the old, it results then from re-establishment of order of whatever sort; the more permanent the new order, the more permanent the relief, and the more stable the person. This finding, like the one immediately following which can scarcely be considered new, is of considerable interest to Dynamic Philology.

The progress of emotional conditions which, like a self-limiting disease, will abate of their own accord without intervention of help, points to the existence of a second factor which again is of fundamental importance in the behavior of language: the preference of Nature for a condition of order in living process rather than one of disorder. Just as Nature's first impulse, when confronted by a laceration which disturbs the organization of physiological functioning, is to re-establish a harmonious arrangement by healing, so too with breaches in the harmonious arrangement of our behavior, Nature's impulse is toward order and away from derangement. If one may designate this impulse as an abhorrence, one may say that Nature abhors a disordered unintegrated condition in biological process, of which language is but one manifestation. In other words, the direction of living is from the amorphous toward the formed, from the unintegrated to the integrated, from the undigested to the digested. Emotional disturbances tend to pass because Nature's impulse is to restore arrangement. Even as Nature roots patterns ever more deeply in habit in a manner described under the term 'the cumulative force of chance,' so too Nature strives to form patterns where there were none, and to remake patterns where they have been disturbed.

The probable correctness of these views of emotion, which will provide us with considerable insight into the nature of sentence-patterns can be established statistically. Inasmuch as they are to be the very foundation of most of our ensuing investigation of language, and since statistical data will be advanced to substantiate their correctness, it seems expedient now to orient ourselves somewhat more securely in the concept.

10. EMOTION

In suggesting that animate process and behavior function in a direction prevailingly toward greater and more crystallized patternness, one is reminded of a parallel in the behavior of physical matter to which many biologists have long called attention. Inanimate material process instead of preferring the patterned and the organized, prefers the disorganized, in the sense that the general direction of inorganic process in the universe is toward complete disorganization, or entropy. For example, coal, a highly organized condition of matter, in burning to ashes is transmuted to a less highly organized condition. The transmutation in matter from high organization to lower organization is attended by the emission of physical energy. It is said that energy has no other source than in the disorganization of matter, and that the disorganization is attended by kinetic energy. A static state of high material organization is potential energy since the prevailing direction is toward disintegration, a process to which the static condition will presumably some day succumb and 'release its energy.' The more rapidly and extensively the disorganization takes place, the more intense will be the concomitant energy.

Now let us for the purposes of illustration and in the interest of clarity of definition equate *emotion* with *physical energy*, and say that, as we proceed from the less complex to the more complex in the totality of our being, emotion is 'emitted.' The more rapidly and the more extensively the change takes place, the more intense is the concomitant emotion. Without change in organization there is no emotion, without emotion, no change; we shall consider that the two are concomitant with the nature of a possible causal relationship not implied. Emotion, then, is like electricity, and the term 'emotions,' sometimes used, would be as meaningless in our usage of the term as 'electricities.'

This progression in animate behavior from the less complex, less crystallized in habit and less patternized to the more complex, more crystallized, and more patternized consists in a redistribution and rearrangement. For one pattern cannot become dominant over another nor be combined with another without a redistribution and rearrangement somewhere in the total being. Let us then assume as a speculation that the greater the degree of redistribution involved, the greater the attendant *intensity of emotion* (i.e. *emotional intensity*). When development proceeds along channels so thoroughly crystallized in habit by the effect of the cumulative force of chance operating through past ages (*instinctive behavior*) that there is practically no choice in rearrangement or re-permutation, the concomitant emotional intensity is so low that one is aware of its existence only by inference. Thus the prenatal life of an individual, which progresses presumably quite without the operation of selection, is presumably also attended by a very low degree of emotional intensity. But when behavior is guided less by unobstructed instinctive patterns and hence is faced by choices subject to trial and error, the amount of potential redistribution and rearrangement is greater, and the concomitant emotional intensity higher. Anything which accelerates the rate of redistribution and rearrangement, or anything that precipitates redistribution and rearrangement by inhibiting the normal functioning of crystallized patterns, automatically increases the intensity. Thus the acquisition of the desideratum by bringing into solution the suspended, and by helping to replace the chaotic with the orderly, accelerates the rate of change and is emotionally intense; when the results are positive in the general sense that organization replaces disorganization, the quality of the emotional experience which is pleasant can be called positive (pleasant). The rearrangement necessitated by inhibition or by the deprival of the usual will in turn be of negative quality (unpleasant) in so far as the rearrangement necessitates a preliminary disintegration or breakage of crystallized pattern. Though this statement of the supposed nature of the process is but superficial, it is, nevertheless, adequate for our immediate purposes, and its more detailed elucidation will later be facilitated after we have proceeded further in our investigation of sentence-dynamics.

Our discussion until now has suggested an explanation of but one side of the picture of emotional conflict and the processes of resolution involved, the optimistic side. Though it is surely in accordance with every man's wish that his unpleasant emotional experiences attendant upon inevitable changes should come to an end as quickly as possible, it is, however, truly unfortunate that what is sauce for the goose is also sauce for the gander, and that likewise our positive emotional conditions which make life so sweet also normally run their course and come to an end. Eager as we are to be rid of the unpleasant, we are equally eager to preserve and augment the pleasant, and hence are constantly confronted by the problem of maintaining what amounts to a condition of equilibrium.

I I. EQUILIBRIUM

The prevailing tendency toward an ever greater crystallization in habit, if unimpeded, would rapidly reduce our existence to a level of complete routine and insufferable dullness in which each event followed its predecessor mechanically as a matter of course. The condition would not only be monotonous, but when confronted by the impelling need for fundamental readjustment, would be truly hazardous because of the intense potential pain which would attend the reorganization. Perhaps in order to avoid more the dullness than the hazard, one automatically strives to spice his life with variety to resist excessive crystallization and monotony. This spicing is accomplished by diversity of occupation and interest. If diversification is carried to an extreme, the result is a condition of emotional instability, which again is hazardous when confronted by the inevitable demands of life for patient unswerving routine. Examples of both extremes are commonplace. On the one hand is the dull existence of the boy, of the housewife, of the husband, of the workingman, of the professional man who is strapped in the traces of routine drudgery; nor are we surprised to hear that such a person frequently 'bolts' or 'explodes,' and that the bolting or exploding is emotionally highly intense, be it positive or negative, until rearrangement of behavior has yielded a more suitable adjustment. On the other hand, there is the instability of the person whose behavior has been so variegated and emotionally intense, positive or negative, that he has not developed stable habits, and who cannot accommodate himself to the inevitable occasions of routine which confront him — the person whose childhood was spent in an unharmonious family circle, the spoiled person who has had too many of the world's goods to distract him, and the rolling stone. One can appreciate the attendant high emotional intensity, and is not surprised to learn of the misery of this person when forced into the daily routine of the office or the household. Examples of behavior between the extremes are also familiar, in which the dullness of routine is mitigated by the variety of social intercourse and recreational activity. Knowledge of this equilibrium and of the opposing forces involved has become common; yet our desire to maintain a contented equilibrium is to a considerable degree, if not entirely, automatic and apparently an innate corollary to our very existence.

This desire on the part of any person to maintain equilibrium can operate, roughly speaking, in two fields. In the first place he can and does change his environment by travel, new acquaintances, etc. with the result that his new reactions to these new stimuli in his environment introduce variety into his life, and interpose new distribution and rearrangement in the ever-increasing crystallization of the patterns of his behavior. In the second place, one can and does change one's mode of activity in the same environment, and by alterations in diet, routine of work, and of social and recreational pleasures introduces variety. It is, of course, difficult to draw the line objectively in every case of change between environmental change and change in the individual, so closely are stimulus and reaction linked. Nevertheless we do know that the monotony of a person's life may be mitigated either by the effort of his friends in introducing diversion into his life, or by the effort of the afflicted in changing his mode of living. Of these two possibilities for change, the former, that is the alterations in environment, are more significant for our purposes because the outsider can on the whole observe them objectively with a greater degree of success than he can the inner personal changes.

Changes in environment to be effective in introducing variety into a person's life cannot be arbitrary: too great a change will disturb the essential patterns too much; too little a change, not enough. For example, to transplant an office-weary stenographer alone into the polar regions, even with a full polar outfit and supplies, though surely a 'complete change,' would so break every shred of daily habit that the consequences would be dire; on the other hand, the mere changing of the pictures on the wall of the office would be too little. There is, then, a mean in the alteration of the environment, in following which the deeply rooted habits are either entirely respected or else modified but slowly, and in which the less deeply rooted habits are changed significantly by gradual modification. There is a balance between too much variegation and too little, between too little respect for the pre-established and too much. It seems that environmental change, to be effective, must follow what we shall term a *normal rate of variegation* to preserve contentment in the life of an average person; this *normal rate* is possibly modified in one direction or the other in order to induce stability or to eliminate dullness in the lives of those whose behavior has been abnormally variegated on the one hand or abnormally mechanized on the other. For the present, however, we are primarily interested in the average person and the normal rate of variegation.

Now, if one could but measure empirically this *normal rate of variegation* in the environment, one would have gained considerable insight into an important aspect of the nature of emotion. For it seems plausible to assume that the normal rate of variegation falls within the limits of tolerable change of rearrangement, that is, the limits of change above which patterns will be broken or changed too much and below which they will be broken or changed too little. In other words, the normal rate of tolerable variegation is an indicator of the normal rate of reorganization or redistribution in maintaining what we shall henceforth term *emotional equilibrium.*

I 2. EMOTIONAL EQUILIBRIUM IN LANGUAGE

The tendency to maintain emotional equilibrium by preserving enough of the pre-established and by introducing sufficient variety is present not only while speaking (Speaker *A*) but also while listening (Auditor, *B*). When *A* and *B* are together, each is part of the environment of the other, and when one talks to the other, say *A* to *B*, *A*'s stream of speech is variegation in *B*'s environment. Where *B* is an average person, *A*'s speech must follow the normal rate of variegation, if *B* is to grant it his attention and to understand it. *B* will not care to listen if *A*'s discourse is too dull, hence *A* must introduce variety into his discourse; *B* will also not listen if *A* introduces so much variety that *B* cannot follow. For we perceive according to established channels of experience and, as is common knowledge, we can appreciate change only against the background of experience; changes are only comprehensible when legitimate, that is, when we see them as new permutations of the old, or as re-permutations of the old, or as modifications (additions or subtractions) of the old. Hence, when A talks to B, A's discourse must be both interesting and intellectually digestible to B if B is to listen, i.e., A's discourse must have a rate of variegation equivalent to B's rate of absorption. If A is successful, the rate of variegation of A's discourse will be an indicator of B's rate of absorption at the time; B's rate of absorption indicates B's tolerable limits of change in maintaining emotional equilibrium.

Now, in the vast majority of instances, every-day speech should represent the average rate of variegation, and should reflect the average rate of tolerable change. If, as a speaker, one does not always attain independently the average rate, nevertheless, as an auditor, one instinctively and stubbornly insists upon its preservation. The auditor's involuntary yawns, drowsiness, wandering attention, dumbfounded queries, nonplussed expressions reveal to the speaker that his discourse is either too much a regurgitation of the familiar or too remote from the familiar, as it is presented to the auditor's ears. And since these symptoms of dissatisfaction, latent in everyone as an auditor, are familiar to everyone as a speaker, the effect of their occurrence is either to silence the speaker (hence no speech) or to force him to modify his speech until it is normal; the average stream of speech, then, must contain with rather close approximation the normal rate of variegation.

Hence the rate of variegation contained in extensive samplings of speech selected at random represents the standard rate of variegation on the one hand, as well as the standard rate of tolerable change for the establishment and preservation of emotional equilibrium on the other. Measure the first and you have measured the second; and it is possible to measure the first (i.e. the standard rate of variegation in language).

The standard rate of variegation in the stream of speech

is, on the whole, the opposite of the average rate of repetitiveness of the elements therein; the greater the variety of the elements, the less the average rate of repetitiveness (see Chapter II) thereof. Since the relative frequency of occurrence of a speech-unit is the measure of its rate of repetitiveness in the stream of speech, the frequency-distribution of the elements in the stream of speech represents the general repetitiveness of those elements; and a standard curve of frequency-distribution represents the standard rate of variegation. Though a standard curve of distribution of phonemes and morphemes is, of course, interesting, the most interesting curve is that of the larger units, for example, words, where the factors of meaning and intensity are more appreciable and where crystallization has not yet reached, on the whole, such a degree as to have eliminated individual choice.

Now we possess and have already presented (Chapter II, pages 26, 27, 28) the necessary data on the distribution of words in present-day American Newspaper English, Modern Peiping Chinese, and Plautine Latin; we have found the distribution of words in these languages to be curiously orderly, representing with a high degree of approximation (in the range of lower frequencies) the inverse square (see page 40). In other words, the variety of words cannot be so great that the exponent becomes greater than the square, nor can repetitiveness (the reciprocal of variety) be so great that the exponent is less than the square — subject, of course, to the findings of more extensive analyses. When variegation decreases below the exponent two, the auditor is bored by excessive repetitiveness; as variegation increases above the exponent two, the auditor tends to be more confused. Hence the auditor's rate of absorption, or rate of tolerable change in organization, is represented by the exponent of the frequency of words, with all its implications, as explained previously in Chapter II.

It was, then, not a complete observation of the total

phenomenon when we stated (page 48) that the speaker selects and arranges words according to their meanings; the meaning of arranged words must, to be sure, always strike the auditor as comprehensible, yet we select and arrange words not only to convey information but also to hold his attention. The curious orderliness which we have found in the distribution of words in Chapter II reflects the orderliness of emotional change — a consideration to which we shall return in the next chapter.

However, when striving to establish the rate of tolerable variegation by analyzing the frequency-distribution of words, one should preferably select written language[1] for analysis, and not a written record of spoken speech; for in spoken speech many other communicative gestures (such as facial and manual gestures) may replace vocal gestures and hence introduce a distortion into the distribution of words. Written language, on the other hand, is without these auxiliary resources of manual and facial gestures and represents communication effected solely by the selection and arrangement of words.*

Now this standard curve of distribution resulting from the nature of the emotional processes of the auditor is naturally ingrained in the speech habits of most speakers, first, because speech is used primarily in communication, and secondly, because most speakers are in turn auditors, at least to some extent. However, it does not happen that every speaker always defers to the limits of toleration of his auditor, and we may well expect, as a result, that his language will deviate from the norm. Since 'abnormal' language of this sort would conceivably shed light on the dynamics of expression, let us briefly turn our attention to this type of language which we may, for convenience, term pathological.

* It is perhaps not by chance that the evenly balanced harmonic series of distribution of words in English (page 46) is found in material taken exclusively from written English, whereas both the Plautine Latin and the Peipingese (pages 26, 27) represent to a considerable degree what was intended to be spoken or what was spoken.

13. PATHOLOGICAL LANGUAGE

Pathological language is language which is symptomatic of a pathological or diseased condition. A symptom is a deviation from the normal, from which, on the basis of the accumulated knowledge of experience, one infers the existence and, sometimes, the nature of disease (abnormal condition). Although many diseases are not revealed by an immediate effect on the normal stream of speech, it is surprising how many illnesses are. Not only do head-colds and sore throats modify the usual configurations of speech, but also swoonings, boils, or deliriums of fever, for example, either by entirely obliterating speech, or by seriously distorting it. Especially in nervous and mental diseases, particularly when functional, as, for example, in anxiety-states, obsessions, manic-depressive psychoses and schizophrenia, distortions of the stream of speech are major symptoms, if not *the* major symptoms. Diagnosis and prognosis in these mental illnesses are often to a very considerable extent effected on the basis of distortions in the patient's speech.

Curiously enough, many of these functional mental disorders are said to reflect an inadequate social adjustment; the patient has not had a satisfactory relationship with his fellow man. Frequently his behavior is antisocial in the sense that it alienates and embitters rather than attracts and endears, even though the patient's chief desire may be the latter rather than the former. It is, then, interesting to note cursorily in a few typical cases the repercussion of this antisocial behavior in the patient's speech. For in these types of speech in which the relationship of the auditor to the speaker is at least presumed to be abnormal (the auditor being held either in excessive esteem or contempt), the normal checks which the auditor exerts on the speaker's discourse are weakened.

In the case of an obsession, for instance, in which the same thoughts are presented again and again and again, articulated in detail with all their ramifications, the consequential and the inconsequential * are offered as of like importance. While the selection, arrangement, and utterance of words are comprehensible, they are abnormal in the sense that variegation is so low that the auditor finally seeks to escape, as he had previously sought in vain to change the direction and contour of the stream. Though his own stream of speech is of great interest and importance to the obsessed speaker, as is also the case with his first cousin, the pedant, it offends the auditor because it is *over-articulated in meaning,* a term to which we shall presently return.

There is, next, the manic phase of a manic-depressive psychosis in which the patient talks all the time and in which the discourse is marked by a flightiness of ideas. Here the subject of discourse changes rapidly with little coherence; the style is telegraphic with the deletion of connecting particles, relatives, conjunctions, even adverbs and prepositions; words are often used metaphorically and frequently suffer in pronunciation from the high tempo of speech. The speaker, as might be theoretically anticipated, is often highly animated. Though the speech may fascinate the auditor, he cannot completely understand its true significance because it is *under-articulated.*

In the language attending schizophrenic disturbances, the auditor often seems rather to be scorned than to be respected.† The patient frequently selects and arranges his words into what are clinically termed 'word-salads,' even enriching his speech with words of his own creation (neologisms), with the result that the auditor can rarely comprehend at all. Both the word-salads and neologisms are instances of new permu-

* From the point of view of the auditor.

† Whether every schizophrenic is *contemptuous* of his every auditor is problematic. Nevertheless his illness is quite generally marked by an exaggerated feeling of independence or even of rebelliousness which would probably have the same effect as contemptuousness on his speech activity.

tations whose formation is not at all clear to the observer; thus the patient increasingly shuts himself off from the help of his fellow man. In extreme cases even the very use of speech is despised, whether from scorn for any social contact or from preoccupation with the patient's self.

Nothing would be more illuminating than a statistical investigation of the frequency-distribution of speech-elements in pathological language — a virgin field of probably tremendous fertility for investigation. It would be interesting to know if and to what extent in pathological English the curve of word-distribution varied from the standard harmonic curve (see page 46); what words and what types of words occupied the different parts of the curve; and to what extent normal words are replaced either by neologisms, or by accepted words with abnormally increased or decreased frequencies. A phonemic count of word-salads might be very revealing. Though pathological language represents deviation from the norms which Dynamic Philology is primarily concerned with investigating, yet, as representing deviations, it is of as much value in testing the validity of our investigation, as any deviation from the norm is in any scientific problem.

Having located and very cursorily inspected deviations from the norm, let us return to a consideration of normal language, and inquire into the devices which are employed in maintaining equilibrium: that is, the devices by means of which the normal stream of speech steers between the Scylla of over-articulation and the Charybdis of under-articulation.

I 4. STYLE

For convenience of discussion let us employ the word *style* as a term to designate the successful charting of the course of speech between dull over-articulation and incomprehensible under-articulation. *Style* implies, then, balance, and no communication is successful which does not contain at least a minimum thereof. Those especially gifted with, or accomplished in, a sense for *style* can hold their auditor's attention and deflect as they will the auditor's stream of thought and its attendant intensity and quality. Style of high degree of excellence is great skill. But he who, through the selection and arrangement of speech elements, can hold the attention of auditors of many different social groups, even long after his death influencing the course of their lives, bringing order where there was no order, effecting permanent rearrangements in patterns of behavior, and deflecting, even by ever so little, what would otherwise be the normal social development, is an artist; for one cannot possess such a consummate perfection in style as measured by its enduring effect without also possessing the depth of insight, the breadth of vision, and the sense of proportion which elevate the stylist to the artist. Thus defined, the difference between the speech of the average man and that of the great artist appears to be one of degree; every person is potentially an artist, just as every artist is but for the grace of God an average man. Though from layman to artist there are many steps, the two differ not in the devices they employ, but in the employment of the devices. And as empirical study of the everyday conversation of the layman may some day shed light upon the products of the artist, so too, a brief study of artistic style will now give at least clues to the devices less perfectly employed by the average man.

In the first place, as is common knowledge, an artistic creation must be new, either in theme, or setting, or treatment; yet on the other hand it must, as is also common knowledge, be familiar in theme or setting or treatment; without the one the auditor will not be attracted, without the other he will not comprehend; likewise in everyday conversation.

Then, too, the artistic presentation must be in terms and

arrangements which are familiar to the auditor so that the auditor's attention will not be attracted to the new in word- or sentence-configurations but to the new in larger configurations of sentences. Here the artist is not limited by his auditor's active vocabulary (i.e. the words which the auditor uses in his speech) but by the auditor's passive vocabulary (i.e. the words which the auditor can understand). Theoretically one may expect that the author will restrict his vocabulary to those words which are found in the passive vocabularies of all to whom his creation is directed; and actually one finds a remarkable simplicity in such artists as Homer, to mention an ancient, or as Goethe, to mention one more nearly modern. The artist in projecting himself into his hearer's place, really borrows his hearer's passive vocabulary; this is true not only of the artist, but of the soap-box orator, and the layman in conversation. The extent to which the artist neglects to borrow his auditor's vocabulary, or the extent to which he selects the groups from whose vocabulary he borrows, is the extent to which the artistic production is esoteric. Since the stump-speaker before the days of radio was obliged to borrow the vocabulary exclusively from his immediate group of auditors, his speech was esoteric and he very wisely rewrote it before publication. Carried to an extreme, the exclusiveness of selection strikes the average auditor more and more as unintelligible; to his mind the difference between extremely esoteric language and the neologistic language of schizophrenic conditions may be so slight that the former runs the risk of being classed with the latter — a not infrequent treatment of the creations of the innovator. Though clinically the difference between the highly esoteric and the pathological may be appreciably great, it is not unlikely that the magnetic compass in esoteric language points in the general direction of that of the schizophrenic.

If the new is a fundamentally different arrangement in patterns of behavior or perception, the artist proceeds gradually step by step. For example, to convince a large group which believes implicitly in the flatness of the earth that the earth is indeed round necessitates a presentation step by step in which accepted patterns are modified gradually to include adduced new data. Once the rearrangement has been satisfactorily accomplished and the group's attitudes and patterns of ideas have become adjusted to the new arrangement, the word *earth* means 'round thing' instead of 'flat thing.' And the simple epithet *earth* conveys clearly to the auditor what may have originally taken a voluminous tome and endless hours of discussion to establish. The author's name is gratefully remembered, but the skillful presentation on which he expended so much thought strikes the average reader a few hundred years later as tedious. For this reader, the single configuration *earth* is sufficient, and the subtle configuration of the tome is over-articulated.

Now, this partial pruning of the old to engraft the new is accomplished by a device which is essentially that of definition. For example, instead of saying *surcingle* one may say *a girth which passes about a horse's back to hold the saddle*, the latter being a configuration with a higher degree of articulation of meaning than the former. The latter may be even further articulated by substituting an even more articulated configuration for each meaningful word. Indeed, this increase in articulatedness may be carried on apparently indefinitely not only until the surcingle has been located in time and space, but until everything in man's entire experience has been correlated with it. Yet, after the degree of articulatedness is carried beyond the immediate needs of the auditor, and reaches a point where it but rehearses the self-evident, the speech is over-articulated, and, if persistent, obsessive.

The statistical effect of over-articulation is a high degree of repetitiveness, since the variety of vocabulary expressions is diminished in favor of more usual words, which are correspondingly over-worked. Though individual speech-configurations of high degree of articulation are (see pages 191 ff.) of low relative frequency, highly articulated speech, on the other hand, is of high average relative frequency or repetitiveness. For in highly articulated speech, one has instead of one word-configuration *surcingle*, the speech-configuration *a girth... saddle*, which is made up of twelve word-configurations in which the proportion of highly frequent words (*a, which, about, back, to, the*) has been greatly increased. The effect of increasing articulation (see page 40 f. and Plates I, II, III) is, then, to raise the peak of the line along the ordinate at the left, and to cause the end of the line to recede along the abscissa at the right (with the result that the exponent will diminish below 2 in the formula $ab^2 = k$ of page 41).

Opposed to the device of greater articulation is the device of abbreviation. If a person is talking about *surcingles*, and after he has made clear to his lay auditor that a *surcingle* is *a girth which passes about a horse's back to hold the saddle*, the speaker cannot continue to employ this entire twelve-word, highly articulated configuration without boring the auditor with excessive repetitiveness. To avoid, then, the effect of dullness he substitutes a configuration which is shorter and which has a lower degree of articulation: he may say *girth* or he may say *surcingle* or he may say *it*. If instead of saying *a girth... saddle* he says *girth*, the process is one of truncation in which one component of the configuration stands for the entire configuration, while the remainder is omitted; if, on the other hand, he replaces the entire configuration by a speech-element not contained in the configuration (i.e. *surcingle* or *it*), the abbreviation is one of substitution. Whether it is one of truncation or of substitution, the abbreviation reduces the degree of articulatedness of the stream of speech and in the long run increases variegation. Excessive abbreviation becomes telegraphic in style, and when pushed to an extreme is incomprehensible because of its incoherence. One would naturally expect that the effect of abbreviation on the curve of distribution would depend upon the relative frequency of the element which was selected to represent the truncated or supplanted configuration. But the total effect of abbreviation, as can be shown, is in the long run toward that of greater variegation and lower average relative frequency. For small words suitable for substitution are few in number, and though they, with their low degree of articulatedness of meaning and low degree of intensity, can tolerate a comparatively high relative frequency, yet their excessive employment is inhibited by a resultant dullness which their very employment in abbreviation is intended to avoid: * speech made up entirely of small and highly frequent words such as pronouns, auxiliaries, etc., granted that it were sufficiently articulated, would, because of the small available number of these short words, constitute but a few different configurations; these few configurations when repeated would become highly crystallized and dull. On the other hand, when selecting the component of a configuration to represent the truncated configuration, we select, on the whole, the one which occurs proportionately most often in the configuration which it is to represent. Though the selection of the most suitable word to represent any given configuration in abbreviated state is a major problem in all composition, nevertheless the total effect of abbreviation is that of greater variegation. The more abbreviated the style, the greater the variety, the lower the average frequency and the larger will the exponent be than 2 in the formula $ab^2 = k$ (see page 41) for the frequency distribution.†

* See discussion of *configuration-carriers*, pages 280 ff.

† How large the exponent may become before the language ceases to be comprehensible to anyone is difficult to estimate; considerable light might be shed on the upper limit to the exponent in language (that is, on the exponent in language with a maximum degree of comprehensible abbreviation) by studying the frequency-distributions of words of telegrams, of which record has been kept, or of the head-lines of sensational newspapers, i.e. tabloids.

The normal stream of speech, then, weaves between excessive articulatedness and excessive variegation to preserve a balance between comprehensibility and intensity out of respect for the attentiveness and rate of absorption of the auditor's emotional organization. Statistical analyses of samples of normal speech reveal in the distribution of words according to frequency that the process is orderly and that, for the lower range of frequency, it follows the inverse square (as explained in Chapter II). Why it should follow the inverse square instead of the inverse cube or some other power is not clear; the size of this exponent, like that of the exponent in the gravitational formula — which is likewise the inverse square — was arrived at empirically.

This simple relationship between the number of different words and their relative frequencies can scarcely exist without constituting an important check on grammatical laws for arranging words into sentences. It would seem, indeed, that no grammatical law of syntax or inflection could permanently exist which regularly necessitated a distribution of words other than that of the standard curve. And we shall see that the preservation of this standard curve of distribution, with all its implications in intensity, degree of crystallization, and articulatedness of meaning, is the chief restraining and impelling factor in the evolution of a language's resources in sentence-patterns.

PART II

SENTENCE–PATTERNS

After a grammarian analyzes a cross-section of the stream of speech for the sake of writing a grammar for the guidance of those who wish to use the language, he propounds rules for inflection and the arrangement of words in sentences (syntax) which are purely empirical and often seemingly arbitrary. The grammatical rules of no two languages necessarily agree, and some in fact are as opposite as can be imagined. Hence the grammarians who have sporadically endeavored to prove the reasonableness of the grammatical rules of their native tongue by appealing to principles of logic or *a priori* laws of clarity or beauty have generally elicited the amused scorn of Comparative Philology whose gaze incorrigibly wanders across borders. The object lesson may be taken to heart by Dynamic Philology: we shall strive to make our explanations appear reasonable without implying that the linguistic habits they describe are or are not peculiarly rational. Our view of sentence-patterns or rules of grammar will be that of linguistic behavior in process of evolution: the sentence-patterns of a language at any time are, on the one hand, the results of evolutionary development in the past and, on the other, represent the foundation from which the evolutionary development in the future will proceed. Limitations in the investigator's time and capacity have prevented him from sampling more than a small fraction of the abundance of actual sentence-patterns in use on the earth; further limitations in space permit presentation of but a few typical examples; yet the findings derived from the evidence presented are advanced in the belief that they will be found of universal validity in sentence-development.

For the sake of clarity let us briefly summarize our main contentions and our method of approach. The fundamental forces presumed to be at play in the development of sentence-patterns are first the ever-growing crystallization of the configuration, and second, the desire for vivid expression. The evolution of sentence-patterns is the result of these two forces in operation to preserve equilibrium. The effect of these two forces in operation over a long period of time is in brief this: (1) as sentence-patterns become increasingly crystallized, they are 'broken' for the sake of greater vividness; (2) the new patterns, being more vivid, are more attractive and hence receive greater usage with the result: that (1) they become more crystallized until they (2) in turn are broken. This general tendency is displayed first in large cycles in which language slowly shifts from a condition of being predominantly positional (and non-inflected) to a condition of being predominantly inflectional (with the positional arrangement of words of less importance). The same tendency is displayed in shorter cycles in which the arrangement within component phrases, clauses, subjects and predicates is constantly shifted. The former cyclic behavior can be measured, in the sense that the extent to which any language is inflected (its *degree of inflection*) can be measured. There appears at present no method of measuring the behavior in the smaller cycles, though it is in the smaller cycles where the operation of the supposed law is more readily apparent.

Before commencing we shall, however, limit the scope of our investigation to languages (the vast majority of spoken tongues) which make use of noun and verb, and we shall take as our first example English.

I. PARTS OF SPEECH

English has what are familiarly termed parts of speech: substantives, adjectives, adverbs, main verbs, auxiliary verbs, pronouns, prepositions, conjunctions, articles, exclamations. These parts of speech represent categories into which the words of the vocabulary are placed empirically according to the probabilities of their behavior in the stream of speech. The members of each part of speech generally have, in their arrangements in sentences, certain definite common usages which are generally denied to members of other parts of speech: the adjective has its usages, the verb has its usages. The part of speech of a word is derived primarily from its behavior or usage, and not its behavior or usage from its part of speech. The allocation of a word to a part of speech reflects the probabilities of its usage rather than all the possibilities of its usage, for one can, for example, use any substantive as a verb, indeed use the word of any one part of speech in the manner of another: e.g. (prepositions as substantives) 'the *ins* and the *outs*'; (verbs as prepositions) 'all *except* John,' 'all *save* John'; (articles as verbs) 'he *the'd* and *a'd* all evening,' etc. In utilizing the categories of parts of speech, then, we shall remember that they are not mutually exclusive in their membership and that they reflect likelihoods in the behavior of their individual members and not the limits of possible usages.

One interesting feature of the different parts of speech is the great disparity between them in the number of members and the average relative frequency of their members. For example let us present the evidence of the French-Carter-Koenig investigation of the parts of speech of the words of 500 telephone conversations in American English:[1]

OCCURRENCES OF PARTS OF SPEECH IN ENGLISH

	Number of Words		Ratio of Total to Different
	Total	Different	
Substantives	11,660	1,029	11.3
Adjectives and Adverbs	9,880	634	15.6
Main Verbs	12,550	456	27.5
Auxiliary verbs	9,450	37	255.
Pronouns *	17,900	45	398.
Prepositions and Conjunctions *	12,400	36	344.
Articles *	5,550	3	1850.
	79,390	2,240	35.4

Although this investigation of English parts of speech would be of even greater use, had the categories of adjectives and adverbs been segregated, and if, in addition to data about main verbs and auxiliary verbs, there were information about

* Computed from data derived from less than 500 conversations.

the occurrences of entire verbs in periphrastic construction,* neither of these short-comings (limitations only from the point of view of our present purposes) are serious.

The curious feature about these statistics is that the parts of speech fall into two distinct groups according to the number of different words and the ratio of total words to different words (average relative frequency). In Group 1 are the substantives, adjectives, adverbs, and main verbs, which have many different words, and a low ratio; in Group 2, consisting of auxiliary verbs, pronouns, prepositions, conjunctions, and articles, are parts of speech containing but a few different words and a high ratio. The members of the two groups differ, then, decidedly in their average relative frequency of occurrence, and this difference has significant consequences.

The first consequence of this difference in average relative frequency is that the actual words represented by the parts of speech in Group 1 will on the whole have a higher degree of articulatedness of meaning than those in Group 2. That is, the words in Group 1 will, on the whole, whether in configurations of phrases and sentences or not, contain independent meaning with a higher degree of specificity and precision of reference (e.g. *house, dog, swim, walk, black, faithfully*) than those in Group 2 (e.g. *he, it, of, for, while, and, the, a*). Though the latter are, strictly speaking, not meaningless, yet the specificity and precision of their reference generally does not appear until they are arranged in larger sequences. Naturally the meaning of every speech-element is modified when arranged with other speech-elements, but the members of Group 1 preserve an independent meaning in their own right to a greater degree in arrangement than do those of Group 2.

The difference in meaning between the members of the two groups becomes more manifest if one views that to which

---

* *Goes, has, walked,* etc. are simple verbs, *shall go, has gone, will have walked* are verbs in periphrastic construction.

the words of the two groups generally refer. The words of Group 1 (substantives, main verbs, adjectives, and adverbs) refer on the whole to the world of our perceptions and our inferences about our perceptions; that is, the world of perception and inferences is their frame of reference. In this frame of reference the meaning of each word of Group 1 is to a very considerable degree stable (e.g. the meanings of *house, dog, swim, walk, black, faithfully*), so stable indeed that at a random occurrence of a word of this group, one is generally in little doubt about its referent. Not so with the words of Group 2, of which the individual words have meaning because of grammatical habits and the nature of the context in which they occur; their frame of reference is the patterns and content of the stream of speech: pronouns, auxiliaries, prepositions, have meaning in the frame of reference of our perceptions primarily because the stream of speech to which they refer has ultimate reference to our experiences. The meanings of *he, while*, etc. are not stable as are those of *house, dog*, and *swim*, nor can one from a random occurrence of a word of Group 2 be as certain of its referent as one can of a word in Group 1.

But the lack of a stable independent meaning in words of Group 2 has compensation in a greater stability or determinacy of usage. Indefinite in reference to our world of experiential data, the meanings of the members of Group 2 are highly stable in their reference to the stream of speech in which they occur. If one cannot tell what man *he* refers to in a given occurrence, one can be sure that it refers to an antecedent in the stream of speech, expressed or implied. The strictly circumscribed usage of the words of Group 2, which we shall henceforth call *articulatory words*, is their meaning, or rather represents that element in them which we term meaning in the words of Group 1. When, however, we turn to the words of Group 1, which for want of a better term we shall call *conceptual words*, we find that the strict circumscription in usage which distinguishes the articulatory words is absent. Conceptual words, being generally of very stable meaning in their frame of reference, have a freedom of usage and arrangement lacking to articulatory words, and any predictability of their usage reposes ultimately upon observed or inferred arrangements in our experiential data. Conceptual words relate our speech to our experience, articulatory words relate our conceptual words to one another; the former may be viewed as the solutes, the latter the solvents; the former may be viewed as the miles of longitudinal and latitudinal track over which expression travels, the latter the switches and spurs which give direction to the traffic and make it coherent. The flexibility in arranging the former permits freedom in expression, while the high degree of crystallization in the usage of the latter assures a coherence in the arrangement. Statistically the differences in these two groups appear closely connected with differences in relative frequency which with all its implications have been discussed in Part I of this chapter. Upon reflection it is not difficult to appreciate why the prepositions, conjunctions, etc. whose chief use is to align words into patterns of common-sense, must be highly crystallized in usage and have minimal variability in the usage of arrangement; whereas the substantives and verbs must have a comparatively highly crystallized definiteness of meaning in reference to experiential data, and a latitude in arrangement. Were the members of Group 1 not to possess a high stability in meaning, the firm usage of the articulatory words would be useless. Were the members of Group 1 not to possess latitude in arrangement, but to have all their combinations completely and firmly crystallized as those of, say, conjunctions, there would be only negligible scope for individualistic expression.

Hence we are not surprised to discover that substantives and main verbs predominantly, and adjectives and adverbs to a considerable extent, loom forth conspicuously in sentences and seem to be that for which the sentence exists, while the *articulatory words* (i.e. those in Group 2) appear merely to modify and orient the others.

Yet language without both the highly stable in articulated meaning and the highly crystallized in usage is unthinkable. Though we assume that in the nominal phrase, *the white house*, the word *house* is the most important element because it is modified and qualified by *white*, and *white house* by *the*, yet one cannot prove logically or empirically that the reverse is not the case.

2. SUBSTANTIVES, MAIN VERBS, ADJECTIVES, AND ADVERBS, AND THE POINT OF VIEW

Since the reference of substantives, main verbs, adjectives, and adverbs, on the whole, is to the accumulated data of perceptual experience, it is not difficult to imagine that the individual words of these categories are primarily indebted to the nature of their respective referents (i.e. that to which they refer) for their membership in one part of speech rather than in another. It is so obvious that we have words for (a) *things* (b) *in change* (c) *with qualifications* because we perceive very generally (a) *things* (b) *in change* (c) *with qualifications* that we are startled to learn that not all languages make, say, noun-like and verb-like distinctions. Yet whether a given phenomenon is to be viewed primarily as a *thing* (described by substantive) or but *the change* in the thing (described by a verb), or as the *qualification* either of a thing or of a change (described by adjective or adverb) depends upon the point of view.

To embark momentarily into general terms: the entire universe, as far as man can perceive it even with his most sensitive apparatus, is in a condition of constant change, either in location or direction, or in speed, or in the organization of its parts. In many phenomena the thing itself seems far more important than the change it is undergoing or the manner or the place of the change, or its relationship to other phenomena; hence its name is substantive: we see

Mont Blanc primarily as a thing despite the speed with which it is passing through space, and the constant erosion which is taking place. In yet other phenomena we see primarily the change, hence the existence of verbs: *to fly*, *to jump*. In still others we see predominantly qualifying factors which relate the phenomena to other phenomena, hence the existence of adjectives and adverbs: *white*, *high*, *slowly*, *East*. Presumably all these factors are present in any phenomenon, and one is as much a primary property of the phenomenon as another, though one factor may stand out in the data of perceptual experience as more significant than another. To designate a phenomenon with a noun means that its features of change and the type of its change seem of secondary importance; so to, *mutatis mutandis* in using a verb, or adjective, or adverb as designation. The use of one rather than another does not imply that the other attributes are lacking in the phenomenon, or in our total apperception of the phenomenon, but rather that in the immediate situation in which designation occurs our selection is prejudiced by our point of view. Hence it is not surprising that the isolated word *swimming* may strike one auditor as a verb ('he is swimming'), another as an adjective ('a swimming fish') and a third as a substantive ('swimming is fun'). So closely associated are the nominal, verbal, and qualifying attributes of a phenomenon in many instances that many languages, such as Sanskrit, have formal suffixes for changing a nominal expression into a verbal or adjectival expression, and *vice versa*; other languages exist satisfactorily without specifying whether a given word is adjective or verb. The latter type of languages in saying what would amount in English to 'oneness houseness burnness downness yesterdayness' conveys the thought quite as well as our 'a house burned down yesterday.' By the sheer force of pre-established sentence-patterns, a language seems able to exist without formal parts of speech, and these sentence-patterns may be nothing more than habitual methods of arranging words in reference to one another without the help of any formal inflectional affixes — the completely *positional* (or analytic) language. Though parts of speech are not essential to sentence-structure, their existence reflects peculiarities of sentence-structure in which they have their origin.

The concept of parts of speech is helpful to analysis by shedding light on potential uses of words in sentence-structure, and parts of speech are convenient labels in discussing sentence-phenomena. By first studying sentence-patterns of languages such as English and German, where parts of speech occur, we are enabled in turn to comprehend the dynamics of sentence-patterns in which categories of parts of speech are unknown. Because certain parts of speech, such as nouns and verbs, loom up conspicuously as sentence-units in English, and other parts of speech show the relationship between these, it is more expedient to approach the study of sentences from this angle.

3. THE SENTENCE-NUCLEUS: SUBJECT AND VERB (VERB-PREDICATE) *

Before continuing further, let us ask what a sentence is. We know, first, that a sentence is a speech-element, or a speech-unit, and we are told rather ambiguously, second, that it is a syntactical unit. Yet neither of these pieces of information is as clear or as helpful as one, a rule rather than a definition, which is familiar from school-boy days: 'Every English sentence must have a subject and a verb, expressed or implied.' This rule, though incomplete, is adequate for our purposes; let us, then, inquire into the evidence on which the rule is based, and the corollaries of the rule.

If we were to record 100,000 sentences from the stream of

* In this section of the discussion the term *verb* will for the sake of simplicity designate both the verb and predicate of a sentence. To remind the reader of this usage of the term it will be followed by (*verb-predicate*).

everyday speech, we should find upon examination that a subject or a verb would occur in more sentences than any other syntactical element, and that a subject and verb would appear as a combination more often than any two other syntactical elements. Even though many sentences would consist of a single word, a decided majority of the sentences would consist of more than one word, and of these a decided majority again would in turn contain a subject and a verb. Without analyzing 100,000 sentences one can easily establish to his satisfaction the truth of the proposition from a half-hour's personal observation of spoken language.

Out of the hypothetical 100,000 sentences let us make a special group of those which have both a subject and a verb expressed; there will be an enormous number of them both actually and proportionately; we shall call them *complete sentences*. From this group of complete sentences, let us select those which consist only of a simple subject and a simple verb, such as 'I do,' 'she can't,' 'he will,' 'I did,' 'John fell'; we shall call them *simple subject-verb sentences*. One cannot determine *a priori* what actual proportion of spoken English consists of simple subject-verb sentences; they probably do not represent a majority, yet their occurrence is by no means sporadic.

It would, of course, be most convenient for Dynamic Philology if all sentences were simple subject-verb sentences, like 'he did.' Indeed this thought suggests the curious question of why not all sentences are simple-subject verb sentences. Since the type is familiar, and the sentences are both short and convenient, the reason we do not use them exclusively is possibly because of one of the reasons suggested in Part I above: either because the resultant meaning would be too little articulated, or the effect too dull. The complete answer to this question will shed light on our use of the more complex sentences.

It by no means follows that a simple subject and verb cannot represent a highly complex and minutely articulated thought. A simple subject consisting of a single word may contain the most elaborate concept thinkable; so, too, a verb. An example of the complexity of meaning of a simple word is offered by a few obvious sentences: 'It must have been funny when John dropped the eggs,' 'It was.' In the sentence 'it was,' the subject *it* does sole but adequate duty for the several concepts contained in the words 'when John dropped the eggs.' In the conversation, 'Why didn't you go to the store and buy the things I wanted,' 'I did,' the verb *did* performs similar duty for 'go to the store and buy the things I wanted.' That *it* and *did* make specific sense only because of the elaboration of the context in the preceding sentences does not alter the fact that *it* and *did* are simple subject and verb and that each represents a highly articulated concept. Hence, in fact, no concept can be found so highly articulated in meaning that it cannot be sufficiently represented by a simple word.

Even aside from considerations of context, many simple words represent highly articulated concepts; not only such words as *thermodynamics*, or *evolution*, but such familiar words as *mother* or *father*. The word *mother*, for example, represents so many concepts that one might spend months naming them all and explaining their connections; yet the bulk of this entire elaboration of meaning is conveyed to the auditor by the single word *mother*. It is no exaggeration to say that every word represents an elaborate complex of meaning.

Nevertheless, not every elaborate complex of meaning has a word exclusively its own. Though nothing prevents our having in English a single word whose denotation is 'a person's uncle's second wife's tenth child,' the fact remains that no such word exists. The reason for our lack of a word for this concept is clearly because the concept does not possess a sufficiently high relative frequency of occurrence. Had its relative frequency been sufficiently high, we should have inherited and preserved a single word for 'a person's uncle's

second wife's tenth child.' Even now, if the relative frequency of this concept were to be increased gradually, first
'hyphens' would begin to appear, as in *brother-in-law*, the
configuration would be run together as it became more
crystallized, and finally, with the attainment of high relative
frequency, its length would be truncated, or a shorter word
substituted for it. And as we have argued of 'a person's
uncle's second wife's tenth child,' which is presumably a
noun, we can argue also of a verb. 'To run down the street
striking a piece of coal along with the foot' is a verbal idea
(though in a sentence we should refer to it probably as a
verb and predicate). If this activity became frequent in
life, we should very likely have a single word for it, as in
fact we have the verb *to kick* meaning 'to strike with the
foot.'

The general phenomenon which we have been discussing
is this: a subject (or any other syntactical unit) is a configuration which may express a degree of articulatedness of
meaning which is high or low, and the degree of articulatedness of meaning will be reflected by a corresponding degree
of crystallization of the configuration, which is equatable
with relative frequency of occurrence. When the configurational arrangement of a subject is sufficiently highly crystallized to be a word, that word is a noun or pronoun; when less
crystallized it is a phrase or a clause. And correspondingly
with the other syntactical units. As for our native feelings
about the complexity of a concept represented by a word,
we are biassed by the word's relative frequency of usage.
'A person's uncle's, etc.' seems more articulated than *brother-
in-law*, and *brother-in-law* more so than *mother*, because this
is the increasing order of their respective frequencies. If the
former had the frequency of the latter, it would be equally
familiar, like *electricity* or *light*. An adequate idea of any one
single thing necessitates theoretically a complete comprehension of everything in the universe; the entire articulatedness
of the meaning of a concept behind every meaningful con-

figuration, that is, its complete relationship in reference to everything else, is, then, theoretically constant.

Now, if we disregard differences in the degree of crystallization of the various configurations, we are justified in saying that every complete sentence in English is a simple $A\ B$ sentence. An example of an $A\ B$ sentence with a low degree of crystallization is: (*a person's uncle's second wife's tenth child*) (*ran down the street striking a piece of coal along with his foot*) $= A\ B$; the same concepts in a higher degree of crystallization of the respective configurations is (he) (did) $= A_t\ B_t$. The difference between $A\ B$ and $A_t\ B_t$ is one of the degree of crystallization (or of articulation) of the configurations of subject and verb (verb-predicate).

But why cannot this argument which establishes the existence of A and B as sole sentence units be extended further? Why as many as two elements? In the sentences 'His house burned down,' 'It was awful,' we observe that *it* really represents the articulation of the entire preceding sentence, and not just the subject or verb. Instead of saying that all sentences are $A\ B$ in English, why can we not simply refer to each sentence as X, saying that X differs from a corresponding X_t in the degree of crystallization (or articulation) of the configuration? We can and we do. X would then stand for the entire sentence which we feel is a unit of language, and which we term sentence; A and B are felt to be units of the sentence which we term subject and verb (verb-predicate). One essential difference between X on the one hand and A or B on the other is a difference in the degree of crystallization; but a difference more significant for our present purpose is that of the extent to which they are dependent.

A sentence, X, is a more independent and self-sufficient unit than either its subject, A, or its verb (verb-predicate), B. The reason for this difference in degree of independence (see pages 191 ff.) is that the variety of different sentences is, by the law of permutations, potentially greater than that of its components, with the result that the average relative frequency of occurrence or degree of repetitiveness is lower; we must, furthermore, remember that independence or self-sufficiency in linguistic expression (pages 191 ff.) seems to stand in an inverse (not necessarily proportionate) relationship with relative frequency. It is this difference in independence which permits the school-teacher to tell his pupils that if a sentence does not actually contain either subject or verb, or both, we must supply them from what is implied. The fact that A or B are each not as self-sufficient as X leads one to suspect, when A or B or a part thereof is tendered in lieu of X, that something is lacking or implied. Just as we should infer, rightly or wrongly, that something were missing if we picked up a fragment of ancient bronze and discovered a single letter, or a single word, so too, we infer from, say, a single subject or a single verb that something is absent. We infer this, because in our experience these speech-elements usually do not stand alone.

Nor is a sentence, in turn, really a completely self-sufficient unit in the stream of speech, for generally it does not stand completely alone. Probably there is no one self-sufficient unit of speech which includes all others as components: for what we perceive, like what we express, reflects change or rearrangement either in the environment of the speaker or in his relationship to it; and change or rearrangement seems impossible except in a medium which knows plurality. Surely experience tells us that the assumption of a minimum of duality is inherent in communication.

Like a phoneme, morpheme, or word, a sentence is a unit; it possesses, expressed or implied, a subject and verb (verb-predicate),* $A B$, which may be viewed, then, as the nucleus of a sentence.

---

* Henceforth we shall refer to A as the subject and to B as the verb, and shall not consider *verb* and *verb-predicate* and *predicate* as in anyway synonymous, since a study of the arrangements of component elements of the subject and of the verb call for a more detailed nomenclature. This nomenclature we shall borrow from

4. SYNTACTICAL ARRANGEMENT
WITHIN THE SENTENCE

The question now arises as to the position of *A* and *B*, both in respect to other syntactical units and to each other. Instead of asking whether the subject should precede the verb or *vice versa*, let us for the present assume that either subject-verb or verb-subject is normal order in a given language and that *A* represents the subject or the verb and *B* the other. The German sentences, '*ich* (subject) *gehe* (verb) *morgen*' and '*morgen gehe* (verb) *ich* (subject),' ('I am going tomorrow' and 'tomorrow am I going'), are examples from a language in which either *A* or *B* may precede.

Now, there is one thing which can be positively asserted about the arrangement of *A* and *B* in respect to each other: regardless of the question of precedence, they may be juxtaposed. No matter what potential arrangements may exist, juxtaposition will be among them because of the abundance of simple two-word *A B* sentences, such as *he did*, in which no arrangement other than juxtaposition is possible. This observation is significant in the matter of syntax. The frequent juxtaposition of *A* and *B* tends to crystallize the two in pattern; and with this crystallization, intensity tends to diminish (see pages 203 ff.). Hence, there is temptation to insert an element between *A* and *B*, because the breach in even a so slightly crystallized configurational pattern will add intensity not only to the inserted element, but to *A* and *B* as well: the configuration will have been rearranged (pages 207 ff.).

the grammar school teacher. Thus in the sentence 'the boy ran down the street,' *the boy* is the subject, *ran* is the verb, and *down the street* is the predicate. The segregation of verb (verb-predicate) into verb and predicate is feasible for practical purposes, even though perhaps philosophically the elements of a sentence not a part of the subject may be considered as a predicate of the subject.

The degree of crystallization of A B is, nevertheless, comparatively slight. Accordingly in infixing an element between A and B care must be taken not to break the pattern of the A B nucleus. The inserted word, Z, must not be too similar to B lest the sentence close at A Z, instead of A Z B, thereby annihilating the nucleus. The danger of breaking the pattern likewise prevents placing too many words between A and B. If, on the one hand, a constant use of simple two-word sentences may become flat and lacking in intensity, a sentence which is too long may, on the other hand, be incomprehensible. The maximum length of a sentence is, as we know, not absolute in number of its words. Both length and comprehensibility depend solely upon the nature of A and B and what is added, as an analysis of the sentence-structure of any language — preferably a foreign language for the sake of objectivity — will show.

German is like English in respect to having the subject-verb relationship (A B) in normal sentence order; furthermore like English, its verb may consist of two or even more elements. Where English says 'I shall go,' German says '*ich werde gehen.*' To represent 'I shall go' or '*ich werde gehen*' symbolically, we may use A b^1 b^2 instead of a simple A B. This A b^1 b^2 pattern — (subject) + (auxiliary + main verb) — has some degree of crystallization of arrangement because of its high relative frequency, being the basic pattern not only of the future active indicative and subjunctive, but also of the perfect and pluperfect active indicative and subjunctive, all tenses of significant frequency. Hence it is understandable from what has gone before, that in adding attributive and predicative words to a sentence of this pattern-type there may be a temptation to break the crystallized order of A b^1 b^2 in the interest of the intensity which will result. Indeed this has been done so often in German that the procedure has become regularly established as a 'grammatical rule.' German grammarians say that the infinitive or past participle (that is, b^2) should come at the end of its independent clause; we have said that the predicate is inserted between b^1 and b^2, which amounts to the same thing.

Since the inserted predicate in an independent clause may and frequently does consist of two or more words, the question now arises as to which should come first in the sequence. To this the grammarians answer, 'the least important word comes first,' forgetting that without a precisely formulated law of linguistic value such a rule, however true, is both meaningless to beginning students, and useless to dynamic philologists.

What one places immediately after b^1 in splitting the coalescing sequence A b^1 b^2 should be that which is least likely to annihilate or prematurely close the basic nucleus. One strives, therefore, to avoid placing, first of all, a word like b^2, — i.e., an infinitive or a past participle. This does not imply that a word like b^2, or like A for that matter, if placed after b^1 would unavoidably and irreparably destroy the sequence; yet it does imply that such a word may lead to a moment of indecision in the mind of the auditor, which will divert his main attention to a word rather than to the sentence. To avoid the risk of even a moment's indecision, words are placed immediately after b^1 which are least independent or self-sufficient or meaningful in their own right. Such words, being also of low intensity, are less likely to break the basic pattern by attracting the auditor's particular attention to them.

The reader may feel that we are scarcely more definite, when, instead of saying that the least important element comes first in the predicate, we say that the least independent element comes first. But we are really far more definite. We know that the least independent elements are also the relatively more frequent (pages 191 ff.); and by the law of abbreviation, that the more frequent are the shorter. It therefore follows that the shortest elements are to follow b^1. Automatically come the pronominal objects, the noun objects or the adverbs, and then the phrases. One must be sparing of infinitive phrases and dependent clauses, inasmuch as the former often contain in the infinitive a word like b^2, while the latter may have a sequence much like $A \, b^1 \, b^2$; either may derange the basic nucleus.

Let us now turn to the position of the adverbs, mindful of the fact that this, like all other questions of syntax, demands especially delicate handling; for where arrangement has such a low degree of crystallization one may at most speak only of tendencies. Yet there is a decided tendency in German sentences for adverbs of time to precede adverbs of place. If our theory be true, the reason for this tendency is that adverbs of time are on the average less independent and therefore shorter than adverbs of place. Of course, many place-adverbs (e.g., *da, hier*) are equally short as, in fact shorter than, many adverbs of time (e.g., *übermorgen, vorgestern*). Yet in the question of usual position within the basic syntactical pattern, it is question rather of the average than the actual length and comparative variety. Although there are unfortunately no definite statistical data on the subject, one's impression suggests that in the average German sentence, the average adverb of time, be it word or phrase, is shorter than the average adverb or adverbial phrase of place. In the average sentence we indicate place with greater precision than time; * hence, place, being usually more articulated, and therefore offering a greater possibility of variety and hence lower average relative frequency tends to be longer. When place does precede time, as it sometimes does, the result is admittedly a slight emphasis, an emphasis which we expect from a breach in slightly crystallized arrangement. It need scarcely be pointed out that in putting other adverbs between time and place, one is but splitting for emphasis the usual and very frequent adverb time-place pattern. This is, I think, the origin of the most salient features of the pattern

---

* Rarely do we indicate time as precisely as *Thursday morning at 10:30, March 27, 1788, A.D.*; yet such a degree of articulation is by no means unusual for designations of place.

of German independent sentence-order. It would be no task to extend the investigation to other little sub-patterns within the sentence nucleus $A\ b^1\ b^2$. *The apple* equals $M\ N$; between these we tuck *big round juicy* ($X\ Y\ Z$), getting *the big round juicy apple* ($M\ X\ Y\ Z\ N$). So, too, with prepositional phrases *at home, at (my) home, at (my new) home.* This tendency to put an element between two crystallized phrasal elements for the sake of intensity is most easily illustrated by the English split infinitive; instead of *really to know* or *to know really*, English speakers often say *to really know.* The sense of the three arrangements is practically identical, the difference residing largely in the intensity resulting from the unusual order in the third.

In German sentence structure, perhaps the most beautiful example of intensity arising from a breach in usual arrangement is the phenomenon called *inversion.* The process of inversion is simple. One puts any organic element of the predicate at the beginning of the independent clause, and 'inverts' the subject-verb order. Applying this, for illustration, to the English sentence, 'I saw the circus yesterday,' we may have 'the circus saw I yesterday' or 'yesterday saw I the circus.' In view of our previous general discussion of intensity and its relation to breach in normal arrangement, it is not difficult to believe the German grammarians when they say that inversion yields emphasis. But why is such a procedure as inversion necessary for emphasis? Why not simply break the order in the predicate? The answer to these questions will be significant for many reasons.

Let us represent the grammatical predicate of a sample sentence by $V\ W\ X\ Y\ Z$, under which we understand objects or predicate adjectives and adverbial adjuncts. A German sentence containing this predicate may be represented by $A\text{-}b^1 - (V\ W\ X\ Y\ Z) - b^2$. Although the original impulse toward this arrangement, if we may accept the general argument thus far advanced, was the desire for high intensity with adequate articulation, yet the very repetition of this pattern has slowly defeated the original purpose. Since millions upon millions of sentences have occurred with an arrangement similar to $A\text{-}b^1 - (V\,W\,X\,Y\,Z) - b^2$, it is not surprising that the pattern has become crystallized and dull. So, too, every arrangement or permutation possible of $V\,W\,X\,Y\,Z$ has occurred in millions of sentences, likewise originally for emphasis. Possibilities of vivid intensity in the predicate, without resorting to unusual words or words in an unusual sense, or an unusual amplitude or softness of voice, are very slight. Hence, it is understandable that to make a common word emphatic, an unusual arrangement is imperative, and inversion is an unusual arrangement. The intensity of inversion does not arise from the fact that it takes place at the beginning of a sentence; a similar effect may be obtained at the end provided the arrangement is unusual. For example, 'er hat seine Frau gesehen *mit einem anderen Mann*'; the normal order for this sentence would be 'er hat seine Frau *mit einem anderen Mann* gesehen' (he saw his wife *with another man*).

This last example, in which b^2 does not occur at the end, leads us to an important observation which is not less important because it also answers the question why do not all other languages follow the $A\ b^1\ (V\,W\,X\,Y\,Z)\ b^2$ pattern of German and put the verb at the end. And this deduction is: sentence-order is always changing, even if only slowly, and not all languages are of necessity simultaneously in the same stage of development. We have seen why part of the verb occurs at the end for the sake of emphasis; we have seen how the resultant pattern may become crystallized with concomitant loss of intensity; we understand the urge to break this order with the result that the subject and verb are no longer at the extremities. Nor are we surprised to learn that in present-day German not only is the verb b^2 beginning to gravitate back toward b^1, but inversion, which has by now been plentifully indulged in, has also lost its original intensity and has really become almost an alternative form of normal order.

There are, of course, many, many other grammatical rules of German syntax which merit investigation to test the validity of our working hypothesis, and German is but one of many languages in which the hypothesis, if true, should be demonstrable. When it was pointed out that a sentence consists of a nucleus *A B*, in whose arrangement, crystallization, and rearrangement with subsidiary elements lies the development of language, it might have been suggested that all other syntactical elements are but nuclei in the development of which the identical factors are involved, whether the unit be a phrase or clause. Of course we have but assumed that the basic simple nuclei, such as *he went* (subject, verb) or *the dog* (article, noun) or *at home* (preposition, object) are statistically and significantly more frequent than the elaborations thereof, and therefore have been considered the nuclei. Whether (as we suspect from our general experience), actual statistical evidence will support our beliefs, can be determined only by statistical analyses of cross sections of language at different periods of its development. The tenor and the methods of application of the hypothesis have been explained and exemplified; we must now wait for statistical data.

In the meantime let us view another aspect of sentence-dynamics, representing the same linguistic phenomena though approached on a different tack.

5. INFLECTIONAL ARRANGEMENT

The foregoing discussion of syntax applies primarily to positional or weakly inflected languages. Although a highly inflected language must also arrange its words in the stream of speech, its use of syntactical devices may be insignificant when compared to the uses made of its abundant resources of inflection. Without some knowledge of inflection we often cannot understand the peculiar syntactical arrangements of primarily positional, that is, of very mildly inflected languages. For example, the reason why German may always put b^2 at the end of the independent clause while English may not, is probably because b^2 in German, whether it be past participle or infinitive, is always earmarked by an inflectional ending that identifies it as b^2 and nothing else. Not so English. Verbs and nouns in English often have identical forms (e.g. *sleep*, *walk*, *run* are nouns or infinitives); past participles are generally marked in English, but not always (e.g. *run*, *come*). Anything potentially so ambiguous as b^2 in English cannot stray too far from b^1 without leading to confusion: hence, a German sentence may be more involved than an English sentence before becoming incomprehensible. The more highly inflected a language is, the greater is the liberty which it may take in positional arrangement. The presence or absence of inflectional devices, and the degree of their usage, modifies the scope of syntactical arrangement.

The chief difference between a primarily inflectional and a primarily positional language is that the former uses inflectional affixes to represent numbers, cases, tenses, persons, moods, voices, etc., whereas the latter frequently uses words — e.g. *he*, *she*, *to*, etc. — words which are to a considerable extent the *articulatory words* discussed on page 229.

If we examine more closely one of these articulatory words, such as *he* or *it* we find, as stated previously, that it has little or no independent meaning of its own. In defining a pronoun the Concise Oxford Dictionary says: 'a word used instead of (proper or other) noun to designate person or thing already mentioned or known from context, or forming the subject of inquiry (used also to include pronominal and other adjectives).' In short, nothing is said in this definition about meaning or intensity, which are derived in each occurrence from that of the referent for which it generally stands. When *it,* for example, occurs impersonally as an expletive, as in *it rains,* without antecedent, the meaning and intensity are in the phrase and not in the *it* whose presence is apparently justified only by the imperative of sentence-pattern that every sentence must have a subject. The pronoun's lack of both independent meaning and independent intensity is presumably explicable from its high relative frequency which in turn accounts for the high degree of crystallization or determinacy of its use, that is, its general lack of independence in usage.

Now it is from these articulatory words that inflectional affixes are supposed to develop; hence the articulatory words represent potential inflections. The reason for this goes back to their general dependence in sentence-structure upon context for sense, a dependence which we sense once the remainder of the configuration is removed in which they are firmly crystallized.

To illustrate the comparative degrees of dependence of words in sentence-structure, let us perform an imaginary experiment. We may take as material a vast number of English sentences, just as they are spoken, say a million of them. Figuratively speaking we shall now dash these sentences on the floor with such force that they will break, and pieces of them will scatter. Of course some of the words, being more crystallized in arrangement than others, will cohere. Definite and indefinite articles will adhere to their nouns, auxiliaries to their verbs, prepositions to following objects. This is but a graphic picture of what grammarians do in reality. And yet, since we understand things better if we draw a picture of them, let us continue with our picture since the absurdities are safely obvious.

Now, among the shattered bits let us search out *he,* and the other personal pronouns of like case, *she, it, we, you, they,* and see if anything has adhered to them. Not only do we find *I'll, you'll, he'll, she'll, we'll, they'll,* but we find *I'm, you're, he's, she's, it's, we're, they're,* and *I'd, you'd, he'd, she'd, we'd, they'd, I've, you've* — for, after all, the million sentences were colloquial. Very likely there are many other combinations, not only of the pronouns but of other words. We might find *United* adhering to *States, so forth* dangling to *and*, but for our immediate purposes the pronouns suffice.

If we were to segregate the pronouns into individual piles, we should not be surprised to find enormous heaps of *I'd* and *you're* and all the others. For these coalescing forms are in very frequent use. If we were to tabulate these piles according to their final elements, we should have

I'll	*we'll*	*I'd*	*we'd*
you'll	*you'll*	*you'd*	*you'd*
he'll, etc.	*they'll*	*he'd*, etc.	*they'd*
I'm	*we're*	*I've*	*we've*
you're	*you're*	*you've*	*you've*
he's	*they're*	*he's*	*they've*

In one sense the above tabulation is not altogether fair, since from the broken sentences alone we could not distinguish between the singulars and plurals of *you'll*, nor be sure, from the sheer forms, whether *he's* represented *he has* or *he is*. The procedure, however, is sufficiently clear for illustration.

The point to observe is that, no matter how vigorously the million sentences are shattered, the above forms will remain intact until the sentences are broken, not into words, but into their component morphemes. *I'll* is one word, even though its degree of crystallization is not so great that we cannot sense the *I will* or *I shall* behind the contraction. However, the only reason we sense the *I will* in *I'll* is because *I will* and *will I* likewise occur in the stream of speech. Without historical study one could no more guess that *I'll* arose from *I will* or *I shall*, than that *bus* was once *omnibus*.

This high degree of crystallization is the beginning of inflection. If we were to dash the million sentences less violently, we should find even more combinations. Not only *he'd*, but *he'd come*, and even *he'd'a come* (he would have come). Numerous other frequent combinations could be segregated and put into piles, more numerous though smaller piles, e.g. *he'll come*, *he'll give*, *he'll buy*, and the like. For, after all the difference between English *he'll give* and Latin *dabit* 'he'll give,' (or 'she'll give' or 'it'll give') is mostly a difference in degree of crystallization; and the difference between English *he* and Latin *t* of *dabit* is chiefly one in the degree of independence. Latin feels that *dabit* is a single word, even though consisting of approximately three morphological units; we, on the other hand, are beginning to feel that *he'll come* is gradually becoming two words, in spite of the transparency of the basic units.

Now the growing degree of crystallization or dependence in arrangement which arises in a purely positional language can slowly but steadily convert the positional language into an inflectional language. The same relative frequency of usage which makes a word more crystallized in arrangement is the same relative frequency which shortens its actual form (page 38), and which so far saps the preciseness of its meaning (page 200) that the word gradually becomes little more than a tag to another word.

But then the question arises whether in *I'd come*, the *I* or the *'d*, or the *come* is the tag; if there are two tags, which two? So, likewise in Latin *dabit*; of *da* or *bi* or *t*, which is the tag, or tags? The answer that linguists give to this is that *t* is a tag to *bi*, and *bi* + *t* is a tag to *da*, and yet this proposition cannot be established empirically without taking into consideration differences in relative frequency of the components. Whatever may be said about the comparative definiteness or distinctness or preciseness of the meanings of *da* and *bi* and *t*, or whatever may be said about the comparative degree of their dependence, or the degree of their coalescence, all this ultimately finds itself standing upon the primary considerations of the relative frequency of occurrence and decreasing variety. Other gates seem to be closed to approach. *With*

*ever-increasing relative frequency, the word becomes the mor-
pheme, which with passing time becomes a phoneme, and finally
the component part of a phoneme, until it disappears:* such appears to be the final statement of all linguistic change.[1]

Now the inflection of any language is much a matter of
degree; not only do we speak of one language as more highly
inflected than another, tacitly assuming thereby some norm,
but we find even in such a low inflected language as English,
which we roughly term positional, unmistakable traces of a
tendency toward inflections (see pages 259 ff.). Inflection, or
tagging, is but one of the two devices for converting the
numerous arrangements of our perceptions into the pure
temporal stream of speech; the other is positional arrangement. In Latin, for instance, one can express 'the dear little
girl is in Rome' by 'puell*a* car*a* parv*a* Romae est,' where the
final *a* indicates that the first three words go together. Mere
juxtaposition would suffice, but the presence of the tag admits of separation, such as 'puell*a* filia fratris mei parv*a* domi
Romae car*a* est.' If we translate this Latin sentence into
English, word for word, disregarding inflectional endings,
the sentence is completely unintelligible: 'girl daughter of
brother of my small at home at Rome dear is.' Incidentally
the fact that every word may not need a tag in Latin (mulier
car*a* parv*a*) or that the tags are not identical (puell*a* car*a*
fort*is*) does not alter the basic fact that these tags partially
take the place of syntax. Nor does the original meaning of
the tags matter, nor does it matter whether they are added
at the beginning (prefix), middle (infix), or end (suffix) of a
word. An inflectional tag represents merely an enormously
frequently used class or category, whatever or wherever it
may be, and nothing more. These inflectional affixes, or
categorizing tags, are made of precisely the same stuff as the
roots of words. Whatever phonetic elements may constitute
the roots of a language, may also constitute the inflectional
affixes of the same language. There is no special category of
phonetic elements reserved exclusively for affixes.

The Latin root *da* 'to give' and the English word *give* each enter into a certain number of primary combinations in its own language. The occurrences of the verb *give* in all its principal parts and forms can be divided roughly into its persons, numbers, tenses, moods, etc. For each of these there is a sign, although one sign may do double duty. *They* is a sign which marks both the plural and the third person; *will* marks the future. *Da* and *bu* and *nt* (in *dabunt* 'they will give') do precisely the same thing, with one difference. When one wishes to designate the third plural more precisely in English, and says for example *the men* instead of *they*, one normally omits *they*, placing *the men* in its stead. But in Latin *nt* is not omitted: *viri dabunt* 'the men they will give.' The *nt* is too crystallized to be omitted. If we remember the general tendency of speech toward vividness (pages 212 ff.) and also the frequent demands of communication for greater precision of meaning (pages 212 ff.), we can understand why the subject frequently demands greater articulation and vividness; the same desire for economy, which maintains *nt* for its brevity and its frequent convenience, is the same desire for economy which tends in the long run to truncate *nt*, (that is, to delete *nt*) as *nt* becomes increasingly redundant because of more precise and vivid subjects elsewhere.

The inflectional morpheme differs therefore from the word primarily in the degree of agglutination, or coalescence, that is, the degree of its crystallization in arrangement. In saying this, we only emphasize the fact that a morpheme is less supple or flexible. If, as is sometimes said, a positional language is of greater value because of its greater opportunity for precise statement, an inflected language is nevertheless more economical, compressing more into one word. Yet both a positional language and an inflected language can and each do express equally adequately the speaker's entire consciousness, to his own satisfaction.

6. DIFFERENCES IN THE DEGREE OF INFLECTION

We have previously said that languages differ in the degree to which they make use of resources of inflection. If we take German, Latin, and Sanskrit, three inflected languages, we find that Latin is more inflected than German, and Sanskrit more so than Latin. At least such is the linguists' feelings about the matter. But wherein, after all, does this difference lie? The difference lies manifestly only in the scope, or the extent of permeation of inflection. A language which inflects both nouns and verbs is more inflected than a language which inflects only nouns, provided that the latter does not inflect its nouns so meticulously as to offset the lack of verbal inflection. So, too, a language which inflects all nouns is more inflected than one which inflects only nouns referring to animate objects, if all other things remain equal. A language whose nouns distinguish eight cases — all other things being equal — is likely to be more highly inflected than one which distinguishes only three distinct cases for a noun. We can easily sense differences in the degree of inflection which exist among languages. Is it also possible to measure with mathematical precision the actual degree of inflection, of any given language? It is.

If we take a million words of connected speech of a highly inflected language, we can say with certainty that there will be a greater variety among inflected words than among the (uninflected) roots of these same words. If we take the inflected word as a unit, for example, Latin *bonus*, *bona*, *bonum*, or English *small*, *smaller*, *smallest*, there are three words, in each case, which, for the sake of argument, occur but once. If we, however, consider the root as the unit, *bon-* in Latin, or *small-* in English, we have in each case only one root, which however occurs three times. It follows, therefore, that the greater the number of different inflectional affixes a language possesses, the smaller proportionately will be the number of different roots occurring in the stream of speech compared to the number of the different words (which are really inflected roots) made up from these roots. To illustrate this point which sounds more abstruse than it really is, let us take English which is relatively low inflected and Latin which is relatively high. English *horse* and *mare* are two different words as are Latin *equus* 'horse' and *equa* 'mare'; the two English words have two different roots, the two Latin words have only one, *equ-*; similarly English *son* and *daughter* and Latin *fili-us* and *fili-a*, and a host of others. English *horse* and *mare* are immediate permutations of phonemes; Latin *equ-us* is first a permutation of morpheme *equ-* and morpheme *-us*, which in turn are permutations of the phonemes *e-q-u* and *u-s* respectively. In the less inflected language, English, *horse* is both a word (the *horse*) and also a morpheme (e.g. on *horseback*) if one will. But in the more highly inflected language, Latin, the word *equus* is composed of two morphemes, and is itself not a morpheme. In a certain sense, of course, the Latin *vir-orum* and the English *of the men* express the same concept, and there is little difference in sense between *dom-i* and *at home*. Indeed, the only real difference between *domi* and *at home* is a difference in the crystallization of the whole, and the predictability of the parts; *dom-* makes little sense alone, and one can more accurately predict the syllable following *dom-* than the syllable following *at* or preceding *home*. A purely positional (i.e. a completely non-inflected) language immediately permutes phonemes into words which, if one will, are simultaneously morphemes: a million words of connected discourse of a purely positional language might contain one million morphemes, one morpheme to a word. But not so an inflected language, which permutes phonemes into morphemes and morphemes into words. Many of the morphemes in a highly inflected language are nothing more than discriminating tags added to roots, like the *-us* of *equus*. In substance, the more highly inflected a language is, the greater use it makes of morphological tags and the less use it makes of a great variety of roots.

7. MEASURE OF THE DEGREE OF INFLECTION

The degree to which any language is inflected, that is, the extent to which it habitually makes use of morphological tags, is measurable with a comparatively high degree of accuracy. Illustration of the methods of measurement of the degree of inflection shed light on the nature of inflection itself.

If one takes samples of 50,000 connected words from the streams of speech of a purely positional language and of a highly inflected language, we have reason to suppose on the basis of the evidence of Chapter II that the frequency distribution of the words in each would follow the formula $ab^2 = k$ (the product of the square of the frequency of occurrence by the number of words possessing the occurrence is constant) for the less frequent words.

In the case of the purely positional language, all of whose words by definition represent permutations of phonemes immediately into words without intervening units, such as roots and affixes, the curve $ab^2 = k$ would also be the morphemic curve; for, the word in this language would be both a morpheme and a word, in the sense that the next larger unit above a phoneme is the word, in the purely positional language and not a morpheme as in inflectional tongues. But the formula $ab^2 = k$ would by no means represent the curve of distribution of occurrences of morphemes (prefixes, base-roots, suffixes, and endings) in the highly inflected language. Since the words of an inflected language represent for the most part permutations of morphemes, the number of different morphemes would be less than that of their permutations. Hence the number of different morphemes in the sample of 50,000 words of the inflected language would be less than that for the words represented by the formula $ab^2 = k$, and the average relative frequency of the morphemes would be greater. The morphemic curve would deviate from that for words; and the section of the curve representing morphemes of lowest frequency would have on the whole an exponent less than 2; that is, the line for morphemes will fall below that for words on a double logarithmic chart.

May we anticipate that the curve for morphemes will be *proportionately* less than that for words; that is, will the section of lower frequency in the morphemic curve appear as a straight line on a double logarithmic chart? We may expect a straight line *provided that the phenomenon of inflection of roots is an orderly process in the stream of speech and not haphazard.* And inflection is an orderly process. When inflection spares a root or a word in a language, as it sometimes does, it spares it consistently. So consistent is inflection at any given moment in any language, that the ancient Indian grammarian Panini was able to formulate the laws of inflection for Sanskrit into a manner or code which held with great precision for the language of his time.

Because, in the first place, the greater the degree of inflection the smaller the variety of morphemes and the greater their average relative frequency, and because, in the second place, the smaller the variety of morphemes (or the greater their average relative frequency) the smaller will be the power of b in the frequency distribution of morphemes in the range of lower frequency, it therefore follows: the degree of inflection of a language is measured by the difference between the exponent of b in the formula for the distribution of morphemes and 2 which is the exponent of b in the formula for word-distribution $(ab^2 = k)$. The smaller the exponent for the morpheme distribution, the larger will the difference be from 2, and the greater will the degree of inflection be of the language from which the sample has been measured.

To illustrate the major points of the preceding discussion

let us present actual data (page 257). Only two statistical investigations have yet been made which will be of service for our present purposes. One, by V. A. C. Henmon [1] represents an analysis of 400,000 words of connected French reduced to a dictionary basis (i.e. lexical units, disregarding inflectional endings such as signs for numbers, tenses, cases, etc.). In reducing connected words to their lexical units before tabulating, Henmon has provided a reasonably accurate * frequency list of French roots (i.e. morphemes of lowest relative frequency). It is inconsequential for our present purposes that Henmon did not include the relative frequencies of formal prefixes, suffixes, and endings since the high relative frequencies of these would place them above that portion of the curve which is of special interest to us. The other investigation is that of 20,000 syllables of modern Chinese, dialect Peiping, already discussed (pages 24 ff.) in another connection. For convenience I present a tabulation of the more important figures of these two investigations.

Let us now plot the data for each of these languages on a double logarithmic chart, representing their curve of distribution by a solid line. In addition let us place a broken line on the Peipingese chart to represent the curve (presented in the chart of Plate I) for the Peipingese words which these 20,000 syllables represent and which follow the formula $ab^2 = k$. On the French chart let us indicate with a broken line, in the absence of data, an ideal curve representing $ab^2 = k$, the presumable distribution of French words, so that we may more readily note the deviation of the curve for roots (solid line) from the probable one for words (broken line).

From the Chinese chart we see that Peipingese morphemes

---

* But not an absolutely accurate one, since some lexical units, e.g. *formidable*, *dangereux*, *épouvantable*, etc. are still felt to contain morphological units. The Henmon material is then presented as an illustration of the application of our method of measurement, and not for the purpose of definitely establishing in numerical terms the degree of inflection of present-day French.

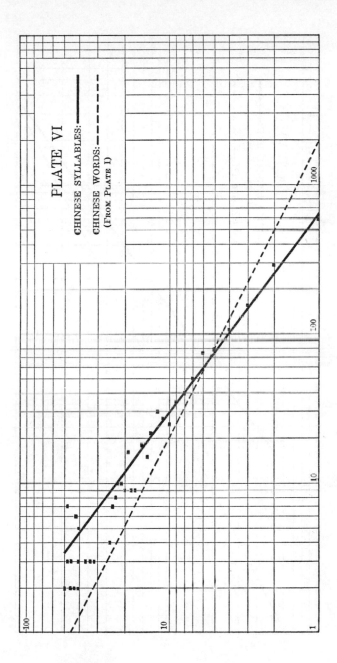

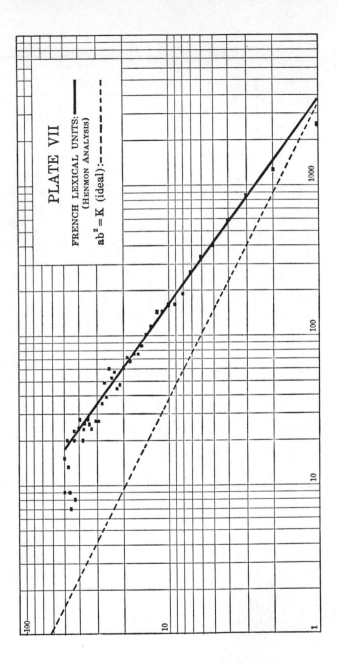

PLATE VII

FRENCH LEXICAL UNITS:
(HENMON ANALYSIS)

$ab^2 = K$ (ideal):

FRENCH		PEIPINGESE	
Number of Occurrences	Number of Lexical Units	Number of Occurrences	Number of Morphemes
1.............	2592*	1.............	563
2.............	1283*	2.............	284
3.............	856*	3.............	154
4.............	594*	4.............	103
5.............	409	5.............	78
6.............	335	6.............	73
7.............	253	7.............	49
8.............	196	8.............	40
9.............	175	9.............	36
10.............	164	10.............	25
11.............	141	11.............	27
12.............	141	12.............	30
13.............	118	13.............	23
14.............	103	14.............	15
15.............	85	15.............	17
16.............	73	16.............	14
17.............	73	17.............	9
18.............	67	18.............	9
19.............	70	19.............	15
20.............	62	20.............	9
21.............	45	21.............	19
22.............	44	22.............	10
23.............	49	23.............	8
24.............	46	24.............	7
25.............	50	25.............	4
26.............	37	26.............	3
27.............	44	27.............	7
28.............	37	28.............	3
29.............	34	29.............	4
30.............	26	30.............	8
31.............	26	31.............	6
32.............	23	32.............	4
33.............	25	33.............	5
34.............	18	34.............	3
35.............	26	35.............	3
36.............	25	36.............	2
37.............	23	37.............	5
38.............	26	38.............	3
39.............	20	39.............	5
40.............	23	40.............	5
41.............	22	41.............	2
42.............	8	42.............	2
43.............	20	43.............	6
44.............	20	44.............	3
45.............	7	45.............	2
46.............	20	46.............	3
47.............	9	47.............	7
48.............	13	48.............	2
49.............	15	49.............	0
50.............	9	50.............	1

* Professor Henmon was kind enough to supply me with the actual number of lexical units occurring 1-4 times in his investigation.

51-912   Total morphemes 19,860 (error of 140 in 20,000 syllables).

in the lower range of frequency follow the approximate formula $ab^{1.78} = k$.   Hence the degree of inflection of Peipingese is .22 on the scale of 2, (the difference between 1.78 of $ab^{1.78}$ and 2 of ab^2 for words).

The formula for French roots appears to be approximately $ab^{1.39} = k$.   Hence the degree of inflection of French, on the basis of our data, is $.61$ (see footnote, page 256).

It would be interesting to know how high the degree of inflection would be numerically in a truly highly inflected language such as Sanskrit, and to speculate upon what would happen in a language as the exponent of b for morphemes diminished more and more toward zero. Additional analyses of the frequency distributions of morphemes are therefore most desirable.

8. OTHER CHARACTERISTICS OF THE CURVES OF DISTRIBUTION

The sections of the curves representing the occurrences of the most frequent elements are presumably also significant. Highly positional languages are, as we know, rich in articulatory words, such as pronouns and prepositions of which they make extensive use; to a very considerable extent the role of articulatory words in positional languages is played by inflectional affixes in highly inflected languages. Hence one would expect that the upper portion of the curve representing the most frequent words of an inflected language would fall below the corresponding portion of the curve for words of a positional language. And indeed if we view the curves (Plate IV), for Plautine Latin (highly inflected) and for American newspaper English (slightly inflected), we find that the former bends below that of the latter in the upper range. Whether this bend in the Plautine Latin curve is to be viewed as solely reflecting a difference in the degree of inflection between the two languages appears to be well worth pondering. In any event study of the upper range of curves of this type will probably be quite rewarding.

A further interesting characteristic of the curve (referring to the graphs of Plates I, II, III) is the major bend between the range of words of lower frequency and those of higher frequency. As previously suggested,[1] somewhere within this general bend in the curve is a section where the formula $ab^2 = k$ would call for fractional words: that is, with k constant, the ever-increasing magnitude of b^2 would reduce a (the number of words having the occurrence of b) to a mixed number and then a fraction. Are there such things as fractional words? Is *the* in English but a fraction of a word? Whether or not *the*, for example, is a fractional word is scarcely worth argument.* The significant point is that *the* is closer in the degree of its dependency to a morpheme than to an infrequent word. The bend in the curve [2] then seems to suggest that words above the curve are becoming increasingly more morphemic, a suggestion which is substantiated by the evidence of linguistic development.

9. LINGUISTIC DEVELOPMENT

Because of the general tendencies (see pages 207 ff.) of language to become increasingly more crystallized, with variety lessening in favor of the increased relative frequency of patterns which have gained ascendency, the general trend of words in a language is, figuratively speaking, 'up the curve.' The articulatory words of a purely positional language will tend in time to become agglutinized to the words they modify, and through agglutinization become inflectional affixes, in a manner illustrated by English (page 247). As they become more firmly agglutinized, they become more formally inflections which modify the meaning of the word to which they are appended. The use of the affix is

* See discussion, page 43.

extended to other words * in order to modify their meaning in the same direction. The language thus becomes more and more inflected. As time passes and frequency of usage increases with a resultant high degree of crystallization, the affix becomes less a meaningful element, and more a conventional appendage; either the morpheme or its independent morphological sense is lost: the result is that the inflected word appears more as an immediate permutation of phonemes than as one of morphemes, and the language passes from a condition of being primarily inflectional back to the condition of one primarily positional. We may call this the grand cycle in linguistic development.

It does not appear that sufficient time has elapsed in the historical era for any one recorded language to have passed through a grand cycle of development, so gradual is the process of change. We may probably assume, however, that primeval man did not commence his speech-ways with a highly inflected tongue and that at least one grand cycle has already occurred. Moreover there seems some reason for belief that we are now completing a grand cycle in certain Indo-European dialects, such as English or French.

The parent Indo-European dialect, it would seem, was probably in the stage of development toward inflection a little more advanced than present-day English (as described in pages 247 ff.). There was a multiplicity of alternate inflectional forms in the earliest recorded dialects which leads one to suspect that a previous time, not too far remote, these were articulatory words with alternate forms † such as English *a*, *an*, *the* (*thǝ* in *the man*) and the (*thī* in *the apple*). Earliest Sanskrit at least in the separability of its prefixes, for example, reflects a trace of positional condition. By Classical Sanskrit, separability had passed and alternate morphological forms had been considerably levelled; a higher

---

* Commonly called suffix-clipping.

† And these supposed articulatory words were probably at first accented when suffixed to roots, even as the prefixes when first prefixed in Latin; see page 163f.

degree of crystallization had occurred, with the result that subsequently the employment of syntactical devices was negligible. In English and some of the Romanic tongues, notably French, the fundamental direction seems to be again turning towards that of inflection.

This consideration leads to an interesting question: is a language ever completely positional or completely inflectional? Is it not a more faithful description to say that, while language is ridding itself of inflection on the one side, it is sowing seeds for inflection on the other, with the result that by the time it has ceased to be inflectional it has already commenced to become inflectional again; by the time it has ceased to be positional it is already commencing to become positional again. To the adequate answering of this question which seems worthy of investigation, there are no statistical data.

I O. SUMMARY

A sentence is a nucleus of subject and verb which in turn are nuclei for subordinate nuclei of syntactical elements. For the preservation of equilibrium discussed in Part I (pages 212 ff.) the degree of articulatedness of these nuclei expands and contracts. First there is expansion and contraction in the articulatedness of individual sentences for the sake of the immediate auditor's comprehension. Next there are shifts in the arrangement of components within the larger nuclei, which take place more slowly and result in changes in grammatical rules. And finally there are changes from positional arrangement to inflectional arrangement and back, which progress at a very low rate of speed. The motivating force behind all these changes is, as far as one can perceive, the desire on the one hand to be comprehensible and the desire on the other to be vivid against the general background of an ever-growing crystallization of configuration and decrease in variegation. The chief device employed is that of rearrangement, either by means of truncation, substitution, or by re-permutation of the old with the new. The arrangement of any given sentence can be comprehended only in light of the prevailing sentence-patterns (grammatical rules of syntax and inflection) which in turn can be comprehended only by investigating the development of the language. The stage of the language in its cycle from positional-to-inflectional-to-positional arrangement will determine whether the grammatical rules will be primarily positional or inflectional. The degree to which a language is inflected (which seems to be a reciprocal to the degree to which it is positional) can be measured statistically.

This entire discussion of the sentence is, however, by no means complete. So peculiarly individualistic is any given sentence that only against the background of the total behavior of the entire person who utters it can it be understood. We have, it seems, investigated the sentence as a unit as far as we can from the point of view of the stream of speech as a frame of reference. Though our results are therefore not completely adequate, they lay a ground-work for investigation of the remaining attributes from the point of view of the individual and his total behavior.

VI

THE STREAM OF SPEECH AND ITS RELATION TO THE TOTALITY OF BEHAVIOR

Now that we have studied the form and behavior of many speech-elements of the stream of speech in isolation, it is necessary, even in an introductory study of the dynamics of language, to consider the total phenomenon of behavior, of which the stream of speech and its elements are but a part. Without the background of the speaker's heredity, physical organization, social groups, and his world of feeling and perception, all of which are part and parcel of all his behavior, many of the phenomena of his speech are not understandable. For in these various portions of his total experience lie the impelling causes of his speaking and the material of his discourse; conversely, the stream of his speech and that of his fellows profoundly influences his total behavior. It is with this larger aspect of Dynamic Philology that we shall be concerned in this, the last chapter, of our investigation.

Since much of the material to be covered is usually considered highly controversial, and since it is inevitable that our conclusions will be somewhat speculative (and hence not to be placed on the same plane with portions of the preceding chapters in which actual data were advanced), we shall proceed with greatest caution in the hope that our conclusions, however bold, may not appear rash. To employ a familiar figure, we shall navigate not on the shortest course through this uncertain sea, but along the coast in sight of familiar landmarks and in depths where at any moment we can take soundings. Hence it may at times strike the reader that we are proceeding circuitously, and that some material, on first presentation, is extraneous and irrelevant. To mitigate as far as possible any feeling of irrelevancy which may arise, it will be well to state the conclusions in advance:

a person and his environment represent an enormous complex in which there is a tendency to maintain equilibrium; because of inevitable changes either in the individual or in his environment there must be constant readjustment in this complex to restore equilibrium; speech is one device for restoring equilibrium and, as a restorative of equilibrium, its course in time and its content are marked by those portions of the great complex of individual-environment where balance has been most disturbed.

I. THE STREAM OF LANGUAGE *
AS A CONTINUUM OF EVENTS

The stream of language, whether spoken, written, thought, or dreamed, whether heard, seen, or remembered is, strictly speaking, a continuum of events. For the acts of expression, perception, and remembering are actual events in this world. Empirically, language is behavior. Any postulates about the existence of language in the intervals between expression, perception, or recollection are inferential. Our adoption of this strictly objective view of language as a continuum of events is actuated by the wish to eliminate at once from preliminary consideration, as far as it is possible, all philosophical speculation about the phenomenal and the noumenal. The virtue of viewing speech-elements as events is that we have in events a common denominator to which potentially every act of perception and experience, and every act of physiological behavior (and anything else that may conceivably not be included in these two categories) can, as we shall see, be reduced. If in adopting this purely empirical view we have deviated from the methods employed by many other investigators of language, who assume that the word has an existence apart from its actual occurrences, we have at least followed the accepted methods of the exact sciences.

* The *stream of language* embraces all language whether spoken or not; the stream of speech includes only spoken language.

2. THE STREAM OF SPEECH AS A CONVERSION OF SPATIAL ARRANGEMENT INTO LINGUISTIC ARRANGEMENT

The chief difference between the arrangements of the events of experiential data and those in speech is that the former contain, at least in part, arrangements in space which are totally lacking to the latter. Limiting our experiential data to visual sense-data, we find objects arranged in space (above, below, nearer, farther, inside, outside). Though additional arrangements may be perceived or inferred in what we see, and though there may conceivably exist experiential data in which spatial arrangement is absent, the fact remains that spatial arrangement is found in sense-data, and in sense-data to which the stream of speech refers. For example, we observe a picture on the wall above a table, and we may and do communicate this observation to another. But though we may perceive the picture on the wall over the table in this spatial arrangement, and though we may manage by speech to indicate this arrangement to another person, we cannot actually *duplicate* this arrangement in the arrangements of the stream of speech. The stream of speech represents purely sequential arrangement, that is, a continuous linear arrangement in the stream of time; there is a before and an after in speech arrangements but no above or below. A striking difference then between the arrangements of experiential data and those of speech is that the former may and frequently do include spatial arrangements which are not found in the latter.

It would seem, then, that one of the functions of speaking is to convert the spatial-temporal arrangements of experience into purely temporal arrangement. The peculiar problems involved in this process of conversion are perhaps best illustrated by a physical model. Imagine a sack full of corn in which is buried, say, a lively mouse whose squirming keeps the grains of corn in motion and constantly changes the arrangement of the whole; imagine an aperture in the bottom of this sack through which only one grain of corn can pass at a time. Now visualize the problem of projecting grains of corn through the aperture in such an order that by their mere sequence one may deduce what is happening in the sack. The sack with its contents represents the world as we experience it, the passing of individual kernels through the hole represents our conversion of the multitudinous spatial arrangements into the purely sequential arrangements of time or speech. It is doubtful whether one could ever devise a system whereby the model of the sack of corn could actually be made to work. In view of the difficulty of conversion one perhaps readily understands why all living species have not evolved speech-behavior, and why even human speech at best is not always as logical and clear as one often wishes.

To digress for a moment in order to integrate our present discussion with that of the preceding chapter on sentences, it might be added that there are only two conceivable devices which may be employed in arranging the succession of kernels falling through the aperture so that their succession will represent the antecedent arrangements in the sack: one is to pass those kernels through together, one after another, in a serial pattern, the other is to distinguish with like tags (say daubs of paint of the same color) the kernels which have arrangements in common. Both of these devices of arranging are employed in speech-ways: the former is positional arrangement (see page 185 f.), the latter is inflectional arrangement (see page 245 f.), which is little more than tagging roots of like usage with common inflectional tags (e.g. pro bono publico).

3. A WORD AS A NAME OF A FREQUENTLY
USED CATEGORY OF EXPERIENCE

It is frequently asserted that a word is a conventional symbol representing an idea. For the purposes of empirical study of speech-behavior this definition is useless and even misleading. Empirically a word is an event in the stream of speech somehow related to the data of experience. In the simplest case a word is a name.

If we view a few words, such as *horse, house, hat,* we find that the name is not necessarily that of one specific precise experience, or a part thereof, but of a category of experience. For instance, though *house* has a reasonably constant primary denotation, the actual experiential data to which *house* has referred in the past year in the lives of all speakers of English would by no means be congruent in use, shape, size, color, value, or any other feature, not to mention all other features. The word *house* like any other word referring immediately to experiential data, represents merely a convenient category in which the data of experience may be arranged. John Brown lives, of course, in a physical environment, but when we name a part of his environment *house*, it is we who have dissected the continuity of his environment by arbitrarily segregating one feature and naming it; and in naming that feature we have automatically compared it with other similar features of environment, similarly segregated. A word, then, in being a name possesses a human factor in its representing, first, a human analysis of experiential data, and second, a comparison of one portion of the data with other portions of the total data of experience. Hence the category which a word names represents both analysis and comparison performed by man, and is not found already at hand in the structure of objective reality. The factor of vital human experience is more clearly evident in words used as action-names, e.g. *run, climb, wish.* Many possible ways of categorizing experiential data have doubt-less not yet been discovered; many of our present methods of classification will doubtless be considered naïve in the future; and some of our categories, for instance, those named by *above, below, high, low* which result from the particular relationship of the perceiver to the perceived cannot be said to exist at all apart from the perceiver.

The question has often been raised whether we truly ex-perience anything new except according to the pre-established categories of experience; an act of perception, for example, is said to be simultaneously an act of arranging into familiar classes. If in countering this statement we remark that we also experience blurs, noises, confusion, and the like which are marked by lack of orderly arrangement, we are told that this very mark categorizes and arranges them among other blurs, noises, and confusion similarly marked by lack of orderly arrangement. If it be indeed true that an act of experience is simultaneously an act of classification into familiar categories, it would appear, then, that all new data of experience are already, to some extent, arranged, and that no experiential data exist unarranged, no matter how inadequate or unsatisfactory the arrangement. If one chooses to believe that all perception and action are made and done through channels pre-established in experience, it must of course be remembered that we can probably never determine empirically (1) whether life exists or ever existed without any antecedent store of experiential data, or (2) what the actual patterns of classification are in the earliest stages of experience.

Fortunately it is possible for us either to observe or to infer what is alone of importance to us in this question at hand, namely the development of experiential categories in the growth of experience of an individual. In the environ-ment of an infant, for example, there occur noises, lights, bodies in motion which he perceives, or which at least appear to attract his attention at a very early age and hence are a part of his experience. To what extent he actually perceives environment *per se* can probably never be established; but he evidently perceives at early age at least to some extent *change-in-environment*, a legitimate category of perception even in adult life. Later he presumably perceives *things-in-change-in-environment*, though probably these things have no individuality aside from the generic category. When he perceives the parts of things in change, then the classes into which he arranges perception increase in number partly through division into parts, at least if we judge from his expression. For example, *bow-wow* 'animal' may be split into *bow-wow* 'small animal' and *moo-cow* 'large animal': *bow-wow* is later split into *bow-wow* 'small quadruped' and *kluck-kluck* 'bird.' Thus with passing time the process of unification, articulation, integration, classification extends more and more into the infant's experiential data. Similarities of dissimilar things are observed; differences in roughly similar things. Naturally this process, which does not necessarily stop at any age, includes perceptual data acquired through the refinements of physical apparatus for observation. If it is conceivably not permissible to aver that all acts of perception are ever attended by simultaneous acts of arrangement in categories, nevertheless it seems reasonably safe to infer (1) that many perceptive acts are thus attended (e.g. we can often see a house immediately as a house without groping for a category into which to fit the impression), and (2) that all perceptual data when referred to in the stream of speech are arranged in experiential data in some manner.

The number of different possible categories into which experience * may be redacted seems unlimited. Since experience differs among individuals, the same thing may

---

* Henceforth, unless otherwise specifically stated, the terms *experience* and *experiential data* refer not to all events happening to a person, but, for convenience of discussion, only to events of which he is aware and which he might express.

appear differently to different individuals. For example, the solution of a given problem or the performance of a given task will appear easy to some, difficult to others, in accordance with their previous experience; what is new to one, may be familiar to another; what is food for one, may be poison to another. Similarly, what appears heavy or hot to one may appear light or cool to another. The position and speed of the observer in reference to the object is also of significant importance; the clouds far above the pedestrian may be far below the aviator; the brakeman walking slowly along the top of a freight car appears moving at a great speed to the hay-makers in the field. The expensive wrist watch for which the shopgirl carefully saves pennies appears less expensive to the heiress. Whether one can ever establish empirically the number of actual categories into which perceptual data are divisible seems doubtful. Furthermore for every two categories there exists potentially a third category which includes the two. There is a category of *horse* and a category of *race* and there is the potential third category of *horse-race*, and indeed a fourth category of *race-horse*. How far compounding of this sort may be continued is not clear; conceivably it may be continued *ad infinitum*, and certainly it may be continued to a number at least far beyond the presumable number of actual formal words in the vocabulary of any known language.

Since the number of available formal words in the vocabulary of any speech-group is by no means so large as the number of potential or actual categories into which experiential data may be, or is divided; and since the language of a given person is commonly supposed to be capable of expressing the entire content of his experience, at least to his own satisfaction, there must then be, it seems, some other device for naming categories than the employment of a single formal word for each category.

The chief device for expressing a category of experience for which there is no single formal word is to locate it

among categories for which there are formal words, just as
one can locate in space the surface of an unknown sphere
by establishing the location of any four points on its surface.
For example, if one wishes to describe a black thorough-bred
three-year-old mare, that is, a reasonably complex category
which is generally named by no single formal word, one can
locate it as the convergence of the four separate categories
of (1) things that are black, (2) things that are thorough-
bred, (3) things that are three years old, and (4) things that
are mares. One may indeed limit it further by adding to the
point of convergence, the categories of (5) future events, (6)
the acts of jumping, (7) the relative position of above, and (8)
single definite fences. The entire complex category would
then be: *a-black-thorough-bred-mare-will-jump-over-the-fence.*
To this ten word arrangement which is a configuration, an
unlimited number of other categories may presumably be
added to locate the category ever more definitely in common
experience; the more numerous the different categories are
into which the datum is located the more articulated is the
datum and, by definition, the higher the degree of articulation of the meaning of the linguistic configuration (see pages
157 f., 195 f., 201 f.) which names the datum.

Now, when we recall our discussion (pages 235 ff.) of the
example 'a person's uncle's second wife's tenth child,' we
remember that the relative frequency of usage may, through
the process of abbreviation, exert considerable influence on
the total magnitude of complexity (e.g. the number of words)
of the configuration. That is, increased usage will by abbreviation decrease both the magnitude of complexity and,
at the same time, the degree of articulation of the configuration. *The different formal words of any vocabulary are then,
it seems, the residues of specific past acts of abbreviatory process,
and are the names of experiential categories which are frequently
referred to in the stream of speech.**

* The frequency with which a category is referred to in speech is, incidentally,
not necessarily directly proportionate to its inferred frequency of occurrence in
experiential data.

4. ARTICULATION AND INTEGRATION; MEANING

The question now arises as to what becomes of the high degree of articulatedness of meaning of a speech-configuration as it diminishes under increased frequency of usage (see pages 196 f., 200 f.). Is there no compensation for its diminution other than that of increased relative frequency?

It would seem that a decrease in the degree of articulation resulting from an increase in relative frequency is accompanied by an increase in the extent to which it is integrated into the basic fabric of experience, either social or individualistic. That is, as a meaningful configuration becomes relatively more frequent, it becomes simultaneously less articulated and more integrated. The magnitude of complexity of a speech-configuration which bears an inverse (not necessarily proportionate) relationship to its relative frequency, reflects also in an inverse (not necessarily proportionate) way the extent to which the category is familiar in common usage. Aside from differences in degree of articulation and integration there seems to be no fundamental difference in meaning between the configuration when elaborately articulated and when abbreviated. For example, when using the single word *surcingle* instead of a *girth or belt around a horse's back to hold fast a saddle*, one does not necessarily describe the object either more accurately or less accurately; both expressions refer substantially to the same data. Similarly, the configuration a *person's uncle's second wife's tenth child*, though more articulated, in the sense that it is located by the employment of a larger number of categories of classification, does not on the whole designate its reference less ambiguously than does the configuration *mother*. The chief difference between configurations of high and low degree of articulatedness, to repeat, is that the latter are more integrated in the collective lives and experiences of the numbers of the speech-group. In articulating we but reduce the unusual to common terms whose use and significance are integrated in common experience; the classification *mother* is a more integral part of our common experience than the classification *a person's uncle's second wife's tenth child*. The more articulated we find a given configuration, the less integrated do we suppose the configuration to be in the collective experience of the group; and conversely. The minimal degree of complexity necessary for comprehensible speech between persons reflects the degree of unusualness (in their group) of the experiences spoken of, or, somewhat more precisely stated, the unusualness of speech about those experiences. For example, if there were a short word, say *dau*, in an American Indian dialect describing the entire activity of a man's climbing a pine tree, plucking cones, kindling the cones into a fire on which to fry rattle-snake meat, we should be inclined to believe that *dau* referred to an activity frequently discussed if not frequently occurring in the life of the American Indian tribe. Of course, the high degree of integration of a concept may not be within the entire speech-group, but within minor social, religious, political, economic, or professional groups (see pages 32 f., 35 f.) which are subsidiary parts of the entire speech-group. Yet within the given group wherein the phenomenon occurs, it seems plausible to believe that a decrease in articulatedness of meaning of a configuration is attended by a corresponding (not necessarily proportionate) increase in the degree of its integration.

It would seem to follow then, that, from the point of view of either major or minor speech-groups, the words of highest relative frequency (and hence lowest articulatedness of meaning) name categories, on the whole, of primary importance in the speech usage of the group or groups, since these terms are the ones into which the less frequent or less familiar experience is redacted.

To summarize, the primary linguistic categories or classes into which experience is redacted are the most frequently used categories, and the names of these categories are both the most frequently used names and the shortest configurations. This consideration, however, leads us to another: change in meaning, either the change in the category which a configuration names, or a change in the configuration which names a category.

5. CHANGE IN MEANING (SEMANTIC CHANGE)
ARISING FROM ABBREVIATION

Semantic change, that is, the change in the meaning of a speech-element is most readily understood when observed from the point of view of its development. If one cannot demonstrate why, for example, the English word *soup* took on the meaning of 'nitro-glycerine' in Racketeer American English, one can nevertheless show how a change of this general type occurs.

Most of the mechanism of semantic change has already been discussed under the heading of abbreviation (page 28 f.) whether the abbreviation be one of truncation (page 30 f.) or of substitution (page 33 f.). When a configuration is truncated so that a component (or components) represents (or represent) the entire configuration, its (or their) meaning is *ipso facto* changed to embrace that of the entire configuration which they represent. So, too, when by substitution a given speech-element outside the configuration represents the configuration, its subsequent meaning includes that of the configuration for which it stands. Let us investigate more closely each of these abbreviatory devices (truncation and substitution) before comparing the similarity of their effect upon meaning.

Any linguistic configuration, because of the sequential nature of its arrangement in time, may be viewed as a sequence of events, and may be represented symbolically by, say, a series of letters, *a b c d e..... n.**

Now, when a configuration, whose parts we shall represent by *a b c d e*, is truncated in future occurrences to *c* (or *a* or *b* or *d* or *e* or a combination of them, say *ad*, or *ce*) the single speech-element *c* has as its meaning '*abcde*' and may be represented thus:

We might represent the *untruncated* occurrence of this configuration in the stream, when preceded by speech-element *y* and followed by speech-element z, as:

In *truncated* form:

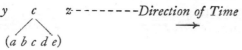

That is, *c* in representing the entire sequence *a b c d e* in truncated form, would be immediately preceded by *y* and followed by z, and the entire sequence *a b c d e* would be implied solely in *c*.

Now, *c* has in these two instances (*untruncated* and *truncated*) two distinct meanings: the first, c^1, has its meaning as a mere component of *a b c d e*; and, the second, c^2, has its meaning as a representative of *a b c d e*, which is '*abcde*.' For example, *tree* has its generic meaning in the configuration *the apple-tree at home*; we shall designate this meaning of *tree* as c^1, which is the *primary meaning* with which *tree* occurs in numerous other speech-configurations. If we sup-

---

* If in addition one cares to designate the subsidiary nuclei (cf. Chap. V) this may be accomplished by enclosing each nucleus in brackets or parentheses: *a b [c d (e f) (g h) i]... n.*[1] We are however now chiefly interested in the configuration as a unit of expression and not as a nucleus of nuclei.

pose, however, that the family in whose backyard this apple-tree grows refers frequently to this tree and to none other, either because the tree is exceptionally fine and useful, or because it is the only tree within miles, they will hardly say 'the apple-tree at home' every time they refer to it, since the single word *tree* (c^2) will normally suffice. Whenever they wish to refer to a different tree, they can specify what amounts to the exceptional tree in their experience, e.g. *the willow tree at the river* ($a\ k\ c\ d\ a\ p$). In this particular family the word *tree* has two meanings, its generic meaning (c^1) and its particular meaning in their own intimate conversation (c^2) in which it means 'the apple-tree at home.' And similarly with *dog, cat, mother, house* and many other words, not only in this family but in every family and in every speech-group of whatever sort, no matter how large or small. If one views the word *tree* in all its utterances by every individual in the entire large speech-community, one finds not only its primary generic meaning, but countless other meanings (c^2, c^3, c^4, c^5,.........c^n) which designate particular trees. And similarly with many other words.

The question now arises, which of the perhaps countless different meanings of a word is to be considered the primary meaning, and which the secondary meanings. By what other criteria may we determine the primary meaning of a word than by the relative frequencies of occurrences of all meanings of the word in the entire speech-community? Though, with one family, *tree* may primarily mean 'the apple-tree at home,' and with another, 'the willow-tree at the river,' yet statistically in the total speech of the entire speech-community, these local meanings are but secondary to the most frequently used meaning, c^1, 'tree in the generic sense.' In the majority of instances the utterances of tree may well refer to specifically localized trees of one sort or another, but the extensive variety of these different local meanings reduces their average relative frequency to but a small fraction of the relative frequency of usage of *tree* in its generic sense. Were the relative frequency of usage of *tree* in a specific sense, say, 'oak tree,' to become so great as to exceed the frequency of usage of *tree* in its generic sense, the primary meaning of tree would doubtless become 'oak tree.' Thus, though *president* primarily means 'an officer who presides over a corporation or assembly,' yet in the United States its primary meaning is probably 'the elected executive of the government of the United States,' with presidents of corporations, clubs, and universities specified more particularly. The primary meaning of a word is then its statistically most frequently occurring meaning in the group for which one wishes to establish the primary meaning.[1] And the more significant the group is as a part of the whole, the more significant are its primary meanings as important meanings in the whole. As the influence of any minor group increases, its secondary meanings may become more and more the primary meanings of the whole group. Primarity of meaning, then, exists only in reference to a group, and is determined by its relative frequency of usage within the group; the more inclusive the group in which a given meaning is primary, the more nearly primary is this meaning in the language.

The effects on meaning of abbreviation by substitution is the same as those by truncation. If instead of *a b c d e* one says *x*, the speech-element *x* has, while representing *a b c d e*, the meaning '*abcde*.' For example, the family calls its beagle-hound (*ab*) by the word *Willie* (*x*), and to that family *Willie* means 'beagle hound'; to another it possibly means 'a white gelding.' Similarly, as in the case of truncation, a meaning gained by a casual substitution may become in time through frequency of usage a strong secondary meaning, if not the primary meaning in a vocabulary.

Thus the individual names of the categories of experiential data may do double or multiple duty. With the passage of time the categories which are named may shift in their arrangement, either the whole configuration becoming but a part of another configuration, or the part becoming the whole, or the parts interchanging, even as the atoms of matter are said to change in their arrangement as time elapses. Whether one views the configurations of speech which name configurations of experiential data, or the configurations of experiential data which are named, at least partly, in speech, we find both regimentation and change either in the wholes or in their parts.

6. THE WHOLE AND ITS PARTS

The question is natural as to the relationship between any whole and its parts, especially in reference to meaning. For instance, when the entire sequence $a\,b\,c\,d\,e$ is represented by c^2 (by truncation) or by x (by substitution), what is the relationship between c^2 (or x) and $a\,b\,c\,d\,e$ for which it stands and from which it derives its meanings?

Now, language is in essence symbolic, and it is quite obvious that a symbol,* in being but a representative of experience, has a larger meaning than that of a mere sum of gestures. Since either $abcde$ or c^2 (by truncation) or x (by substitution), each refers to substantially the same, their meaning is substantially the same and we may probably believe that the magnitude of c^2 or x represents proportionately more experience than any part of $a\,b\,c\,d\,e$ of similar magnitude.

However, there is a danger in thus adding and subtracting the parts of a configuration. It is almost self-evident that in one sense a configuration represents more than the agglomerative sum of its parts; for example, the sentence is more than the sum of its words, or a word more than the sum of its phonemes. Were a configuration but a sum of its parts, then the configurations, *the bull charged the woman*

---

* A discussion of the symbol and its referent, and of the symbolic and the real will be found on pages 287 ff. below.

and *the woman charged the bull*, or the configurations, *cat* and *act*, would be the same. In brief, configurational arrangement is as vitally important a factor in our behavior as the parts, even as the arrangement and proportions of sodium and chlorine in common table-salt are as vitally important a factor in the chemical configuration, salt, as the sodium and the chlorine.

However, it may not be overlooked that the independent parts of a configuration generally exist in experience before the configuration. Thus, the words *America, of, states, the, united* existed in the speech of the English-speaking group before the configuration *the United States of America*. It seems no exaggeration to say that the parts of any configuration are more archaic than the configuration which contains them. Furthermore, attention does not usually pass to the entire configuration (whether it be a painting, a melody, a statue, a building, a poem, or a scientific study), until it has satisfied itself as to its familiarity with the essential parts, or with the subsidiary nuclei of which the whole configuration consists. Many a new configuration, say a musical composition, is appreciated only after the lapse of years in which the auditor has matured sufficiently to grasp it as a whole and not as an agglomeration of parts.

Furthermore, it may not be overlooked that the formation of a configuration may in some cases be emotionally pleasant or painful; [1] that is, not infrequently in experiencing something new, an individual is at first but aware of the parts and only with the lapse of time does he become ever more aware of their configuration until the whole stands forth as a unit. This deepening of awareness which may be termed *insight* is frequently attended by emotional intensity, either of positive or negative quality, according to the pleasure or pain of the realization, or insight.

Of course, once the configuration is perceived or expressed or otherwise experienced as a whole, it seems usually impossible ever completely to perceive, express, or otherwise experience its isolated constituent elements except as potential parts of the whole. And the more we experience the configuration as a whole, (1) the more crystallized are its parts in the configuration, (2) the more we see the configuration as a whole rather than as an aggregation of parts, and (3) the more we consider an isolated part as belonging to the whole configuration (i.e. the more immediately we *associate* the entire configuration with its part). Thus, given a few essential lines and we see the tree under which we played as children; 'four score and seven years ago' and the American school-boy supplies the remainder of Lincoln's Gettysburg Address; the few opening bars of music and we know that the national anthem is being played — so crystallized are these configurations in experience, so determinate in arrangement are their parts.

7. CONFIGURATION-CARRIERS

As isolated events become configurational with the passage of time (see pages 207 ff.), and as the configuration becomes increasingly more crystallized, conditions become ever more ripe for abbreviation. It is naturally of some importance to know which elements, in the event of abbreviation, will either survive in truncation or be selected as representatives in substitution; for these surviving or representative elements will be in the long run, it would seem, the foundation of future evolutionary development. Since the problem involved in the telescoping of parts into the whole is largely one of complicated prediction, we must be content if we can shed but a little light on its essential nature from the angle of truncatory acts.

One may reasonably expect that the elements preserved in the truncation of a given configuration will be those most peculiarly characteristic of the configuration; we shall term them, by definition, the *configuration-carriers*. For example, in truncating *the big white house* to a single element, we should normally delete, it would seem, *the*, *big*, and *white* rather than *house*; for, though all four elements are significant, the latter appears most peculiarly characteristic in most cases.

Since many, if not all, of the components of a configuration occur in other configurations, the *configuration-carriers* of a given configuration seem to be those which occur more frequently in the given configuration than in any other. This is not necessarily the commonest word in the configuration (for *the*, the commonest word, is not the significant element in *the big white house*). If we determined the relative frequency of occurrence of each component of a given configuration (say the components *a*, *b*, *c*, *d*, and *e*, in the configuration *abcde*) in all the configurations in which they occur, we should have an idea, not only of the total frequency of that component in the entire sample studied, but also of its relative availability as a carrier of some one or more of these configurations. If some one element in the configuration *abcde* occurs with decidedly greater frequency in *abcde* than in any other configuration, it may serve as the configuration carrier of *abcde*. If no one element qualifies as a single configuration-carrier, then the best two elements, in the configurational order in which they occur in the configuration. If there are no two elements, then the best three, or the best four. If no portion of the configuration can be found which occurs more often in that configuration than in others, the configuration has no subsidiary configuration-carriers, but is itself the minimum of possible organization and cannot be further truncated without risk of incomprehensibility.*

If we consider the long history of language and the tendency toward truncation of unnecessary elements, it seems

---

* If the entire configuration itself is insufficient as a configuration-carrier, it is underarticulated and is generally expanded, i.e. located in additional categories: e.g. the configuration *the war* in American English of the period of 1865 has subsequently been expanded at least to *the Civil War* in American English of today.

probable that in persistent configurations of high relative frequency there is a minimal difference between the configuration and the configuration-carriers. Since the users of a language tend to perpetuate by actual use those elements of most significant meaning (the configuration-carriers rather than the full-fledged configuration), it is the totality of *configuration-carriers* which constitutes the *matrix* from which the future evolution of a language emerges. An interesting study of the development of the matrix of any language, say English, could be made by comparing analyses of cross-sections of the language as it appeared at intervals of a century apart, in which the stock and relative frequencies of phonemes, morphemes, words, etc. of one period were compared with those of preceding and subsequent periods; a study of this sort would give a remarkable insight into the dynamics of pattern in its generic sense.[1]

The question arises as to the necessary length of a sample of language sufficient for the determination of its configuration-carriers. In short, what is the proper length of a sample of speech for statistical analysis?[2] With the constant changes occurring in the stream of speech, the probabilities of future behavior clearly alter as the future becomes present; what was a configuration-carrier a year ago may not be one today; moreover the probabilities vary in some cases if the sample is short or long. This moot question as to proper length of a sample cannot, it seems, be answered for all configurations either in terms of minutes or years of speech, or in terms of the number of speech-elements (e.g. phonemes or words) in the sample. However, it is reasonable to assume that the sample taken must be antecedent to and include language up to the moment in the stream for which information about configuration-carriers is wished. May it not be tentatively suggested that the sufficient, indeed, the proper size of a sample of speech for determining the carriers of a configuration is the period of speech from the time the configuration first appeared in an individual's experiential data until the time for which information is wished? Without this information the course which the configuration will probably take in future truncation cannot be safely estimated. Hence the size of the sample will vary directly with the degree of crystallization or the relative frequency of occurrence of the configuration in question. The more crystallized the speech-element, the more precisely and the more remotely into the future can one predict, first, because of the smaller variety and, second, because of the greater stability or inertia of habit. But the total prediction of future development of language as effected by possible truncation presents a dilemma: the more predictable the material, the more enormous the amount of material necessary for analysis to predict. It is of some value, however, to envisage the problem even in the abstract; for such a view presents a background for the clearer understanding of the fact that, among the magnitudes to be studied in the dynamics of language, frequency of use and rate of change are of utmost significance.

8. ABBREVIATION: THE BASIC DIMENSION OF SPEECH

The chief difference between abbreviated and unabbreviated speech is that the latter is more articulated in its meaning. We may represent an unabbreviated portion of the stream of speech by some such sequence as *abcdefghijklmnopqrs* in which each letter stands for a given word. Abbreviated, this same portion of the stream of speech may be represented, say, by *CFILOR*, — that is, six elements instead of nineteen. The abbreviated portion refers to whatever the unabbreviated portion refers to, only it is shorter and, if all else is equal, makes the reference more swiftly. The abbreviated portion might be represented alongside the unabbreviated portion thus:

$$\rightarrow C \longrightarrow F \longrightarrow I \longrightarrow L \longrightarrow \text{etc.}$$

$$\underset{a\ b\ c}{\diagup\diagdown} \quad \underset{d\ e\ f}{\diagup\diagdown} \quad \underset{g\ h\ i\ j}{\diagup\diagdown} \quad \underset{k\ l\ \text{etc.}}{\diagup\diagdown}$$

That is, while the more fundamental meaning is the stream *abcdefghijkl, etc.*, the actually occurring stream of speech is *C F I L, etc.* in which each capital letter (e.g. *C*) refers to a configuration of small letters (e.g. *abc*).

Now, assuming that both the average magnitude of complexity and the average rate of utterance of each speech-element, whether abbreviated or unabbreviated, is the same, we may view the abbreviated stream as a short-cut through the unabbreviated stream, whether the abbreviation is one of truncation or substitution. Abbreviation is then actually a short-cut; and moreover, since the stream of speech knows no other arrangement than that of time, *an abbreviation of speech is a short-cut in time.*[1] Furthermore, since by means of abbreviation ground is covered more rapidly than in the absence of abbreviation, the belief is plausible that *the more extensive the abbreviation, the greater is the velocity of the stream of speech*. Though the actual minutes consumed may be the same both for 100 connected words representing abbreviations of more articulated language, and for 100 words of unabbreviated articulated language, the former is moving at a greater velocity than the latter from the point of view of effective communication. If the speeds of the two appear the same, they are nevertheless no more the same than those of an airship flying a mile high and a bird flying in the same direction at a lower level and at the same apparent speed; though the bird in its flight may remain in the line of sight between the observer and the airship, the actual speeds of the two are different.

For the phenomenon of abbreviation, convenient analogies can be found in the field of mathematics. When, for example, in the stream of speech *y c² z* serves as the abbreviation for *yabcdez*, one may conceive of *yabcdez* as an arc on the circumference of a circle, whose extremities, *y* and *z*, are connected by the straight line *yc²z*. This manner of representation is descriptive of the isolated phenomenon though its employment would be difficult in describing subsequent abbreviations. More adequate analogies could be drawn from spherical geometry.[1] Perhaps the most extreme use of abbreviation is in algebra, where a single letter may be used, at the arbitrary choice of the mathematician, to symbolize a whole paragraph of verbal description.

In saying that the stream of speech has a rate of velocity which varies according to the extent to which it is abbreviated (i.e. the more abbreviated, the greater the velocity) we do not mean that one necessarily utters words more rapidly in the stream of high velocity, but that one covers more ground in effective communication in less time. Furthermore, no matter how abbreviated the stream of speech may become, it can, theoretically at least, always be more abbreviated because any two or more events in sequence may be represented symbolically by a third. Conversely, no matter how great the degree of articulation and concomitant slowness of the stream of speech, it may, theoretically at least, be ever more articulated and of slower velocity. Manic and obsessive language (pages 217 ff.) represent unusual velocities, the first above average, the second below.

There seems to exist nothing in the observed nature of speech which permits one to deduce an absolute and constant velocity, in terms of which differing velocities may be measured. The velocity of one stream of speech is fast or slow only in comparison with that of another. The velocity of any stream of speech is then relative; and any language pattern or speech-element is, in terms of the velocity of its occurrence, relative.

Moreover, since the function of language in actual communication depends upon the representative use of symbols, the relative velocity attained through abbreviation is the basic dimension in language development. Our examples have mostly illustrated the abbreviation of a configuration of words; the same principle applies to the abbreviation of any other speech-configuration, no matter how large or how small, whether the components are articulatory sub-gestures, phonemes, morphemes, words, sentences, etc.[1] The most fundamental unit of speech may well prove to be a unit of velocity. However, that there may be no confusion, let us view in somewhat greater detail what is meant, first, by a dimension of speech, second, by velocity as a dimension of speech, and finally, by a unit of the dimension of velocity.

Now, a *dimension* is a measurable extent of any kind, as length, breadth, thickness, area, volume; in algebra it may also be each one of a number of unknown quantities contained as factors, say, in a product (e.g. the product *vwxyz* may be viewed as possessing five dimensions). The mathematical comparison of two automobiles, for example, may include not only the three conventional dimensions of space, but a fourth for weight, a fifth for speed, a sixth for power, and so on. Each dimension may have its unit (e.g. the foot a unit of the dimension of length, the horsepower a unit of the dimension of power, a mile per hour the unit of the dimension of speed). Similarly the stream of speech may have many dimensions (e.g. pitch, amplitude, etc.);[2] but it also has the one that we have mentioned — velocity.

That is, the stream of speech is representative of experience, but it consumes far less time as a symbolic representation of experience than occurred in actual experience. For example, Caesar's *ueni, uidi, uici*, 'I came, I saw, I conquered,' represents in a few seconds a portion of Caesar's experience of such duration that the few seconds of the symbolic representation are but an almost infinitesimally small fraction. And the more abbreviated speech is, the more is time telescoped or compressed or condensed; and it is this telescoping of time which is a fundamental characteristic of speech, and which is also probably the significant dimension of speech. The unit of speech is the ratio of the time of experience to the time of the gesture (i.e. configurations thereof) in conveying the experience adequately in communication. In other words, the basic unit of speech is a unit of time, and not one of meaning or phonetic articulation.

If this conception of a speech-unit in terms of speed is valueless as a practical measure, it seems nevertheless to be the only measure obtainable by empirical study and may be serviceable in exposing the fallacy of the easy belief that some particular speech-element (such as the phoneme, word, or sentence) is the basic unit.

9. THE SYMBOL AND ITS REFERENT; GENES OF MEANING

It is clear that in the stream of speech either the full configuration *abcde* may occur, or its abbreviation c^2 (or x), but not both simultaneously. While c^2 (or x), which, for convenience, we shall term a symbol,* occurs in place of *abcde*, it means '*abcde*' which we shall tentatively † term the *genes of meaning* of c^2 (or x). It would seem that every meaningful speech-element has *genes of meaning* which, when they occur more nearly in full in place of the symbol, represent a greater degree of articulatedness of meaning than that of the symbol; the *genes* (*abcde*) may be also viewed as representing more nearly primary categories of meaning than the symbol (c^2 or x) does.

Many different symbols have many genes in common and conceivably every symbol has genes in common with some other symbol. Though there is no certain way of establishing empirically the genes in common in two symbols, yet the commonness of genes alone accounts for two linguistic phenomena of frequent occurrence: (a) substitution, and (b) analogic change.

---

* This use of the term *symbol* is restricted to the particular discussion at hand. For a discussion of the problem of the *real* and the *symbolic*, see pages 290 ff.

† Later, pages 301 ff., we shall see that these tentatively termed *genes of meaning* are but complex elaborations of *genes of meaning*, even as any speech utterance refers to categories of experiential data in very complex elaboration.

a. Substitution; Primary and Secondary Meanings

It is a curious phenomenon that a speaker may call the moon a candle, or a man a dog, and still be understood, for neither is really what the speaker has termed it. This seems possible only because the supplanted and supplanting words have elements (our hypothetical *genes of meaning*) in common, a statement which is scarcely new in spite of its unfamiliar wording.

Not any word may be substituted for another with equal propriety. In calling the moon a candle we feel that the two have the element of light in common. Were one to term the moon a rattle-snake the connection would not be as immediately apparent, though a fugitive from a posse might on a moonlight night find that the two had certain unpleasant elements in common. Theoretically it may be expected that every word has some element or elements in common with every other word, since no matter how humble the category named, the rest of the world must be relative to it, and, no matter how humble the category named, an adequate idea of any category is probably possible only with a complete knowledge of many other if not all other categories. In practice, however, one substitution may be more felicitous than another if we judge from the differing degrees of approval which different substitutions elicit. To predict in advance the most suitable word for substitution appears impossible because of the many variable factors involved in the given situation, in the content of the vocabulary at the given time, and in the experiential data of the given speaker and auditors involved.

Nevertheless, the act of substitution (whether abbreviatory, or indeed articulatory) is scarcely comprehensible except with a hypothesis of underlying elements in common, even though we cannot immediately perceive the actuality of these underlying elements.

b. *Analogic Change*

The first time one word is used instead of another in the stream of speech, the supplanting word in its unexpected usage may be termed a *metaphor*. The unusual arrangement existing in metaphoric expression is usually attended by greater vividness, as we may anticipate theoretically from our previous hypotheses (page 212), and probably this greater vividness is an important impulse to the substitution.

But as a given substitution is repeatedly made there is a curious effect on the meaning of the supplanting word (see page 274 f.). The moment that *candle* has once been substituted for *moon* the word *candle*, on the basis of past performances includes in its meanings 'moon.' The primary meaning of candle will presumably remain 'a roll of tallow or wax with a wick in the center to give light,' yet in addition to this primary meaning there has arisen by metaphor a secondary meaning, 'moon.'

Which meaning of a word is to be termed primary and which secondary or tertiary appears to be solely a matter of relative frequency of occurrence of meaning (see page 276). Neither the original meaning * nor the etymological meaning † of a word is necessarily its primary meaning; the meaning which has the most frequent usage is the primary meaning. Hence it is not only conceivable but quite possible that the meaning 'moon' may ultimately become the primary meaning of *candle*, just as the primary meaning of the word for *cup* has become 'head' (i.e. *Kopf*) [1] in German, and the primary meaning of the Latin word for *pot* has become 'head' (i.e. *tête*) in French.

---

* The primary meaning of *to prove* is, today, 'to show or demonstrate the correctness of'; its original meaning was only 'to test,' as witnessed by the old proverb 'the exception proves (i.e. tests) the rule.'

† The etymological meaning of *write* is probably 'to cut' and of *read* 'to consider or discern.'

Now, if candle were gradually to receive the primary meaning 'moon,' the astronomical satellite which revolves around earth would have two names, *moon* and *candle*, the primary meaning of which would be identical. Would this condition persist? The history of language reveals many instances of the development of two names for the same thing, yet it is by no means frequent that two completely congruent synonyms exist together long in the usage of a given speech-group.* Supposed synonyms often differ in this that one is generic, the other special, or the one abstract and the other concrete, or the one collective and the other individualistic, or, like *dormant* and *sleeping* in English, the supposed synonyms refer to different categories within the common category.† The consequence of the simultaneous existence of two different words of congruent meaning would probably always be the leveling or deletion of one by the other. For example, in the minds of many speakers the words *forceful* and *forcible*, *masterly* and *masterful*, *contemptuous* and *contemptible*, *pitiful* and *pitiable* have become synonyms of congruent meaning. And it is of interest to note in the language of close associates how one person has preferred and given complete usage to one form, and another person to another.

The phenomenon of analogic change from the time when two or more words enter into the same sphere of influence through the period in which they gravitate toward one another until one has completely supplanted the other, if that point is ever reached, is scarcely comprehensible without the hypothesis of genes of meaning in common. To repeat,

---

* They may of course exist concurrently, one in one geographical or minor group, one in another; e.g. what is called *doughnut* in one portion of America may be called *cruller* in another, yet he who has doughnuts for breakfast does not have crullers, and *vice versa*. Preferred words in couplets of this sort are interesting in indicating the geographical, economic, professional, or social origins of the speaker; not only preferences in words but in accent and in the articulation of phonemes.

† In English a person is *sleeping* and a plant is *dormant*; *dormant baby* and *sleeping rose-bush* sound bookish or poetic.

although what we term genes of meaning cannot be directly perceived or isolated, one is almost forced to postulate their existence if only as explanations of abundant instances of substitution and analogic change. We shall return to this subject later (pages 301 ff.) when the chief utility of the postulate will become apparent.

10. THE MEANING OF EXPERIENTIAL CATEGORIES AND THEIR RELATION TO LANGUAGE: A SUMMARY

It may be useful to summarize here the preceding discussion of the relation of the stream of speech to the experiential data to which it ultimately refers. It has been suggested that both speech-data and experiential data reveal to analysis the presence of classification into categories, and that a major problem of formal speech is first, the naming of categories found in experiential data, and second, the representation of categories of experiential data by arrangements in the stream of speech. Small speech-elements, such as words, become, through the processes of abbreviation (either of truncation or of substitution), but convenient labels for frequently used and often highly complex configurations into which experiential data are classified. The saving of time by such a system of symbols is one of its fundamentally useful features; hence, abbreviation, or accelerated velocity of experience, may be considered the basic dimension of speech. In the actual process of abbreviation, the behavior of a speech-element is determined in part by its total reference to experiential data, and in part by its contextual arrangement. The description of the behavior of a speech-element is greatly facilitated by the postulation of the existence of genes of meaning as the subsidiary categories represented by a linguistic configuration; though these genes of meaning are apparently imperceptible, their existence is revealed by their effect in modifying the course of the stream of speech, especially in the phenomena of metaphor, of abbreviation, and of analogic change.

I I. A SPEECH-ELEMENT AS A COMPLEX OF GESTURES IN A UNIVERSE OF BEHAVIOR

Until now we have viewed language as but a stream of gestures in linguistic arrangement with the presence and action of subsidiary physical * gestures tacitly assumed. Since we should expect to find that a bee by stinging the orator Demosthenes both in the middle of an oration and in the middle of his back, would seriously influence the course of the oration, even to the extent that the laughter-loving Greeks might decide not to send troops against Philip, it is clear that the stream of speech is connected in an important way with other physical functions than those of the conventional vocal organs.

Any speech-element represents an enormous complex of gestures including not only the peculiarly linguistic gestures of the conventional vocal organs (e.g. lips, tongue, teeth, etc.) but also the essential acts of living process, such as the acts of respiration, alimentation, and the like. It seems reasonable to infer that any part of the body which upon disturbance or removal will modify or inhibit the production of the stream of speech, whether temporarily or permanently, is to that extent a speech organ, and its normal behavior is a part of the normal gesture-complex represented by a speech-element.

To be more explicit, let us imagine that we have a slow moving picture, taken with the help of X-rays, covering days and days of a person's conduct, whether speaking or

---

* To avoid potential ambiguity inherent in the terms *mental, physiological, physical*, and *material*, we shall use the word *physical* in the sense of 'physiological' unless otherwise qualified.

not. All we could perceive in this picture would be matter in the process of human behavior, and this behavior we might view either as a continuum of acts, or, in so far as it is contributory to speech, as a continuum of gestures. From the point of view of the speech production we might divide all observable acts into three categories: (1) the necessary common activities such as the acts of respiration and alimentation which seem to be common and essential to all behavior; (2) the gestures peculiar to speech, such as the phonetic gestures of the vocal organs, which seem to be essential and peculiar to speech-behavior; (3) the *incidental* acts, such as combing the hair or filing the finger-nails, which, however essential or peculiar to other behavior, seem to be neither essential nor peculiar to speech-production, and from the point of view of speech-production may be termed incidental. A cross-section of the total behavior of a person during the utterance of a speech-element would then be roughly divisible into necessary common activities, gestures peculiar to speech, and incidental acts. Though the necessary common activities and the gestures peculiar to speech must be present in speech-production, it apparently makes little difference whether many of the common activities are doing much else than functioning normally, according to their most probable course, which is generally highly determinate. When the normal course is disturbed, as by the intervention of physical disease or injury, the total behavior, including, of course, the production of speech, may well be altered.

From the point of view of comparative philology, the only places where changes may occur which are truly significant for speech are in the combinations of articulatory sub-gestures, into phonemes, phonemes into morphemes, into words, into sentences, etc. All else is generally viewed as constant either because it proceeds in a firmly fixed course, or because it is always fortuitous or random as a concurrent phenomenon from the point of view of speech. Probably the reason why this viewpoint has been so eminently useful in the drawing of comparisons and in the establishing of formulae of correspondences is because, for practical purposes, it is sound. A medium of communication for young and old, wise and foolish, sick and well, and one serviceable in daylight and in darkness, at close proximity and over great distances, might well be expected to consist of gestures peculiar to speech which, on the one hand, are not incompatible with other necessary common activities, yet which, on the other hand, are not stringently dependent upon activity incidental to the individual speaker in his individual situations. Yet this viewpoint seems justified only for the practical purposes of comparative philology.

When, however, it is further said, more strictly speaking, (1) that everything is a speech-organ, the removal or disturbance of which will temporarily or permanently effect the production or course of speech, or (2) that all subsidiary physical arrangement of behavior is constant for one reason or another, in either case we presuppose the existence of the stream of speech as a course through a vast universe of acts. Having in mind this stricter view of speech as a course through a universe of acts of behavior, we may reasonably inquire both into the nature and history of this universe of behavior in which the stream of speech with all its phenomena has its foundation, and into the connection between this universe and the stream of speech. Let us, now, approach this question in reverse and consider first the effects of language, as a part of behavior, upon the more general behavior of the persons concerned.

I 2. LANGUAGE, AS A REPRESENTATIVE OF EXPERIENCE, IS AN EQUILIBRATING DEVICE

As has often been repeated, language is primarily a representation of experience. It may represent experience as a report of direct perceptual experience, such as in an account of a football game or in a description of some scene or event. Or it may represent tendencies to act and may be viewed as representative of potential activity, such as in an oration to persuade others to modify their behavior in accord with the wishes of the speaker. The stream of speech of a truly impartial witness on the stand exemplifies language as a representation of direct perceptual experience with little or no respect for the potential action involved. The stream of speech of a politician desirous of winning votes for himself exemplifies language as a representation of potential action often with little or no respect for the direct perceptual experience involved.

Now it would seem that certainly in the case of potential action, and often, though not necessarily always, in the case of direct perceptual experience, a function of the linguistic representation is to preserve or restore equilibrium. This equilibrium may be of two types: (a) *inter-personal* and (b) *intra-personal*.

a. Inter-personal Equilibrium

It is not without significance that the old and established English name for a congregation of delegates from various sections of a country, who meet to reconcile conflicting aims and needs, is the word *parliament* (from the Old-French *parlement* meaning 'speaking'). The cause of the congregation is *conflict* which has disturbed the harmonious balance or equilibrium between the parts of the country; the chief if not often the sole device for attempting to restore harmony and equilibrium is *talk*.

To understand the existence of inter-personal equilibrium as the presumable goal of common verbal action we must remember that all the delegates in the parliament as well as all those whom the delegates represent possess a great deal of experience in common, whether one views the totality of

experience from the angle of the mental, the physical, or
the material. In fact it may be stated as a seemingly universal truth that when two individuals have not a truly
enormous proportion of their experience in common they
cannot even converse, for the symbolization of speech is
conceivable as a practical device in communication only
when words or other symbols refer to corresponding portions
in the common experience of all the individuals engaged in
conversation. Thus, with a parliament, the delegates and
constituents agree to an amazing extent in their manner of
perception, in their instinctive reactions to pleasant and
unpleasant situations, in their wish for particular types of
security, in their habits of behavior; their physiological or
physical organization is closely similar, as are their physical
reactions to stimuli both beneficial and injurious; their needs
for particular material substances, their classifications of
much of matter into the valuable, the valueless, the beneficial, the necessary, the deleterious, correspond to a very
high degree. In brief, no matter how experience is defined,
an extremely large amount of human experience is common
property.

Of course, some individuals possess more experience in
common than do others. What we have hitherto referred
to as racial, national, social, political, geographic, professional, or family groups are each distinguished primarily
by a commonness of much definite experience not present
in the experience of persons not members of the particular
group. The commonness of group experience, whatever the
cause of the grouping, is doubtless the reason why the individuals of a given group have common assets and common
liabilities, and frequently seek, in communication, a common
solution to their common difficulties which block or disturb
the harmonious functioning of the group.

The preservation or restoration of supposed equilibrium
may demand at times drastic action, as is witnessed by our
battle-fields, gallows, jails, whose use is primarily to restore

equilibrium; or by our armaments, our codes of law, our systems of justice, which seek primarily to preserve equilibrium. But whether the action is drastic or merely casual, whether preservative or restorative of equilibrium, it is marked by rearrangement and reorganization (page 209 f.) in which the course of experience of the various individual members of the different groups in conflict is modified, painfully or pleasantly, or painfully in part and pleasantly in part, to effect a balanced compromise.

In all the activity which attempts to preserve or restore inter-personal equilibrium, language is a highly useful means, especially when it is representative of potential action (see page 295) though possibly too when representative of only direct perceptual experience (see page 294). Indeed it is a moot question whether today we could exist without the employment of language to preserve or restore equilibrium between us in the face of conflict. Furthermore, it is conceivable that very rarely, if ever, does inter-personal communication occur without being in any way an attempt to preserve or restore inter-personal equilibrium which is likely to be, or has been disturbed in someway, however slight. And this seems true regardless of whether we view human behavior from the point of view of mind, or of body, or of matter, or of all three.

b. Intra-personal Equilibrium

The occasions of inter-personal conflict are often occasions for intra-personal conflict as well. Most individuals are members of many different groups whose best interests are by no means always the same and are often radically different. Thus, in time of war, the most suitable action for every adult male of physical fitness may well be to enter the armed forces; yet from the point of view of the family or economic groups in which this person is a vitally important factor, this course of action may equally well prove to be disastrous. It may indeed be stated as a seemingly universal truth that when a person's inter-personal activity is in more than one group (of whatever sorts), there exists potential intra-personal conflict, indeed probable intra-personal conflict, since the chances are practically negligible that the interests of these different groups to which he belongs will be equally well served by the same course of personal action. The device of 'talking it over,' so useful in restoring and maintaining inter-personal equilibrium, serves at the same time for the clarification and adjustment of the intra-personal conflicts simultaneously concerned.

But language has an even more personal use in preserving or restoring a condition of harmonious equilibrium within the life of a given individual. Not only do presumably all persons converse with themselves, either aloud or silently, but very generally the content of the self-conversation is a discussion of possible or probable eventuations in environment and of available modes of action to be adopted in encountering them. By means of self-discourse the loose ends of a person's experiential data are frequently integrated into his whole personality, and problems are analyzed, and plans of conduct formulated, to a degree which seems often unattainable without the aid of intra-personal language. Not only may a person 'write himself clear' but he may 'talk and think himself clear' in meeting the daily problems of his life upon whose solution his continued well-being, if not existence, may depend.

The source of intra-personal conflicts may be the conflicting interests of groups to which a person belongs (e.g. the intra-personal conflict of a fearsome person who feels it his duty to enlist during war-time). Other sources of conflict may be within the person himself, whose urgent wishes may in serious respects be mutually contrary (e.g. the man who wants children but loathes contact with women). The presence of injurious animate or inanimate interference in the functioning of his bodily process may derange the harmonious equilibrium of his daily life and cause conflict. In all these intra-personal conflicts the use of intra-personal language is almost admittedly an important device in preserving or restoring a condition of harmonious equilibrium.

c. Summary

In summary, the employment of language may be shown to play a serviceable role and to be an excellent device at times in preserving or restoring equilibrium in the face of conflict, whether inter-personal or intra-personal.

13. ORGANIC BALANCE; ACTEMES AND GENES OF MEANING; MENTAL BEHAVIOR

Under this heading we shall seek to extend to a deeper level the discussion of language in its relation to equilibrium. To do so, we must deal with the terms mind, body, and matter. This involves the ontological problem of the nature of ultimate reality, and the epistemological problem of our ultimate sources of knowledge. These questions confront the investigator in every field; an attempt at their solution may be made from the point of departure of the findings in any field; and their successful solution would seem possible only after the combined findings of all fields, together with the loose ends of human knowledge, had been successfully integrated into one system. Surely the findings of Dynamic Philology are not yet sufficient to provide a final metaphysics. Yet, on the other hand, inasmuch as our field is in that of symbolism and of mental and of physical activity, the connection between mind, body, and matter might, perhaps, be viewed as a primary problem, the solution of which should be attempted before any other step is taken. Without attempting in any way to arrive at the ultimate truth, we shall but seek to present now merely a working hypothesis.

If we ignore for the moment the epistemological problem involved in the relationship of ourselves as 'observers' * to the universe 'observed,' and consider simply the body of 'knowledge' thus produced, we find among the 'objects' of knowledge two types: animate and inanimate. It is doubtless true that we, as observers, become aware of these objects only through 'experience,' i.e. by means of reactions occurring within ourselves, whether it be reactions of the retinal cells, reactions of the striated or unstriated musculature, or of whatever else the physiological organization may be. Any knowledge of inanimate objects involves an animate process in us. But we do find it useful, in general, to discriminate in some way between the animate and the inanimate. Various empirical criteria for this distinction might be noted which could be roughly indicated by the statement that animate things react in organized modes not directly deducible from the known chemical or physical characteristics of their constituent materials, and in some ways running apparently contrary to the general rules, as in their reversal of the usual entropy direction.

These organized modes of reaction of animate things are patterned. For examples, we experience this patterning in ourselves as habit, we see it in the behavior of certain insects as instinct; and patterns of reaction are also characteristic of the intimate details of the cellular activities in our bodies, although we may have no immediate awareness thereof, and though it may require delicate instrumental means to bring them to our knowledge. This patterning of response, however else it may be viewed, is ultimately an act of classification. Whatever may be added or abstracted

* Quotation marks indicate that the term is taken, without specific definition, from general usage.

in the phenomena called 'mental,' we can only become aware, in experience, of that to which we react, in whole or in microscopic part, according to some more or less definite pattern. The nature of our final awareness is therefore pre-conditioned by the potential patterns of activity inherent within our system of organization.

Consider a stimulus of one quantum of light falling on the retina of the eye. We may say that this quantum of energy passes from the inanimate universe into another universe of activity at the retina where it elicits animate response. This statement should, of course, be somewhat qualified. There are no special reasons for supposing that the energy 'escapes' the physico-chemical 'laws' of the inanimate universe. These laws appear also to hold for the inanimate materials of the animate organization. But the ensuing response within the retina is *also*, nevertheless, conditioned by the animate organization of that tissue. It is this more or less specific potential activity of the retinal tissue which already *classifies* for the organism its most elementary experience of the light. Since all animate experience happens by means of such reactions of organized animate tissues, more or less patterned in their potential activity, all experience must undergo at least that preliminary classification. All animate experience occurs therefore in *a frame of reference* or *a frame of meaning*, determined by the animate organization of potential behavior.

We need a term to designate the minimal unit of behavior-classification. Since a quantum seems to be the smallest unit of inanimate energy, our reaction to a single quantum is probably the smallest unit into which animate activity may be divided, and for convenience we may term this smallest unit of animate activity an *acteme*.[1] The *acteme* is not only the minimum of animate action but also the minimum of experiential classification, which we may henceforth for convenience term a *gene of meaning*. An *acteme* is then a minimal animate reaction in classifying external material reality; a *gene of meaning* is a minimal amount of patternness into which animate acts may be classified. All of our acts, other than those which are the hypothetical *actemes*, are configurations of *actemes*, no matter how large or small the acts, nor how short or prolonged; and by the same token all these same acts, no matter how large or small, nor how short or prolonged, are configurations of *genes of meaning* in the data of experience.

Thus, for example, the utterance of a word is in truth an enormous configuration of *actemes*, or of *genes of meaning*, the choice of terms depending upon whether we view the utterance primarily as action or as classification.

In describing thus the hypothetical relationship of animate and inanimate, have we not also sufficiently described the connection between mind and body? Is there necessarily any difference, except in degree of specific patternness, between animate reactions which are loosely termed mental and those which are loosely termed physiological? Would not our consciousness perhaps disappear if all our present conscious processes became as completely regimented and determinate as our cellular processes presumably are? We have been using the expression 'more or less specific patternness.' It is in the 'more or less' that the mental character appears. May we not assume, as a working hypothesis, that consciousness as a characteristic of animate behavior appears when the configurations of actemes (or genes of meaning) are looser and less determinate? For a philological analogy, conscious mental activity is to unconscious physiological activity as sentences are to phonemes.

In human behavior, as compared to the activities of other animate beings, the relative prominence of the mental reflects the less rigid patterning; furthermore, mental activity is most evident in those aspects of the behavior of an individual person which are least patterned, rather than in the more stereotyped physiological reactions — but not exclusively so. We tend to become aware of the presence of disturbance to many of our processes of behavior which function normally without our awareness of them.

The line of phylogenetic evolution away from stereotyped action patterns, culminating in the relatively free man, is not systematically recapitulated throughout the life of an individual man. Rather the reverse. We pass from conscious and less determinate activity to the greater inertia of habit, from the *may* to the *must* (see pages 197 ff.). From the great number of available different *mays* of today are taken those which are to belong to the matrix of *musts* of tomorrow.

To gain a more complete picture we should probably be obliged to assume that a person is not only a universe of actemes, but that each subsidiary organ or unit part of him is a universe of actemes, which are ever more highly determinate in order. Similarly we should be obliged to assume that the individual person and his universe is but a part of larger universes: the inter-personal groups.

However, it is not necessary to pursue our almost dangerously speculative hypothesis further than this point, namely, that inter-personally and intra-personally, materially, physiologically, and mentally there is a supposed condition of organic balance which we seek to maintain by analyzing and rearranging new experience as far as possible into pre-established classes and patterns. This condition of equilibrium may be deranged permanently or temporarily, irreparably or reparably, either by changes originating in the material (e.g. electrocution), or in the physiological (e.g. cancer, diabetes) or in the mental (e.g. the loss of one's dear ones, one's wealth or one's prestige), or in the inter-personal (e.g. warfare). And unless the derangement incapacitates the processes of speech, speech is a help in preserving or restoring a condition of equilibrium.

14. THE SYMBOLIC AND THE REAL; DEGREES OF REALITY

Man, having two hands for dealing with the world of experience, is fond of antitheses in language — the mental and the physical, the animate and the inanimate, the true and the false, the real and the symbolic, and so forth. We have already expressed a tentative working hypothesis in respect to the apparent antithesis of mental and physical; we must now consider the symbolic and the real. Of course, up to now, we have not hesitated to make practical use of the terms *symbol*, *symbolic*, and *symbolization*, whenever convenient, on the basis of the common understanding that a symbol is that which stands for, or represents, something else. However, we must not forget that the 'something else,' represented by a symbol, may itself be a symbol. Thus, when x stands for, or represents, *abcde*, this latter (i.e. *abcde*) is in turn itself a symbol. All speech, being an abbreviatory gesture-activity, serves a symbolic role, because it is representative of larger configurations of experience.

Now, there is a belief, by no means uncommon, that behind the screen of symbolic representation, and even beyond the utmost limit of experience, there exists an ultimate objective reality. Since, however, we can have no knowledge of that of which we can have no experience, we mention this naïve concept of absolute reality only to dismiss it from further consideration.

Nevertheless, the fact does remain that we recognize varying degrees of reality among our experiences. Though we may not properly erect a notion of absolute reality, and say, comparatively thereto, 'more nearly real,' we do have need to say 'more real' and 'less real,' for vital practical consequences flow from such classificatory behavior. Not to seek examples beyond the field of language, we note that speech gestures may express nonsense as well as fact. To say 'abracadabra' is of course an actual experience, though its representative value, beyond that particular experience, may be relatively slight; but to shout 'the house is on fire' may state an important fact, with numerous practical implications of meanings verifiable by others. In some other speech utterances it may be difficult to judge the degree of reality, as when the prophet says, 'I saw a new heaven and a new earth.' The apparent antithesis of real and symbolic resolves itself into the problem of evaluating the degree of reality. One might do better to say *degree of actuality*, to emphasize the *behavior* implications, because experience is at bottom an affair of actions; but the thing-oriented characteristic of human mental life has been in many ways a useful prejudice, and to this we defer when designating 'reified actuality' by the name 'reality.'

In the actual business of evaluating degrees of reality, one commonly uses a statistical criterion which can be expressed, as a first approximation, in the statement that those portions of total experience are most real in which there has been the greatest agreement of the largest number of individuals over the longest time.

The statistical criterion for degree of reality is especially evident in the field of inter-personal communication and other social behavior, but let us also consider briefly its more elementary use. If we view all experience as classificatory behavior (configurations of actemes) our criterion would lead us to say that a portion of one's total experience (behavior, or reaction) is more real in so far as it is in better agreement with the rest of one's experience. Thus, the inanimate physical possesses for us in general the highest degree of reality, because the genes of meaning, into which the actemes of animate process classify our most immediate reactions to inanimate materials, not only are the basic materials of all other behavior, but also have the highest relative frequency of occurrence.

But configurations of meaning of a much more complex type may acquire by frequent repetition such a high reality-significance as to produce curious 'distortions' of the reality-evaluation. As a simple example one may recall the returned ocean voyager who finds the sidewalks rolling under his feet. A more complex example is provided by the veteran soldier on leave of absence who, against his recent background of repeated war experiences, finds the once-familiar scenes and events of civilian life curiously unreal and devoid of significance.

15. THE DEGREE OF REALITY AS A FUNCTION OF THE GROUP, AND LANGUAGE AS A MECHANISM THEREFOR

If we do not restrict our survey to the individual but consider human experience in general, our statistical criterion would imply that experiences shared with others are evaluated as more real than individual reactions. Indeed, the common practical test of knowledge is agreement of experiential report by different observers. Into such a judgment there often enters an estimate of the reliability of individual observers, but this apparent exception to the apparent statistical rule is not an exception but only an individual application; for, the 'weighting' of personal testimony is based upon frequency of agreement in the past.

There are other less tangible but equally important implications in the statistical-reality criterion which we have set forth. Thus, public sentiments of long and accepted standing are patterns of action of a higher degree of reality than those of individual personal beliefs. For example, the belief in the divinity of a given person, if popular and of long and accepted standing in a community, is a basic social reality of the community, even though it may be found by some to be nonsensical. Persons may prosper or lose their lives because of the presence of this social reality, which may also materially modify the course of art, science, and daily life. Those social patterns of animate process, which we may call *sentiments*, represent correspondences of individual *beliefs* or *feelings* and have their power and high degree of social reality not because they necessarily truthfully interpret in the best possible scientific manner our experience with an 'absolute reality,' but because they represent a consensus of opinion or purpose, and are the matrix of social action from which future social evolution is to emerge.

It would seem, broadly speaking, that the great realities of tomorrow are but fantasies today, and that in the process of maturation during which the developing individual orients himself ever more in his social, occupational, and physical environment, the individual's behavior becomes ever more patterned both in conformity with the accepted patterns of his social group and along independent lines. Though some may place an exaggerated weight on the value of the approved sentiments of group action, even to the annihilation of that which is independently personal and individualistic, and though others may proceed unduly along their independent way, and thus cut themselves off from the stabilizing security of the group, the rank and file develop both as social animals and as individuals.

Since, however, the group is apparently but an aggregation of individuals and since group sentiments are but a rough consensus of opinion and purpose of individuals, the degrees of reality of behavior are probably constantly in change as the group influences the individual, and as the individual influences the group. The chief change in the degree of reality of our ideas results from the integration of the personal into acceptable terms of the social or inter-personal. No matter how sublime the idea of *Lear* or *Faust* was in the minds of Shakespeare and Goethe, these ideas attained their high degree of reality in their respective groups only after they had been converted into the commonly accepted terms of communicative language of the time. Not until after their conversion into common terms were they capable of exerting a modifying influence upon the behavior of any other individual or of the entire group.

Language is, then, the device *par excellence* by means of which human beings equalize the degrees of reality of their reactions, acquiring on the one hand the strength and security which seems quite generally to attend upon membership in the group, and in turn providing variegation for the whole by redacting into common terms highly personal experiential data. Though it is, of course, possible for an individual to depart far from the realities of the group until, in the hallucinatory realities of his inner personal life, he seems to have lost all contact with his fellow man, yet his lack of contact is never complete, and most of his reactions, including language, continue to show some degree of similarity to those of the more nearly average persons.

Indeed, were we not all so similar in our reactions to environment, possessing by and large the same needs for the same kinds of support and defense, and in a like manner evaluating the degrees of reality of these various needs, language would not be serviceable in restoring or preserving equilibrium, even if it could conceivably exist, a proposition which can scarcely be too often repeated.

When we speak, it is in a sense, the auditor who speaks, and the problems we discuss, no matter how personal to the speaker, are in some way the auditor's problems or he would not listen. For the reaction to a perception of speech is itself an expression. Though we have much experience in common, we scarcely have enough completely corresponding experience that one person can convey a portion of his experiential data with all its roots and associations to another, as one would convey a marble statue intact from one place to another. In conversing we but mould or modify our auditor's course of action, enticing him to crystallize or analyze common experience in a common way.

Of course the discourse of some may be far more original than that of others. Some are more gifted with intelligence and can analyze and arrange experiential data in more fruitful configurations; some are more imaginative in conceiving potential interrelationships; some are wiser in having a richer awareness of experience. Though the proportions of these gifts in gifted individuals may vary, all can express themselves in some fashion, and thus influence the reality-evaluations of the group. But of greatest social value is he who has all these gifts to a high degree and can also communicate his experience to the motley crowd, holding their attention and interest and moulding their future inter-personal and intra-personal behavior for long years to come.

16. CONCLUSION

All experience is reaction, patterned at its source. All reaction is expression, once we become aware of it. And all expression is language, once we can decipher it. What we have been terming language is only that particular portion of behavior for which the code is pretty generally known.

In concluding this introduction to a field of possible scientific inquiry, we may well be reminded that the actual speech-gestures, together with their meanings and patterns, are but accidents when compared to the close-knit relationships of the stream of events in the total universe of behavior (biological, psychological, sociological) in which these accidents occur. Yet, in their *recurrences*, these accidental speech-gestures have found acceptable use by human groups as time-saving representants of the larger universe of experience. A record of the recurrence of these gestures constitutes in fact the chief and almost the only record of human experience available for empirical study.

In this book we have considered, in a general review, the

results thus far obtained from the empirical study of some of these language-records by the method of relative frequency, and we have sought to place the results of these studies in some rational perspective relative to the more general universe of behavior. It remains to be seen whether further empirical studies will completely substantiate our findings, and, if so, how far they will limit, modify, extend, or reinterpret what appears already to have been found.

3. The cuneiform writing of the ancient Mesopotamians reached the stage of being largely syllabic.

4. See *Bloomfield*, pp. 285 f.

CHAPTER TWO

22   1. *Bloomfield*, p. 277, gives interesting discussion of problem.

2. *Kaeding*, p. 24.

23   1. *Kaeding*, p. 24, fn.

24   1. The 15 most frequent words in Kaeding's analysis represent 25.22% (i.e. ¼) of the total occurrences of all words, and are all monosyllabic. If, instead of taking the 15 most frequent, we take the 66 most frequent, (according to Abteilung A 1., *Kaeding*, pp. 53–54), which represent 50.06% or ½ of the language examined, we find 54 monosyllables and only 12 dissyllables. As the frequency becomes less, the number of syllables becomes greater. Proceeding to the next most frequent words, numbering 254, and making with the above 66, a total of the 320 most frequent words which (1) include all words occurring more often than 5000 times, and (2) account for 72.25% (nearly ¾) of the occurrences, we find that in these 254 words, there are 115 monosyllables, 130 dissyllables, and only 8 trisyllables. That is, the monosyllables are fewer, the dissyllables on the ascendency, and the trisyllables commencing to appear. These 8 trisyllables have a total occurrence of 57,812 among the 10,910,777 words, and yet represent only 4% of the occurrences of all trisyllables. All the words occurring less often than 5000 times each account for only 27.75% of the occurrences; 20.78% out of these 27.75%, or approximately ¾ of words occurring less than 5000 times, have three syllables or more.

2. *Selected Studies*, p. 23, and pp. 31–51.

3. *Idem*, p. 23, and Appendix C.

4. *Eldridge*.

32   1. *Volt* (named after Alessandro *Volta*, the Italian electrician) is tendered as an example, not of truncation, but of a short word rarely used in the speech-community as a whole. The *volt* was defined by the International Electrical Congress in 1893.

35   1. For illuminating examples presented entertainingly cf. H. T. Webster, 'They don't speak our language,' *The Forum*, xl (Dec. 1933), pp. 367–372.

36   1. *Selected Studies*, pp. 15 f.

43   1. *Eldridge*, pp. 22–29, 30–36, 37–42, 43–48.

2. *Eldridge*, pp. 49 f.

NOTES AND REFERENCES

In the notes which follow, additional material and discussion are presented which have been referred to in the main text but whose inclusion there would unnecessarily mar the continuity of discussion.

In view of the large amount of literature on the general subject of linguistics, the author will consistently limit his references as far as possible to three standard works in each of which will be found copious illustrative material and in the first and third of which will be found extensive bibliographical material:

1. Leonard Bloomfield, *Language*, New York: Henry Holt, 1933.
2. Karl Brugmann, *Kurze vergleichende Grammatik der Indogermanischen Sprache*, Strassburg: Trübner, 1902–04.
3. Otto Jespersen, *Language; its Nature, Development, and Origin*, London and New York: Henry Holt, 1933.

These three works will henceforth be referred to simply as *Bloomfield*, *Brugmann*, and *Jespersen* respectively. With the use of these, the reader will encounter little difficulty in orienting himself in almost the entire literature of linguistics.

The chief sources of statistical data referred to in the main text will be found in the following four studies:

1. R. C. Eldridge, *Six Thousand Common English Words*, Buffalo: The Clement Press, 1911.
2. F. W. Kaeding, *Häufigkeitswörterbuch der deutschen Sprache*, Steglitz bei Berlin: Selbstverlag des Herausgebers, 1897–98.
3. G. K. Zipf, 'Relative Frequency as a Determinant of Phonetic Change,' *Harvard Studies in Classical Philology*, XL (1929), 1–95.
4. ——, *Selected Studies of the Principle of Relative Frequency in Language*, Cambridge, Mass.: Harvard University Press, 1932.

These will henceforth be referred to as *Eldridge*, *Kaeding*, *Relative Frequency*, and *Selected Studies* respectively. The complete reference to other publications will be given on first mention.

CHAPTER ONE

PAGE

4 1. *Jespersen*, Chaps. 2 and 3.
5 1. *Idem*, pp. 89–96.
   2. *Idem*, p. 98, ll. 22 ff.
   3. *Jespersen*, p. 99.
15 1. The conventional alphabet of Czechish is phonemic.
   2. The writing of Peipingese Chinese is chiefly morphemic. A *morpheme* is usually defined as a minimal unit of meaningful form, a definition from which I do not depart in my treatment of the morpheme.

PAGE

44 1. Nevertheless in *Kaeding's* analysis of nearly 11 million words of connected discourse, (page 44), 126,862 words occur only once; 34,523 occur twice; 17,072 occur thrice; 11,144 occur four times; 7850 occur five times. (The remainder are not in a form susceptible to statistical treatment.) Even with 11 million words, then, there seems to be no diminution in the accessions of new words.

CHAPTER THREE

50 1. *Bloomfield*, pp. 283–296 for a discussion of written records; *ibid.*, pp. 85–92 for a discussion of phonetic transcription.

2. *Ibid.*, pp. 75 f.

3. *Ibid.*, pp. 78 f. I do not follow *Bloomfield*, pp. 90, 91, in the use of the term *Compound Primary Phoneme* to designate diphthongs because I believe it a misleading designation of the dynamic aspects of the phenomena involved. See my treatment of all *groups* of phonemic elements, see pp. 97 ff. above, and the entire ensuing discussion of the skewness of a phoneme. In my treatment of statistical data, diphthongs have for consistency been handled as single simple phonemes.

53 1. See *Jespersen*, p. 166, §4, for similar analogy.

2. Illustrative material, *Bloomfield*, pp. 77–85.

55 1. *Bloomfield*, pp. 77–81.

56 1. Vedic *r* generally corresponds to Indo-European *r*, though also not infrequently to *l*. See *Brugmann*, pp. 117–118 (i.e. §175) for illustrations and some slight statistical data. See also W. D. Whitney: *Sanskrit Grammar*, Cambridge, Mass.: Harvard University Press, 1923, p. 19, §53 b.: 'The semi-vowels *r* and *l* are very widely interchangeable in Sanskrit, both in roots and in suffixes: there are few roots containing an *l* which do not show also forms with *r*; words written with the one letter are found in other texts, or in other parts of the same text, written with the other.'

2. *Bloomfield*, pp. 78–79.

57 1. The *t*, as well as *p* and *k*, of French may be accompanied by a simultaneous glottal stop as a non-distinctive variant. See *Bloomfield*, pp. 99 f.

59 1. For a discussion of many different types of phonemes see *Bloomfield*, Chaps. 6 and 8.

61 1. For a discussion of Chinese phonetics see Bernhard Karlgren, *Etudes sur la phonologie chinoise* (Leyden and Stockholm, 1915), pp. 223 ff.

2. Other equally valid terms are sometimes used for the particular

phonemes which we shall term *stops*; the term *stop* will be employed in this investigation merely because it is found used in *Bloomfield*. In *Relative Frequency* and *Selected Studies* the author employed the terms perhaps more familiar to Comparative Philology, i.e. *tenues* and *mediae*, the *tenues* being *voiceless stops* and the *mediae* being *voiced stops*.

62 1. See Bernhard Karlgreen, *op. cit.*, pp. 223 ff.

63 1. Some South-German dialects distinguish voiceless unaspirated fortes and lenes (cf. *Bloomfield*, p. 100) but there appear to be no available statistics for these.

2. *Bloomfield*, pp. 99 f.

3. *Ibid.*

64 1. *Ibid.*, pp. 94 f.

66 1. Specific instances are known where the voiced stop appears to represent the voiceless stop plus *voicing*, e.g. *d* and *t* in some positions in modern Albanian, cf. G. S. Lowman: 'The phonetics of Albanian,' *Language*, VIII (1932), 274, 'the voiced dental plosive [e.g. *d*, ed. note] is the voiced counterpart of the breathed [t].' The term *counterpart* thus used seems to imply that on the whole Albanian *d* thus described represents primarily an Albanian *t* plus *voicing*.

68 1. The phonetic transcriptions themselves are presented in *Selected Studies*, Appendix B. The percentages of frequency for all the different phonemes in the transcription are given *ibid.*, pp. 6, 7. The method of transcription used is explained *ibid.*, p. 5: i.e. the aspirated fortes stops were transcribed as the simple *t*, *p*, *k*, etc. and the nonaspirated stops as *d*, *b*, *g*, etc. This method of procedure was followed, instead of the one in our present text, because the employment of digraphs or of diacritical marks in a transcription of any length introduces an additional opportunity for error. In our present text digraphs are used so that the reader will not confuse the Chinese stops, in which *voicing* is very probably not present (cf. Karlgren, *op. cit.*, pp. 261, 269, 288, etc.), with the voiceless and voiced stops of, say, English. See also *Bloomfield*, p. 100.

69 1. Henri Forchhammer with preface by Otto Jespersen, *Le danois parlé* (Heidelberg: Jules Groos, 1911), pp. 14–48, center column. The transcription of the Danish stops is phonetic in the sense that Forchhammer subdivided the aspirated fortes stops into two seemingly variant forms: (1) the strong aspirates (indicated by a following[h]), and (2) the aspirates in which the aspiration, though present and phonemically significant, is less forceful; for these

latter the simple symbols *t*, *p*, and *k* were employed. We have presented the sum of these two variant forms of each aspirate occurring in the text (cf. footnote, p. 74 supra). Forchhammer transcribed the lenes stops by *d*, *b*, *g*, yet he made clear (p. 5) that they were voiceless and not to be compared with either the French voiceless or voiced stops.

2. The glottal stop in Danish is significant. Thus the pairs of Danish words written *mord* 'assassination,' *moder* 'mother'; *hund* 'dog,' *hun* 'she,' *et. al.* are phonetically indistinguishable save for the presence of the glottal stop in the pronunciation of the first word of each pair. Cf. Forchhammer, *op. cit.*, pp. 1 ff.

70 1. Some may feel that the aspirated and non-aspirated voiceless stops of Danish are precisely identical with those in Peipingese. Though not desiring to enter this controversy, the present author wishes, nevertheless, to point out that the two languages are not compared in our investigation, and that neither the statistical data nor our interpretations thereof for Peipingese and Danish will be invalidated if it is subsequently discovered that the corresponding stops of these two languages are or are not identical.

71 1. Daniel Jones and Kwing Tong Woo, *A Cantonese Phonetic Reader*, London: Univ. of London Press, no date.

72 1. L. E. Armstrong and Pe Maung Tin, *A Burmese Phonetic Reader*, London: Univ. of London Press, 1925.

2. *Ibid.*, p. 12.

74 1. The phonemic transcriptions of modern colloquial Dutch used in the statistical analysis are presented in E. E. Quick and J. G. Schilthuis, *A Dutch Phonetic Reader*, London: Univ. of London Press, 1930, p. 25, l. 19 through p. 59, l. 17.

2. See *Relative Frequency*, p. 45.

3. See *ibid.*, pp. 42, 43; also see p. 116 n. 1a below for further statistics on French voiced and voiceless stops.

4. See *Relative Frequency*, pp. 44–52 and pp. 57–60.

5. *Idem.*

75 1. See Quick and Schilthuis, *op. cit.*, p. 5, ll. 6–10.

77 1. See *Journal of the American Oriental Society*, x (1880), Proceedings at New York (October, 1877), pp. cl ff. We must remember that Vedic Sanskrit has long been dead and that the two phonemes may have differed in other respects than that of duration. The same criticism applies to all other Sanskrit phonemes, cf. note 1, immediately following.

78 1. *Ibid.* The percentage 27.97% for Vedic *ă* represents the sum of 19.78% for *ă* and 8.19% for *ā*.

2. *Kaeding*, p. 645, col. 24.

3. There are in addition some further data on vowels to which the attention of the reader is called.

(*a*) In his *Experimentelle Untersuchung der Laut-und Silbendauer im deutschen Satz*, Bonn diss., 1931, Dr. K. Weitkus reports his extensive investigation of the duration of sounds and syllables in the German sentence. Although the entire monograph rewards the most careful study, p. vi of the appendix in which the average duration of vowels and diphthongs is given, is especially interesting to us now. Arranged in the order of increasing average duration (for which he gives figures in columns 4 and 5) the short vowels, 'unterlange' vowels, long vowels, 'unterlange' diphthongs, and long diphthongs are presented, according to phonetic, *not phonemic*, differences. Weitkus is aware that this series may well be in the order of diminishing relative frequency. Interesting light might be shed on the role of duration in the form of vowels and diphthongs if the average duration of the individual vocalic and diphthongal *phonemes* of a dialect could be ascertained and compared with the relative frequency of their occurrence in that dialect. Cf. note *b* immediately following.

(*b*) In respect to the relative frequency of English vowels mention must be made of the important statistics of N. R. French, C. W. Carter, Jr., and W. Koenig, Jr., *The Words and Sounds of Telephone Conversations*, Bell Telephone System Technical Publications, Monograph B–491 (June, 1930), [published also in *The Bell System Technical Journal*, IX (1930), 290–324]. On page 23 of the monograph are presented the average occurrences of speech-sounds in telephone conversation for all words (except articles). Since the articles were omitted, and since the samplings were made in a manner radically different from that employed for the statistics of consonants, which we have presented in Chapter III, the French-Carter-Koenig statistics for consonants are not comparable to those presented in Chapter III above though they clearly point to the same prevailing tendency discussed in Chapter III. But, if we take all the short vowel-phonemes presented in this monograph (excluding as incomplete the vowels represented by the vowels of the articles *a*, *an*, and *the*), and arrange the short vowel phonemes (as spoken in Cambridge, Massachusetts) in the order of decreasing relative frequency, we have:

i (pin)	10.27%	of all vowels recorded.
e (pen, pair)	7.69	
ε (pan)	6.89	
a (pot, par)	6.52	
o (pawn)	4.15	
u (pull)	2.96	

It will be noticed that this order of decreasing relative frequency is also the order of the position of articulation of vowels proceeding from the high frontal position and progressing to the high back: on the basis of these statistics one may say that the more nearly frontal the short vowel is, the higher the relative frequency, or, the more nearly back the short vowel is, the lower the relative frequency. (For a discussion of the vowels of Central-Western American English cf. *Bloomfield*, pp. 103 ff.)

We should expect then on the basis of our findings in Chapter III that the order of our tabulation above represents one of increasing magnitude of complexity. And this order seems understandable if we take the closed mouth in repose as zero and view the series in English of *i, e, ε, a, o, u* as a progressively more complex modification of the mouth, first in the direction of wider aperture and then (with *o* and *u*) in the direction of an additional and ever more pronounced rounding of the lips. May the reader, if unfamiliar with phonetics, notice his formation of these vowels before a mirror. Since the production of these vowels includes gestures of vocal organs (e.g. the tongue) not otherwise measurable, this explanation of the dynamics of this curiously orderly correlation is of course speculative. The vowel *ə* as in *pun, about, China* has a relative frequency of 28.78% of all vowels recorded (and occurs also in the articles which were not recorded); this is not only the most frequent vowel, but also, almost admittedly, the vowel most close to zero (i.e. the position of complete repose).

It may well be remembered that in clear cases of vowel 'weakening' (i.e. loss of magnitude of complexity) resulting from loss of accent, the weakening is in the general direction of *a e i (ə)*. See the discussion of this phenomenon in Latin, page 179 supra. Hence there is considerable justification for our present speculation.

The long vowels: *ī* (peel) 6.44% (not including the frequently used *ī* of the article *the*); *ē* (pane) 4.78%; *ō* (pole) 4.74%; and *ū* (pool) 6.26%, show the same relationship between frequency and position with the exception of *ū* which is too frequent. Since the pronunciation of the article *a* is frequently *ē* the percentage for *ē* is really inconclusive. In the phonemic system of Cambridge,

Massachusetts, the length of a pure *a* (e.g. *par*) does not seem to be phonemically significant.

For statistics for long and short vowels and diphthongs in present-day Icelandic derived from printed material in which letters and digraphs were counted see note 4 immediately following.

4. Following are some statistics for vowels and diphthongs in modern colloquial Icelandic from a sampling totalling 25,000 letters and digraphs taken from Guðmundur Kamban: *Sendiherrann frá Júpiter* (Reykjavík: Arsaels Arnasonar 1927), p. 50, l. 1, through p. 86, l. 23. The *short vowels* are *a*, 9.724%; *e*, 5.728%; *i*, 7.028%; *o*, 1.488%; *u*, 4.336%; *ö*, .600%; *the long vowels*: *á*, 1.560%; *é*, 1.612%; *í*, 1.476%; *ó*, .632%; *ú*, .524%; *diphthongs (long and short)*: *æ*, .904%; *ei*, .984%; *íu*, .004%; *au*, .196%; *ey*, .124%; *ja*, .468%; *já*, .364%; *jæ*, .028%; *ji*, .052%; *jö*, .112%; *jó*, .128%; *ju*, .080%; *jú*, .040%. In addition *y*, .996%; *ý*, .112%. In each case the short vowel is decidedly more frequent than its corresponding long vowel; the diphthong is decidedly less frequent than its simple vocalic element.

5. *Relative Frequency*, p. 67.

6. See *Relative Frequency*, p. 65 f. for a discussion of these statistics except for those of Dutch, Peipingese, Cantonese, Burmese, Danish, and Singhalese, the source of which is the same as for the stops. For Singhalese see note 1b to page 116 below. For Old High German, Old English, and Icelandic see note 1, p. 120; note 2, p. 124; and note 4, p. 78, respectively.

79   1. The Chinese dialects of Peiping and Canton are sufficiently different to be classed, for practical purposes, as different languages, perhaps, in fact, more different than French and Italian.

81   1. *Bloomfield*, pp. 349–355.

2. *Jespersen*, p. 269.

85   1. *Ibid.*, p. 391; *Jespersen*, p. 329, also p. 281.

2. *Bloomfield*, p. 390.

87   1. For illustrative material and illuminating discussion see references under *phonetic change* in index to *Bloomfield*, p. 560; see also *Jespersen*, pp. 255–301.

89   1. *Jespersen*, pp. 284, 285.

2. See: *Jespersen*, pp. 191 ff., pp. 255 ff.; *Relative Frequency*, p. 87.

90   1. *Bloomfield*, p. 308, pp. 357 ff.; *Jespersen*, p. 195, pp. 197 ff.

91   1. *Brugmann*, pp. 39, 225, 235, 238, 256, 278, see also references under *assimilation* in indices of *Bloomfield* (in first reference, read 373–381 for 273–381), and of *Jespersen*.

2. *Brugmann*, pp. 39 f. See also pp. 209, 214–215, 225, 239, 244, 255, 275, and 292. See also *Bloomfield* under *dissimilation*.

97 1. But not always. See the able investigation, P. Menzerath and
A. de Lacerda, *Koartikulation, Steuerung und Lautabgrenzung*, Berlin and Bonn: Ferd. Dümmlers Verlag, 1933.

105 1. See also Greek ἄξων, Old Church Slavonic *osə*, Lithuanian *aszìs*,
Latin *axis*, Old High German *ahsa*. Cf. *Brugmann*, p. 78, §120.

106 1. After this assimilatory change had taken place in English, the *sk*
of loan words subsequently adopted into English has remained
stable even until today. Thus, the *sk* of the loan word *skirt* corresponds to the *sh* in its English cognate *shirt*. Similarly English
ship and the loan word *skiff* (taken from the French *esquif* which
was borrowed from the Italian *schifo* which was borrowed from the
Old High German *skif* before the *s* and *k* had coalesced).

107 1. *Bloomfield*, p. 81. In some dialects of American English intervocalic *t* and *d* are indistinguishable, the intervocalic *t* having become
voiced.

2. The case is not altered if the phoneticist also takes into consideration the position of the vocal organs in the production of phonemes
in positions where differences are subliminal, for it is by no means
always possible to deduce the aim (i.e. norm) from the approximation (see p. 108).

112 1. E.g. the English voiced stops are less fully voiced than the French
(cf. *Bloomfield*, p. 99).

115 1. Bloomfield seems to have overlooked the fact that the determination of absolute limits from statistical data is not easily possible
(cf. *Bloomfield*, p. 389, l. 28); and most certainly the person to
whose research he there refers had only statistical thresholds of
tolerable frequency in mind. Bloomfield's remarks in the last nine
lines of page 389, though suggesting interesting problems, seem to
be somewhat irrelevant to the matter at hand because the Principle
of Relative Frequency, thus far advanced, does not pretend to be
able to predict the course a change will take. See p. 283 *supra*.

2. E.g. footnote, page 38 *supra* and *passim*.

116 1. Thresholds of tolerable frequency have other possible uses than
the ones given in the text (pp. 116 ff.). Two of these other possible
uses for which illustrative statistics are available are presented
here, lest their inclusion in the main text lead us too far afield.

(*a*) There has been considerable theorizing about the effect of the
speed of utterance on phonetic change (see *Jespersen*, p. 258 f.).
In shedding light on the question of the effect of speed of utterance, our thresholds of tolerable frequency *may* be of help. For
example, in Paul Passy, *A French Phonetic Reader*, London:
Univ. of London Press, 1929, are given phonetic transcriptions

of (1) slow conversational pronunciation (p. 1 ff.), (2) careful pronunciation (p. 15 ff.), (3) oratorical pronunciation (p. 19 ff.), (4) rapid colloquial pronunciation (p. 23 ff.). We are interested of course primarily in the slow conversational and rapid colloquial texts since these are more representative of the stream of speech. Though the transcriptions are broadly phonetic, they are reasonably phonemic in the slow material, at least in respect to the consonants for which statistics are about to be given. The texts of slow conversational material are 13,000 phonemes in extent (and hence valid); the rapid colloquial material is but 2446 phonemes in extent (and hence really not adequate). If we put the percentages·of relative frequency for the slow conversational above the rapid colloquial we shall observe some quite interesting differences.

	t	*d*	*p*	*b*	*k*	*g*	*m*	*n*	nasalized vowels
slow	5.23%	4.48%	3.30%	1.47%	3.27%	.66%	3.12%	2.60%	5.70%
rapid	6.09	3.10	3.67	1.10	3.18	.57	3.96	2.00	6.99

In all cases the percentage of voiced stops is decreased in the rapid colloquial material; in all cases but one (e.g. *k*, perhaps the effect of truncation of *que* in rapid speech) the voiceless stops became relatively more frequent in the rapid material; the *m* increased in the rapid; the *n* decreased but the nasalized vowels increased. Though we remember that the statistics for the rapid are not sufficiently long to be reliable it is nevertheless interesting to note the effect of increased speed: voicing seems on the whole to suffer. It would be interesting to know what part, if any, of the increase in voiceless stops result from the unvoicing of voiced phonemic stops; it would also be interesting to know how much of the increase in nasalized vowels results from the lowered percentage of *n* in the rapid material (see *Relative Frequency*, p. 66). In the case of nearly all the stops, the percentages from the rapid material seem more in accord with what we might expect from our thresholds, p. 75. Investigation along this line may be very rewarding in helping to determine what we may call the normal speed of utterance (i.e. the speed in which the thresholds are likely to be most readily perceivable, or the speed in which the more permanently truncated and modified phonemes are either absent or modified). But see the discussion of 'Allegro' and 'Lento' forms in H. Hirt, *Indogermanishe Grammatik*, Teil 1 (Heidelberg: Winter, 1927), p. 129, §120. On the other hand see *Brugmann*, pp. 212, 220, 252 for forms which in the opinion of Brugmann are explicable only as the result of accelerated speech tempo and hence are 'allegro forms.'

(*b*) The frequency thresholds of toleration *may* also reveal interesting information about phonemic differences. For example, in Singhalese there are two voiceless and two voiced dental stops which are said to be phonemically different and which we shall term t_1, t_2, d_1, and d_2 respectively. Let us view the statistics of pertinent phonemes from a phonemic transcription of Singhalese, 5000 phonemes in extent, taken from H. S. Perera and D. Jones: *A Colloquial Singhalese Reader* (Manchester: University Press, 1919), pp. 21 ff.

t_1	t_2	d_1	d_2	p	b
4.04%	2.58%	2.80%	1.28%	2.32%	1.18%
t_1 *plus* t_2 = 6.62%		d_1 *plus* d_2 = 4.08%			

k	g	m	n	c	j
5.00%	2.56%	3.12%	7.40%	.22%	.06%

Now, in all these cases the voiceless stops are more frequent than their corresponding voiced stops. Furthermore, the percentages of all agree on the whole with our findings on p. 75 above, except for the dentals t_1, t_2, d_1, and d_2. The stops t_1 and d_1 are true dental stops, and the former is below what we might infer to be its lower threshold. The stops t_2 and d_2 are cerebral (pronounced like the *t* and *d* in *heart* and *hard* in some dialects of American English). The cerebrals are said to be phonemically distinct from the dentals. But if we add the dentals and cerebrals together, the percentages for t_1 *plus* t_2 and for d_1 *plus* d_2 are quite right for the dentals. Are these dentals and cerebrals phonemically distinct in every respect as we are lead to believe? Will perhaps our thresholds in time not be able to yield quite adequate information alone in many cases about what is phonemic? There may conceivably be such a thing as a binary phoneme, i.e. one phoneme which is a pair of distinct variants which may indeed at times keep otherwise homophonous words apart and is the result of some syntactical or morphological factor no longer present, such as tone or pitch.

117 1. Not an *absolute* threshold of tolerable frequency.

  2. Cf. T. Navarro Tomás, *Manual de Pronunciación Española*, Madrid, 1918, pp. 75 ff.

PAGE

118 1. Cf. D. Jones and K. T. Woo, *op. cit.*, p. xi, bottom.

119 1. See discussion and references, *Jespersen*, pp. 261–264.

120 1. Eduard Sievers, *Tatian*, Paderborn, 1892. Diphthongs were counted as 1 phonemic element, double letters (e.g. *hh*, *ll*, *rr*) as 2; *ch*, *sc*, *qu*, each as two phonemic elements. That these statistics might also be used in an unrelated study of *Tatian*, the selections were small amounts scattered throughout the entire work, totalling, however, 50,000. The selections are as follows:

Chap.		count		Chap.		count	
	2.2		1,500		109.1		750
"	4.9	"	1,000	"	113.1	"	700
"	13.6	"	750	"	116.1	"	750
"	13.18	"	750	"	116.4	"	800
"	16.1	"	700	"	117.1	"	500
"	17.1	"	300	"	121.1	"	1,600
"	18.1	"	500	"	123.2	"	900
"	20.1	"	1,500	"	124.7	"	1,500
"	22.7	"	750	"	131.9	"	2,500
"	25.4	"	1,800	"	133.1	"	1,000
"	43.4	"	450	"	138.1	"	1,000
"	54.1	"	750	"	139.2	"	1,500
"	68.3	"	250	"	145.4	"	1,000
"	49.1	"	1,500	"	148.1	"	1,500
"	72.1	"	1,500	"	154.1	"	500
"	82.1	"	1,500	"	165.4	"	1,000
"	84.5	"	1,000	"	190.1	"	1,000
"	87.4	"	1,000	"	155.3	"	1,500
"	88.7	"	1,000	"	177.4	"	1,500
"	92.1	"	1,000	"	212.1	"	900
"	97.2	"	500	"	217.1	"	1,000
"	99.1	"	500	"	222.1	"	500
"	94.1	"	1,000	"	224.1	"	1,100
"	104.4	"	750	"	239.3	"	1,500
"	106.1	"	750	"	132.5	"	500
							50,000

124 1. *Relative Frequency*, pp. 69 ff.

   2. W. J. Sedgefield, *King Alfred's Old English Version of Boethius de consolatione philosophiae*, Oxford: Clarendon Press, 1899. The following two (*A* and *B*) selections were taken, each totalling 25,000 phonemic elements: *A* page 74, line 15 to page 92, line 16. *B*, page 103, line 23 to page 121, line 32.

126 1. *Relative Frequency*, pp. 80 ff.

PAGE

128 1. The dialects of present-day German still seem to be in the process of seeking equilibrium. A statistical analysis of 5,000 connected phonemes of intimate family letters transcribed phonemically for me according to the speech of a native educated person (Bergisches Gebiet) by Dr. Werner Frowein of the Phonetisches Institut, University of Bonn, yields the following percentages: t, 7.78%; d, 4.08%; p, .704%; b, 2.88%; k, 1.62%; g, 2.04%; n, 10.32%. Here we find t and d in possession of quite standard percentages, but in all the other stops the voiced stops are appreciably more frequent than the voiceless, and appear to be at their upper thresholds even as the voiceless at their lower. Hence, equilibrium is disturbed. The pronunciation of the material of these statistics is reasonably close to that which is accepted as standard German pronunciation. If we observe other typical dialects of German (for which phonemic statistical analyses are unfortunately not available, though urgently needed) we find in some (notably in the North) that the voiceless stops are becoming aspirated as in Danish (the t following by analogy?); in others (e.g. the dialect of Alsace) the voiceless and voiced stops have fallen together; in still others (e.g. many South German dialects, cf. *Bloomfield*, p. 100) the phonemes have all become voiceless, the phonemic difference residing in a lenis and fortis unaspirated pronunciation (see p. 63 above). Statistics of the frequency of phonemes of these dialects would be invaluable in showing to what extent a condition of equilibrium had been achieved by these devices.

CHAPTER FOUR

130 1. *Jespersen*, pp. 271 ff.
     2. *Ibid.*, p. 272.
     3. It would seem that the effect of any deliberate appreciable deviation from the customary norm of amplitude, pitch, or duration in the utterance of a speech-element would be one of accent, since this deviation would tend to attract the auditor's attention to it. This deviation may be in the direction of a decrease below the normal as well as an increase above the normal. Thus, either to whisper or to shout a speech-element in a conversation of average amplitude and pitch will often equally well attract attention to it, or 'accent' it, perhaps even when the deviation is unintentional. These probably very significant aspects of accent are not considered in this study. It might be suggested, nevertheless, that the degree of accent (i.e. the degree of attention attracted to a speech-element)

may well bear some inverse relationship to the relative frequency of occurrence of the element when thus accented, no matter in what way attention becomes attracted to it, or whether intentionally or accidentally; for (1) that which is accented is also that which is unusual, almost by definition, and (2) the additional effort expended in modifying or deflecting an act of behavior from its normal patterned course may well be more than sufficient to off-set any saving resulting from a smaller total magnitude of configurational complexity; and hence the effect of *any* decided deviation from normal pattern may well prove to be the same as that of a greater magnitude of complexity, regardless of the nature of the deviation. The factors probably involved in this question can perhaps be more clearly illustrated by an example from a comparable situation in a phonemic system. For example, let us assume that a language exists like ancient Sanskrit which possesses the labials *bh*, *b*, *ph*, and *p*, but no *f*. Let us assume that in many languages which possess these labials, the customary articulation of *f* represents a smaller magnitude of complexity than that of any of the other above four labial stops. Nevertheless, for the speakers of the language like Sanskrit, the production of *f* in lieu of any of its labials would represent a greater effort because its production involves a deviation from the normal pattern. Thus the weak palatal or velar voiceless spirant of German (written *ch*) though essentially a very simple sound and quite unobtrusive in a German conversation, looms up conspicuously both to the speaker and to the auditor when the American student tries to speak German. Similarly with the German articulation of the English voiceless spirant written *th*. It is not clear to the present author how this problem, which may be of fundamental importance in dynamic studies, may best be investigated empirically. Discussed somewhat more extensively in *Relative Frequency*, pp. 3 ff.

131 1. *Eldridge*, p. 49.

2. *Kaeding*, p. 53.

132 1. Bloomfield prefers to view stress as a secondary phoneme (cf. *Bloomfield*, pp. 90–92). The present author has not been convinced that there is any gain to our knowledge or convenience by substituting the term *secondary phoneme* for *stress* (in our case, *accent*), and, believing that the phenomena of the phoneme and of stress may be essentially different, feels that the term *secondary phoneme* may be misleading. Of course it is true that otherwise homophonous words of different meaning are frequently differentiated solely by difference in accent (stress or tone), e.g. English

próduce and *prodúce*, or *it* (3d sing. neuter pronoun) and *it* 'sex appeal' as pronounced in colloquial American English. Nevertheless, though frequently of comparable use and effect, phonemic and stress phenomena are not for that reason necessarily of like structure and nature.

133 1. *Jespersen*, p. 272, bottom of page.
  2. Jespersen does not say that psychological value is the only factor but the *chief* factor in sentence-stress (*ibid.*, p. 272). Furthermore he says, not that value plays the only role in syllabic accent, but 'a not unimportant role.' We shall later (pp. 161 ff.) find considerable empirical evidence in support of these beliefs which at present seem impossible of statistical treatment.

139 1. Cf. Charles Rockwell Lanman, 'Noun inflections in the Veda,' *Journal of the American Oriental Society*, x (1872–80), 325 ff. Discussed in *Relative Frequency*, pp. 9 ff.
  2. *Relative Frequency*, pp. 10, 11, 12.

140 1. Cf. W. D. Whitney, *Sanskrit Grammar, cit. supra*, §552 ff. (pp. 208 ff.). For further discussion of Sanskrit accentuation see references under *accent* in Whitney's index.

141 1. Cf. John Avery, 'Contributions to the history of verb-inflection in Sanskrit,' *Journal of the American Oriental Society*, x (1872–80), 220 ff. See also discussion of my use of the Avery statistics in *Relative Frequency*, pp. 10–13.

144 1. Cf. W. D. Whitney, *op. cit.*, §§ 585–589 (pp. 220, 221, especially the first eleven lines of p. 221). In Homeric Greek the augment was by no means invariably and completely crystallized to the same extent as in later Attic.

145 1. For a more complete and more fully exemplified discussion of the Sanskrit accentuation of verbal stem formatives cf. *Relative Frequency*, pp. 19–23.

146 1. *Ibid.* See also John Avery, 'On the formation of present-stems of the Sanskrit verb,' *Journal of the American Oriental Society*, x (1872–80), cxli ff. from which these statistics have been taken.

148 1. *Kaeding*, p. 464.

151 1. *Ibid.*

156 1. *Ibid.*

163 1. The pre-Plautine accent [cp. C. Exon, *Hermathena*, xiv (1906), 117] seems to have been an intermediate stage in the transition from the first syllable accentuation to the accentuation of Classical Latin. In brief, it differs from the accentuation of Classical Latin essentially in this one respect, that when in pre-Plautine Latin, both the second and third syllable from the end were short, the accent

seemed to rest on the fourth syllable from the end. Since this was probably only a transitional stage, and since there is not an abundance of Latin material from that time suitable for analysis, we shall not be able to investigate it. That the pre-Plautine accentual phenomena seem not to vitiate our ensuing conclusions on the subject of analogical accent in Latin cf. *Relative Frequency*, pp. 30, 31. Cf. also F. Sommer, *Handbuch der lateinischen Laut-und Formenlehre* (Heidelberg: Winter, 1902), pp. 95–108.

165 1. Lane Cooper, *A Concordance to the Works of Horace*, Carnegie Institution of Washington, 1916.

2. For the list of compound words whose frequencies are presented for each of the simplexes, cf. *Relative Frequency*, pp. 27 f.

167 1. For a complete and well illustrated discussion of Latin vowels, and their mutations since Indo-European times, cp. Ferdinand Sommer, *op. cit.*, pp. 37–167. For the effect of accent on the quality of Latin vowels see *ibid.*, pp. 94–125.

171 1. That this ratio of 3700 to 2141 (or approximately 5 to 3) is sufficient to effect an analogic change in Latin seems reasonably certain from a statistical examination of the Latin nominal *s*-stems whose behavior in early Latin (*ca.* 4th and 3d centuries B.C.) almost surely involves analogic influence; the results, presented in detail in *Relative Frequency*, pp. 31, 32, 33 are not repeated here, except to say that the effective ratio derived from the samples selected was 72.7 to 27.3 (i.e. approximately 8 to 3). In the *s*-stems there were only two homogeneous alternatives, whereas in the 'natural' and 'analogous forms,' there were 5 different classes, the successful one (4) being over twice as frequent as its closest competitor (5); the ratio of 5 to 3, hence, seems valid. But, see also R. G. Kent, *Language*, VI (1930), pp. 87, 88, who offers a somewhat different explanation of the phenomena discussed in *Relative Frequency*, 31 ff. [Kent believes that when the stem vowel was the same throughout all cases, e.g. *labōr*, *labōris*, the following stem consonant was the same, e.g. *labōr*, but when the stem-vowel was different, e.g. *tempus*, *temporis*, the stem consonants were also different, e.g. *tempus*, *temporis*. Kent gives further illustrations. This is a very ingenious explanation which merits careful consideration. But we must not forget the well established fact that intervocalic *s* became *r* (e.g. **temposes* became *temporis*) in the 4th century B.C. probably over 100 years before final *os* became *us* (e.g. **tempos* became *tempus*), cf. Sommer, *op. cit.*, p. 210 who places the change of intervocalic *s* to *r* at the middle of the 4th century B.C. but (*ibid.*, p. 157) that of final *os* to *us* toward the end of the 3d century. Kent's suggestion is

tenable only if the analogic change, e.g. *labōs* to *labōr* occurred after final *os* became *us*, because, before that time, there was no vowel differentiation in many stems, e.g. *tempos* and *temporis*. Should Kent's explanation be found correct, which is possible but not, I think, likely, I do not believe that even he would believe that analogy played no role; cf. Kent, *op. cit.*, p. 87, ll. 37–40.]

173 1. *Kaeding*, p. 464 f.

178 1. Cf. Sommer, *op. cit.*, p. 114.

2. To summarize the effect of pre-historic first syllable accent in Latin upon the quality of monophthong vowels in unaccented syllables (cf. Sommer, *op. cit.*, pp. 108–122), it may be said in general that all long vowels remained unchanged (e.g. **éxmānō* > *emānō*, **cónfēci* > *confēci*, **cóntrītos* > *contrītus*, **cóndōno* > *condōno*, **empūros* > *impūrus*). Similarly short *i* remained generally unchanged (e.g. *aditus*) except when assimilated to *e* before *r* (e.g. **cinises* > *cineris*) cf. *ibid.*, p. 109. Short unaccented *a* became short *e* in closed syllable and became short *i* in open syllable (e.g. *facio*, *factus*, but *conficio* and *confectus*). Short *e* remained stable in closed syllable (e.g. **ádemptos* or **óbsessos* and historical *ademptus* or *obsessus*); short *e* changed to *i* in unaccented open syllable (e.g. **óbsedeo* > *obsídeo*, **cónteneo* > *contíneo*). Of course there were further assimilations of *i*, *e*, and *a* in some instances. With short *o* and *u* the assimilations seem to have been the most conspicuous part of the total change.

CHAPTER FIVE

185 1. The reader may profitably read *Bloomfield*, Chaps. 10, 11, 12, 13, and 14 which contain considerable illustrative material either on the sentence or on important elements in sentence structure; a knowledge of this material is not, however, prerequisite to an understanding of the present chapter.

2. *Bloomfield*, p. 20.

199 1. For discussion of the history of the word *mandrake* in English see Adolf Taylor Starck, *Der Alraun, ein Beitrag zur Pflanzensagenkunde*, Baltimore: J. H. Furst Co., 1917.

204 1. Cf. *Selected Studies*, pp. 21 ff.

215 1. On the other hand, in written language, the opportunity for erasure and re-writing (cp. *Selected Studies*, p. 24) may artificially distort what would otherwise have been the normal course of speech-events.

227 1. N. R. French, C. W. Carter, Jr., W. Koenig, Jr., *The Words and Sounds of Telephone Conversations*, op. cit., p. 5.

250 1. To be sure all words do not become phonemes ultimately, for clearly some are lost in the process. However, some words do, though not sufficient historical time seems to have elapsed to provide an abundance of examples. For example, the Classical Latin word-morpheme *ex* 'out of' was both an independent word and an inseparable prefix by classical times. Though crystallized in *expensa* 'expense' as a morpheme, it also occurred in the language as a word. From Latin *expensa* through Italian *Spesa* through the borrowing into German represented by the present-day forms *Spesen* and *Speise*, we see the transformation of a word-morpheme into a simple phoneme. One need not add that no German feels the morphemic origin of the *s* in *Spesen* or *Speise*. The English adjectival suffix *ly* (OE *lic*, OHG *-lîk*, from Germanic *-liko* from the word *lîkom*, 'form') meaning 'having qualities of,' e.g. *kingly*, *scholarly*, was clearly once a word and probably will some day be but a phoneme.

256 1. V. A. C. Henmon, *A French Wordbook Based on a Count of 400,000 Running Words* (Madison, Wis.: Bureau of Educational Research Bulletin No. 3. Sept., 1924), pp. 7 ff.

259 1. *Selected Studies*, p. 24.
      2. *Ibid.*

CHAPTER SIX

275 1. For the use of parentheses in the description of the present-day German stream of speech for the sake of correlating otherwise seemingly unrelated phenomena and of reducing them to a single 'parenthesis-law' (i.e. *Klammergesetz*) which merits the most careful consideration by Dynamic Philology, see A. Debrunner, 'Das Gefühl für grammatische Gesetze,' *Indogermanische Forschungen*, vol. L (1932), 177–203.

277 1. See also *Selected Studies*, pp. 10 f.

279 1. To be compared with the discussion of patterns and emotional equilibrium in Chapter V, Part i, above.

282 1. In the near future I hope to have finished for publication studies of the historical development of English and of German from the viewpoint of Dynamic Philology. These two languages are especially interesting, among other very important reasons, because: English, through extensive truncations of suffixes and endings, evidently restored balance among the stops only to disturb balance among vowels with a resultant lengthening and diphthongation thereof; German, in preserving inflectional end-

ings, has presumably kept a reasonably stable vocalic system but an unbalanced consonantal system.

2. Cf. N. R. French, C. W. Carter, Jr., Walter Koenig, Jr., *The Words and Sounds of Telephone Conversations, op. cit.*, p. 19 ' ... to measure a vocabulary by recording spoken words involves the risk of gross underestimation unless the observations are exceedingly prolonged.'

284 1. For a somewhat more complete discussion, cf. *Selected Studies*, Part ii (pp. 8 ff.).

285 1. The author attempted in *Selected Studies*, pp. 19 ff. to apply this analogy to linguistic phenomena by assuming that the common unit of speech-elements in the stream of speech was of the nature of a time-triangle.

286 1. Discussed somewhat more in detail in *Selected Studies*, p. 22. [I have subsequently been informed that the common Scandinavian *bil*, Icelandic *bill*, the abbreviation of *automobile*, was not a natural abbreviation, see K. Malone, *Modern Language Notes*, XLVIII (1933), 395; the English abbreviation *bus* for *omnibus* or any other similar abbreviation may be used in place of *bil*.]

2. In *Selected Studies*, Part ii, the dimensions were *intensity, determinacy of order, preciseness of meaning*, and *quality* in addition to relative frequency. *Quality* as a dimension seems understandable only when the phenomena of semantic change and abbreviation are studied from the angle taken in *Selected Studies*, which seemed necessary at the time because the phenomena were on the whole viewed in isolation, and because limits of space in *Selected Studies* prevented the presentation of the material now presented in Chapters ii-v which leads rather to a discussion of the basic dimension of speech (pp. 283 ff.), than to that of the above four dimensions. The author has, however, neither found, nor been apprised of, any reason why *quality* should not be considered a dimension, nor why the method of presentation of *Selected Studies*, Part ii, is invalid, although he is convinced that the method of analysis there adopted is by no means as adequate scientifically as the one adopted at present.

289 1. From the late Latin *cuppa*, whence Old French *cope*, Italian *coppa*, etc.

301 1. Should it be subsequently proved that more than one quantum of energy are requisite for a minimal animate reaction, our theory of the *acteme* will scarcely be invalidated, since the *acteme* is defined in terms of minimal animate classificatory action and not in terms of physical quanta.

INDEX

INDEX

THE M.I.T. PAPERBACK SERIES